The Bloomsbury Introduction to Postmodern Realist Fiction

The Bloomsbury Introduction to Postmodern Realist Fiction

Resisting Master Narratives

T. V. Reed

BLOOMSBURY ACADEMIC
LONDON • NEW YORK • OXFORD • NEW DELHI • SYDNEY

BLOOMSBURY ACADEMIC
Bloomsbury Publishing Plc
50 Bedford Square, London, WC1B 3DP, UK
1385 Broadway, New York, NY 10018, USA
29 Earlsfort Terrace, Dublin 2, Ireland

BLOOMSBURY, BLOOMSBURY ACADEMIC and the Diana logo are trademarks of
Bloomsbury Publishing Plc

First published in Great Britain 2021
Reprinted in 2021

Cover design by Eleanor Rose
Cover image: © Nota Bene Visual

A catalogue record for this book is available from the British Library.

A catalog record for this book is available from the Library of Congress.

ISBN: HB: 978-1-3500-1081-9
PB: 978-1-3500-1080-2
ePDF: 978-1-3500-1083-3
eBook: 978-1-3500-1082-6

Typeset by Deanta Global Publishing Services, Chennai, India
Printed and bound in Great Britain

To find out more about our authors and books visit www.bloomsbury.com
and sign up for our newsletters.

For Noël, always

Contents

Acknowledgments

I want to begin by thanking those responsible for the first visible manifestation of this book, the cover. The *Nota Bene* collective of Istanbul provided me with the image from their brilliant installation, "In Order to Control."

Like all books, this one has been a collective endeavor at every stage. Its origins can be traced back to the many versions of courses I taught over the years on postmodern fiction at Washington State University, York University, and elsewhere. I thank the students in those courses who inspired me and helped bring forth many of the ideas that have made their way into this volume.

The particular shape of this project started with an email from David Avital when he was an editor at Bloomsbury Academic. His patience and thoughtfulness over several years as the book evolved were vital and the book would not have come into existence without him. When David passed the project on to Ben Doyle and Lucy Brown it landed in capable and helpful hands. I thank them both, along with Angelique Neumann and all the other folks at Bloomsbury for their stellar work in the editing, proofing, production, and dissemination of *Postmodern Realist Fiction*.

Finally, and most importantly, though she wisely early on turned down an offer of co-authorship, I wish in addition to the dedication to express the deepest gratitude to the individual most responsible for making this a better book, through her research, voracious reading of fiction, numerous discussions, editorial comments, and encouragement, Noël Sturgeon.

A Note on Usage

I have tried throughout this book to use the currently preferred self-descriptive terms from the communities discussed in the readings, terms like "LGBTQIA2S+," "Latinx," "transgender," "Indigenous," and "First Nations," while recognizing that there is not always one standard agreed-upon usage in those communities. At times I have used older terms when they were used in the novels being analyzed.

1

Introduction

There is no such thing as postmodern fiction. But that doesn't mean I can't write and you can't read a book about it. Postmodernism is not a thing. It does not exist, at least not the way a tree, or a building, or even a book of fiction exists. It is a concept, a way of organizing disparate things into a category, and it is a notoriously slippery category at that. There are hundreds of magnificent literary works published during the postmodern era, roughly from the 1960s to the present. There is considerable disagreement about which works get to count as postmodernist, however. This is partly due to the fact that critics have often sought one narrow definition of a postmodernist style or approach. In my view, anyone seeking to write about postmodern fiction needs to note that in practice there is not one postmodernism, but many different postmodernisms. Postmodernism is also a global phenomenon, with writers hailing from all continents (with the exception of Antarctica, though that might be an excellent place to write without disruptions). In one sense there are as many postmodernisms as there are postmodern authors, or even postmodern works, since the same author may do very different things in individual works.

The existence of this myriad of possibilities allows for quite different generalizations about what postmodernism is, and thus quite different possible introductions to postmodern fiction.[1] Virtually every aspect of postmodernism has been subject to intense debate: not only which particular artefacts of culture are or are not postmodern but also what its political or cultural origins are, what its key features are, whether it is progressive or regressive politically, when it began, and whether or not it has ended. Indeed, there are those who argue that postmodernism never made sense as concept at all.

This all points to the fact that the label "postmodernist" is very much a category of convenience, one that allows literary critics and literature professors to organize their scholarship and teaching. That is a perfectly reasonable thing to do, but it can also be misleading. Few of the actual producers of various works of fiction labeled "postmodernist" embrace the concept. This is hardly surprising. Most fiction writers of any era hate to be placed into literary categories or schools. They believe, rightly, that being grouped in such a way tends to move away from the particular, even unique, qualities of each author, each novel. Perhaps the best way to think about these issues is to imagine looking through an adjustable telescope; the scope lets you focus far out and see broad patterns, or close in to see the uniqueness of each piece of writing. In this book I am primarily interested in broad patterns, but I try to strike a balance by acknowledging the unique ideas, sensibilities, and styles of particular writers and works.

Postmodernist fictions range from ones that seem to seek the pure aesthetic joy of wordplay with little apparent connection to world play, to texts that attempt precisely to find ways to engage the social world through the force of their narratives. There are dozens of texts of each type, and many other types that could be elaborated. Any book about postmodernist fiction is therefore itself a fiction, a necessarily selective, invented collection. The selection I have chosen represents what I call *postmodernist realism*, works that use the realism-disrupting techniques of postmodernism in order to treat substantive social issues in the real world.

Postmodernist fiction is part of a broader body of phenomena labeled "postmodern." More ill-informed and totally misleading things have been written about postmodernism than about almost any aspect of contemporary culture. Some of this stems from legitimate confusion arising from the obscure style of some postmodern theorists and fictionists. But much of it, especially in the last decade or so, is a politically motivated attack on aspects of postmodern thought and practice because they challenge elements of religious, political, and cultural authority.[2] Attacks on distorted versions of postmodernism, often joined to attacks on certain forms of multiculturalism, have sometimes played a role in the rise of new waves of right-wing pseudo-populism and the revival of white supremacist, misogynist, anti-immigrant, anti-Semitic, and Islamophobic discourses. In that context, a book seeking to introduce postmodern fiction bears a special responsibility to address not only aesthetic but also political issues swirling around this body of work.

The bad rap on postmodernism, that it consists of obscure and cynical wordplay, lacking both substance and moral values, strikes me as deeply mistaken. Postmodern fiction writers have offered some extraordinarily rich explorations of the social conditions of the late twentieth and early twenty-first centuries. They have addressed the challenges of forming a coherent identity amid the massive information overload provided by TV, the internet, and other forms of mass communication; they have treated the immense dislocations of people caused by war, famine, poverty, climate change, and political repression; they have explored the psychic roots of terrorism and religious extremism; they have celebrated the emergence of social groups previously marginalized by gender, sexuality, and race; they have raised the issue of what it means to be human in an era when the rise of biotechnology and the prospect of artificial intelligence profoundly challenge the borders of our bodies and minds—indeed they have addressed virtually all aspects of life in this era in ways that deal concretely with the world as more than a collection of words. Postmodernist fiction is certainly not the only, or in all cases, best form of writing through which to explore each of these issues, but as a body of work it does provide unique perspectives that can prove vital to a fuller understanding of how these phenomena shape our lives. These works do for our era what fiction has always done; they get beyond theoretical and sociological generalizations to address social conditions at the level of our daily emotional and intellectual experience.

Terminal Confusion

Before I outline my chosen approach to postmodern realist fiction, it is important to separate out three aspects of the term "postmodern" that, when not separated, account for a good deal of the confusion surrounding these concepts. These three distinct aspects of the postmodern, while interrelated, refer to quite different things: *postmodern theory*, a set of philosophical arguments; *postmodernist aesthetics*, a set of forms and styles in literature, film, music, theater, architecture, and the visual arts; and *postmodernity*, a set of claims about the particular social issues defining the last several decades.

Each of these aspects of the postmodern *shapes and is shaped by* the others. But they do distinct things. Our immediate subject, postmodernist fiction, is both a reaction to earlier aesthetic style and a reaction to social conditions that form postmodernity as a distinct era, and some (but not all) postmodern fiction is influenced by postmodern theory. In turn, fiction has had an influence on some strands of postmodern theory, and has not only illuminated but also helped to shape postmodern social conditions.

I outline the characteristics of postmodernity as social conditions, and the typical elements of postmodernist style, in the next chapter. So let me very briefly here point to the third part of this triad, postmodern theory. While postmodern theory informs some of the interpretations I offer in this book, I explain the relevant concepts in context so that substantial knowledge of this often philosophically dense, not to say obscure, body of work isn't necessary for readers to understand my analyses. But it can perhaps be useful at the outset to at least acknowledge who some of these figures are. Postmodern theorists include a number of writers associated with the intellectual terrain known as poststructuralism, especially Jacques Derrida, Michel Foucault, Julia Kristeva, Jacques Lacan, and Roland Barthes. In addition, prominent theorists associated with postmodern theory include Giles Deleuze and Felix Guattari, Jean-François Lyotard, and Jean Baudrillard. There is also an influential school of postmodern theorists collectively known as the French feminists, including Luce Irigaray, Hélène Cixous, and Monique Wittig. In the English-speaking world, prominent theorists associated with postmodernism include Judith Butler, Donna Haraway, Fredric Jameson, Stuart Hall, David Harvey, Brian McHale, Linda Hutcheon, and Richard Rorty, among many others. Each of these authors offers a different set of conceptualizations of things postmodern, and each has been influential on at least some postmodern fiction writers.[3]

While it is impossible to find commonalities among all these varied theorists, Arkady Plotnitsky has offered a useful triad of concepts that cover a rather large portion of the terrain of postmodern thought: "1) *irreducible multiplicity*; 2) the *irreducibly unthinkable* in thought; and 3) *irreducible chance*."[4] I take these to mean, first, that no single belief system can encompass all reality, or contain all of the truth; second, that no system of thought (including postmodern theory) can fully get outside itself to understand its own limits; and third, that because reality always has an element of randomness, our notions of historical and social causality should always contain an element of cautious doubt. What should be underscored about these three principles is that far from the stereotype of postmodernism as an "anything goes" philosophy, each is about recognizing limits, about the impossibility of perfect knowledge.

These principles also stem in large part from the position that languages offer not a transparent window on the world, but rather a set of self-enclosed, culturally variable systems for constructing representations of an ultimately only imperfectly knowable reality. Virtually all the common complaints about the nature of postmodernism are off the mark. The claim that postmodernism is godless, or atheistic, misses the fact that there are postmodern theologians representing every major faith group. The claim that postmodernism is all about the new, that it claims to be some unprecedented historical phenomenon was already refuted by the first major book written on the subject. Jean-François Lyotard makes clear in *The Postmodern Condition* (1979) that postmodernism is a recurring historical phenomenon dating back to at least the ancient Greeks, a phenomenon that arises whenever segments of a culture develop an intense self-consciousness about language as a force in creating the world. Likewise, claims that postmodernism arrogantly sweeps aside all previous cultural expression are nonsense given that postmodernism's commitment to pluralism means that it can make no claim to be superior to the realisms and modernisms that preceded it, but must instead be seen as one of the many alternative forms of representing reality that coexist in this or any other era.

At base, postmodern theory is about challenging all absolutes, all fundamentalisms—religious, philosophical, and political. It is not a denial of reality as some mistakenly claim; it is a call to take responsibility for the social processes through which we construct (imperfect) interpretations of reality, rather than claiming to know some unchallengeable truth. Rather than try to summarize further this large, complicated body of theories in the abstract, I try in each of this book's thematic chapters to introduce, where relevant, some aspects of postmodern theory, while noting that those theories never tell the whole story of the fictions represented.

Postmodern fiction has at times critiqued poststructuralist and other forms of postmodern theory, and postmodern theory itself was from the outset influenced by a number of different fiction writers especially early-twentieth-century modernists, some of whom were clearly forerunners of postmodernism. Indeed, some of the perceived obscurity of postmodern theory stems from the fact that many of these theorists mix experimental literary form with more traditional forms of philosophical discourse.[5] Among poststructuralists, psychoanalyst Jacques Lacan was immersed in literary avant-garde movements, especially surrealism; Roland Barthes and

Julia Kristeva were part of a circle of experimental writers in France, the "Tel Quel" group, that produced an influential strand of postmodern fiction (*le nouveau roman*); and Michel Foucault, Jacques Derrida, and Gilles Deleuze were deeply influenced by avant-garde French modernist writings and by other proto-postmodernist figures like Czech-German Franz Kafka, American Gertrude Stein, and Argentinian Jorge Luis Borges. Likewise, US postmodern theorist Donna Haraway has acknowledged her deep debt to feminist science fiction, to cite just a few examples.

While postmodern theory has undoubtedly influenced some postmodernist fiction writers, many others seem unaware of, indifferent to, or even hostile to elements of these theories. There are works of fiction that seem virtually to illustrate aspects of theory, but others that parody, challenge, or sidestep issues deemed central to postmodern theorists. To the degree that postmodern theory has become part of the repertoire of literary critics, it has illuminated some works of postmodernist fiction, but also obscured other aspects. The strengths and limits of postmodern theory arise from the high level of abstraction that characterizes it, as well as an almost exclusive focus among some on language as a determining force in social life to the neglect of material realities that while inevitably shaped by language also exist outside of it. Much postmodernist fiction, on the other hand, approaches some of these same concerns from the level of everyday, lived experiences that ground, complicate, and often challenge some elements of theory. Put differently, when theory is applied too broadly to the fiction, when fiction is seen as simply echoing aspects of theory, something vital is lost. Fiction itself has theoretical dimensions, but it is usually a different kind of theorizing, one that brings an equal or even greater self-awareness regarding the nature of language in touch with the material world and lived particularities that generate different kinds of knowledge embedded in different kinds of experience, thought, and feeling. In this light, it is important to see theory and fiction as generally having very different roles to play in the ecology of discourses, even if sometimes those roles overlap.

An overemphasis on certain strands of postmodern theory can obscure the ways in which a whole host of writers were engaged in thinking in ways related to postmodernism long before poststructuralist theory rose to prominence. This includes writers from marginalized social groups like African Americans and First Nations/Native Americans who were in many ways postmodernist before the term arose. African American postmodern novelist Ishmael Reed, for example, was deeply influenced by the deconstructive art form that is jazz music. Long before Jacques Derrida coined the term "deconstruction," jazz musicians were engaging in something very much like that process. Before Derrida showed that the seemingly stable surface level of a text, fiction or nonfiction, belied instabilities and even contradictions within itself, jazz musicians were taking seemingly simple popular melodies and revealing in them complexities, including full-fledged contradictions (a sweet song with hidden depths of anger), that at some level existed within the text. And with regard to a different set of cultural traditions, Anishinaabe fictionist and critic Gerald Vizenor has made a strong case that Indigenous/Native American Indian storytelling *trickster figures* have been postmodernists for centuries.[6]

I will endeavor throughout this book to keep these three dimensions of the postmodern—theory, aesthetic style, and social conditions—clear to readers. I want to note here that there is also a related terminological confusion that can arise around the term "modern." When theorists are talking about being postmodern, what is the modern they are posting? If we are talking about postmodernity as a social condition, the modern that is being talked about is several hundred years of the *modern era*, a period of European history usually said to have begun either with the sixteenth-century Renaissance or the seventeenth-century Enlightenment. By contrast, when the subject is postmodernist fiction, the modern being posted is usually the era of *modernism in literature* and the other arts, a period from the late nineteenth to the mid-twentieth centuries. Postmodern theorists do sometimes reference modernism in the arts, and postmodernist fiction has relevance to the longer modern period, but generally, the former are talking about the *long* modern era and the latter are concerned with the *short* modern era.

Admittedly, the complex interplay among postmodern theory, postmodern historical conditions, and postmodernist aesthetic approaches is seldom easy to sort out, but at least keeping these basic elements of terminology in mind can hopefully provide threads to follow through the labyrinth of things postmodern.

Postmodernist Realism

As I have suggested, there are many different ways to slice and dice the larger body of postmodern fictions. This can be done, for example, chronologically, in which case there are now at least three or four generations of postmodern fictionists. This makes some sense if it is linked to an approach recognizing the evolving nature of postmodern conditions over time (i.e., the growth of a digital culture from a marginal to a central force). A second way to characterize these works looks more at the question of form, characterizing works perhaps in terms of the degree of their departure from "realist" traditions in the novel in favor of more experimental forms (i.e., how far does a given novel go in disrupting our expectations as to what a novel should be?). A third way can take the form of creating a canon of the allegedly most important works of postmodernism. And a fourth method organizes texts thematically rather than chronologically around key issues or topics.

Which of these techniques for herding postmodernist texts, which principles of selection, have I employed in this book? To some extent I draw upon all four approaches. But the simple answer is that I have organized the book thematically, highlighting novels and stories that use *postmodernist style* to address key *social concerns arising in postmodernity*. While I have included discussion of works by well-known, canonized postmodernists, I have used a broad strategy that also includes works by less often-cited, but relevant, writers. In order to avoid too many spoilers, my approach has been to minimize plot summary and instead focus on the social issues the chosen works seek to illuminate.

In one of my earlier works, *Fifteen Jugglers, Five Believers: Literary Politics and the Poetics of Social Movements* (1992), I called the writing that emerges from these political and critical positions *postmodernist realism*.[7] This names at once a mode of writing and a mode of reading, one that features self-reflexive, realism-disrupting techniques identified as postmodern, but places those techniques in tension with real knowledge claims and with realistic, radically pragmatic political needs. It is a mode of reading in the sense that any novel is given to multiple interpretations, and thus the selection of elements to emphasize is a critical and political choice.

There are works using postmodernist style that seem to have little concern for social issues, and there are contemporary works of fiction that show concern for social issues but that use more traditional ("realist") aesthetic styles. I have respect for both of these other broad tendencies, but my focus will be on works that show how *postmodernist aesthetic forms can be used to illuminate social conditions and social issues* particular to our time. This approach is supported by the observation that even some writers like John Updike and Philip Roth, who often wrote in more traditional veins, chose a postmodernist style when addressing certain aspects of postmodernity.[8]

The great Russian literary theorist M. M. Bakhtin argued that a key feature of the novel was that it could draw into itself every other kind of discourse, including the languages and jargons of journalism, sport, science, business, philosophy, historical writing, cultural criticism, and any other arena of life, as well as all the other verbal arts like songs, poetry, and drama. And through this process he called *heteroglossia*, the novel can put these various linguistic expressions, and usually discreet areas of social life, into dialog in ways they seldom are in daily life.[9] The novels I survey in this book employ various techniques to show up the ideological limits of what passes for the real in society and realism in literature in order to contribute to the construction of a different world.

As Linda Hutcheon argued in her influential book, *The Politics of Postmodernism*, much postmodernist fiction uses formal innovation to critique and undermine the cultural "master narratives" of the West. In the case of postmodern neo-slave narratives by writers like Ishmael Reed, Toni Morrison, Octavia Butler, Paul Beatty, and Colson Whitehead, the attack on master narratives is literally and literarily an attack on slave masters.[10] But a myriad of other narratives that favor the wealthy, the powerful, the normative, and the privileged also receive their comeuppance from postmodern fictionists. That is a key reason that postmodernism has been under attack, an attack intensified during the rise of Donald Trump in the United States, Brexit in the United Kingdom, and other manifestations of right-wing, nationalist pseudo-populism. Of late, the masters (patriarchs, misogynists, racists, xenophobes, homophobes, Islamophobes, anti-Semites, and economic exploiters, among other authoritarians) have been reasserting themselves more openly. Questions can be raised, and I will raise them in the course of this book, about the wisdom and effectiveness of some postmodern political strategies, but in general the fiction created in this era has been on the side of radically democratic work for racial and gender equality, recognition of multiple forms of sexual identification and expression, economic fairness, pluralism in religious expression, and in support of those forced to emigrate due to terrorism, religious intolerance, political repression, poverty induced by corporate globalization, and the impact of climate change. The premise of this book, then, is that postmodern fiction includes interesting, important, and aesthetically exciting things and politically important things to say about this world. Novels alone do not change the world, but they can play a role in shaping the sensibility of those who resist master narratives, those who engage in social movements and the other forces that bring about real change.

Where some postmodernist art opens itself to randomness and formal eclecticism solely to undermine what authors see as outdated literary forms, postmodernist realism breaks the illusion of aesthetic autonomy for a different reason—to point out the political logic through which even oppositional art has been turned into a commodity under late capitalism. In the face of such incorporative power, only an explicitly political analysis of the ideological stakes of this formal play can make form effective in challenging entrenched power. Postmodernist realism is based on the premise that politically effective texts today need both the self-conscious play of "literary" forms that open up new ways of seeing and being, and an analytic framework that articulates the social, political, and economic forces that play through and around texts. Sometimes these texts do this work quite explicitly. At other times, these politics are more subtle and I bring them forth through interpretation and contextualization.

Much critique of postmodern fiction has focused on radically experimental writing by a wave of 1960s writers, most of whom were white males (Ronald Sukenick, John Barth, William Gaddis, William Gass, and Donald Barthelme, among others) who were the first to be identified as a group of postmodernists. Much of the criticism of postmodernism as a kind of empty formalism focuses on this generation, a group dedicated to breaking each and every rule of fiction writing. And while some of these works verge on the unreadable in their endless formalistic self-reference, these works too contributed in important ways to the general task of dismantling master discourses. They also freed subsequent writers to more selectively and pointedly apply disruptive techniques that challenged politically regressive elements of narrative.

To take but one example, novels labeled as self-indulgent aesthetic exercises full of randomness might well be helping readers learn to live with, and even enjoy, the randomness generated by a world supersaturated with random information. If, as postmodern theorists have argued, we are kept in our place, kept from questioning our role in a clearly imperfect set of social systems, by narratives, by the kind of stories we tell ourselves and each other, then every breaking up of the standard storytelling methods can have some liberating impacts, both socially and personally. As postmodern electronic fictionist Shelley Jackson suggests,

> The purpose of the innovative is, I think, to wake us up. We are not quite alive, most of the time; we occupy a sort of cartoon version of our lives, its lines made smooth by repetition. Writing can open the seams in that world, reintroduce us to the real lives that we have forgotten. Maybe all good writing

is innovative in some sense, in that it shows or tells or makes you feel something you never felt before—something for which you have no cartoon ready.[11]

Put differently, if our lives have become bad, formulaic novels, then formal fictional innovation can make us more alive to the world's possibilities.

In any event, a number of literary critics recently claimed to have found a lessening of interest in radical experimentalism, and more concern with referencing the "real world" among twenty-first-century writers. Mary Holland, for example, in her important book, *Succeeding Postmodernism* (2014), argues that especially after the turn of the new century, the radical experimentalism that somewhat narrowed audiences, and made direct engagement with social issues more difficult, has lessened among a new generation of postmodernists, as well as in the careers of some postmodern authors from earlier generations.[12] She argues that in some writers there is a shift from the problem of language (how we make meaning) to a greater concern with the question of what meanings we need to make in an era where truth is hard to find. This tendency is less about embracing older forms of realism, she argues, than about finding the realism in the postmodern.

I find Holland's argument generally compelling. But in order to make it, I think she exaggerates the lack of socially relevant engagement by earlier postmodernists. As I have suggested, I believe there has been from the beginning of the postmodern era a strand of *postmodernist realism*, a strand that uses postmodernist techniques to tackle the kind of questions Holland raises. Like many critics, Holland evokes without citing allegedly "nihilist" tendencies in early postmodern fiction. While there may be elements of "nihilism" in some strands of postmodern fiction, I think critics often confuse nihilism with skepticism and authors with their characters. Some postmodernists have given us portraits of nihilism, have illuminated aspects of nihilism in the era of postmodernity, but that is not the same as embracing nihilism. Indeed, it is hard to know why any nihilist would bother to write a 200-page novel, let alone a 1,000-page one, as did some of the experimentalists who are presumably the target of these claims.

Many first-generation postmodernists worked to radically sweep aside every possible literary convention, assaulting every norm of literary construction and readerly consumption. They include amusing and amazing tour de force works, defying even the basics of grammar and syntax, such as Donald Barthelme's story, "The Sentence," a several pages-long unpunctuated single sentence in which the sentence itself becomes a kind of character. But lest we believe that such experiments no longer apply, Lucy Ellman's novel

Ducks, Newburyport (2019) takes Barthelme's task to the tenth power, since it consists of a single 426,100-word sentence covering 1,000 pages. Her novel is a rich exploration of dozens of troubling topics facing contemporary citizens, and the form is itself very much a commentary on the rapid, chaotic flow of discourse in this internet-driven era.

But, as Holland and several critics have recently elaborated, while exceptions like Ellman's novel and the equally experimental Mark Z. Danielewski's rich *House of Leaves* (2000) continue to be written in the twenty-first century, there has been a general tendency over time for the most wildly experimental forms of postmodernism to give way to ones that, while still critical of "realism" as a conservative ideology, tend to retain more recognizable elements of traditional fiction. This proves true not only for later generations, but for the careers of writers whose works span several decades. In a sense, all writers who have written since the experimentalists, however realistic or traditional their styles, are postmodernist because their use of these older forms proceeds in light of, or in the shadow of, their thorough dismantling by their recent predecessors.

I would also add that among the factors leading to somewhat less extreme forms of postmodernist stylistic play among some (but clearly not all) twenty-first-century writers is some sense that postmodernism has to a large degree done its work in popularizing the idea that realism is an extremely slippery concept. And, more important, that at a time where truth seems harder and harder to come by, we need an accessible and clear presentation of postmodern truths, truths rooted in fact and revelatory of the processes by which facts can be manipulated untruthfully.

Is Postmodernism a Zombie?

As I have noted, every aspect of things postmodern has been contested, even the spelling (to hyphen, post-modern, or not to hyphen?). This includes starting points and ending points for both postmodernity as a condition and postmodernism as a set of aesthetic choices. Many of these questions are academic, in the sense where academic is a synonym for nonsensical. But some consideration of the starting and possible ending points for postmodernist fiction can help clarify certain aspects of the approach taken by this book. Postmodern theory acknowledges that origin stories are a particularly powerful, in many respects, determining, kind of fiction, so it is important to ask what power plays are at work in such stories.

What critics call *periodizing* can be a complex issue, though again, less so if one remembers that it is only a convenient concept, not some creature that must be captured and caged (an especially difficult task since postmodernists are more like the Yeti or the Loch Ness Monster than a tiger or lion). In terms of postmodernity as a set of social conditions, in his influential book, *The Postmodern Condition*, Jean-François Lyotard argued that postmodernity began in the wake of the Second World War. That makes sense in general, given the way that war broke the twentieth century in half, though one would add that awareness of specifically postmodern conditions emerged only over the next several decades and the label "postmodernity" did not gain wide acceptance until the 1980s, and always controversially.

In terms of periodizing the fiction, the first question that has troubled some critics trying to cage the phenomenon, is that there appear to be postmodernists writing before the postmodern era. There are (at least) two equally plausible solutions to the fact that there seem to be postmodernists avant la lettre, before the time, let's say April 1, 1960, when the postmodernism this book is primarily concerned with began.

One type of answer is also given in *The Postmodern Condition* which addressed postmodernism as a cultural style too, arguing that it is not a unique style or set of styles but rather a recurring one, an attitude toward language and the real that has occurred in various historical periods of intense societal self-consciousness (at the end of the Greek and Roman empires, for example). That makes a good deal of sense, especially given the suspicious approach of postmodernists to claims of absolute newness or originality.

Or, second, we can argue, as some critics have, that when a new literary movement arises it creates its own progenitors. In this view, the fact that many aspects of a postmodern sensibility and style can be seen in authors writing before the era of postmodernity is a kind of retrospective projection, rather than a contradiction. That would mean, for example, that certain writers like Gertrude Stein, Jorge Luis Borges, Franz Kafka, and the James Joyce of *Finnegans Wake*, as well as many s/f novels, seem postmodern only after postmodernism proper has emerged in the era of postmodernity.

For our purposes, given the parameters I have laid out above in which a specific historical period is matched to a particular set of literary techniques and attitudes, either of these explanations works fine. It matters not whether those writers whose postmodern style seems to precede postmodernity by decades are seen as particularly sensitive to, or prescient about, trends that became more readily apparent after the Second World War, or if it is only the rise of postmodern criticism that allows us to see hitherto less visible aspects of postmodern style in earlier writers.

What about the question of an endpoint for postmodernism? In one sense, postmodernism has been dying since it was born, given that few have ever embraced the term wholeheartedly. (And, as that postmodernist Nobel Laureate Bob Dylan once sang, "he not busy being born is busy dying.") As one exasperated critic put it, "Surely no one would argue seriously for retaining the words Modernism and Postmodernism if we could think of anything better. And what does it say about us that we can't? As terms, Modernism and Postmodernism are something we have to live with."[13] We do seem to be stuck with these terms, even if no one is particularly happy about that fact. Despite many attempts to declare it dead in every decade since it was first proposed, postmodernism just doesn't seem to want to die. Reports of its death have accelerated in the twenty-first century. Even the critic who has arguably done the most interesting work elaborating the kind of politics of postmodern fiction embraced by this book, Linda Hutcheon, jumped on the death of pomo bandwagon.[14] But the problem has been that none of the terms suggested for a successor movement, and there have been lots of them—critical realism, hypermodernism, altermodernism, digimodernism, metamodernism, speculative realism, even, horror of horrors, post-postmodernism—has stuck. Some of this seeking out the new is interesting in specifying certain bodies of work, but much of it just seems like critics worried that they need a new product, a new brand, to sell in the academic or artistic marketplace.

There have now been dozens of these "death of postmodernism" essays. But clearly, postmodernism makes Lazarus look like a cheap trickster. No matter how often it is killed, it rises again. Given this fact, one critic has suggested that it is now a "zombie concept," continuing to act alive though actually dead. This is an interesting solution, though many would note that given the discomfort that has always accompanied the term, we might have to argue that it was born a zombie. Or perhaps it is time to remember that concepts are not in fact subject to life and death. They are just concepts. True, some seem to "outlive" their usefulness. But few ever actually die.

There is also a worry among many critics that postmodern style, like modernism before it, has become commodified, tamed, made to serve the very forces it seeks to critique. There is certainly truth in this. The rise of things calling themselves "postmodern advertising," "postmodern management," and the like surely suggests this, as does the use of the term as a modifier for every pop culture trend coming down the pike. But unlike the modernists, postmodernists seem to realize that to abandon a concept because it is misused is to misunderstand concepts, misunderstand that they can always be misused. That is the reason postmodernists do not simply trash modernists, but rather seek to use and partially redirect what is best in their predecessors' work. Likewise, the popularity of postmodernism as an idea, in such things as the adoption of "meta" as a term applied to any pop culture text alluding to another pop culture text, can be built upon as a basis for digging more deeply into the problem of the real. If truth and the real have become increasingly difficult to locate in the era of postmodernity, it may well be that certain kinds of postmodern writing that has long dealt with these questions may be our best route to real, useable truths.

In any event, this book is premised on the notion that while postmodernism is/was not one thing, not one agreed-upon thing, there is enough agreement as to some of the things it was/is that its path can be traced over many decades and that its footsteps are still traceable in works of fiction well into the twenty-first century. Perhaps the best way to answer periodizing questions is to say that postmodernism began when critics started using the term, and postmodernism will end when critics stop using the term altogether.

How to Use This Book

In this book, for the sake of space and coherence, I have limited myself to works written in English. I have chosen to emphasize texts that speak in important ways to the lived complexities of life in the twenty-first century, and that lend themselves to the struggle to achieve a more just set of social relations. Where many books of this type focus on a few well-celebrated writers of the twentieth century, I have also sought to focus on a number of writers who emerged in the twenty-first century (after the alleged death of postmodernism), and to write about not only the most well-known, canonical postmodern writers but also those who have not received as much critical attention.

Any summary of a book is deeply inadequate. If a book can be adequately summarized, it need not be a book. This inadequacy is much deeper when the book in question is a novel. In novels, form and content, style and substance are utterly entwined, rendering character descriptions and plot summaries deeply misleading. As one frustrated reviewer put it, "If plot were the crucial measure, there'd be no difference between a story about the fish that got away and *Moby-Dick*." Novels have plots and ideas, but novels are not made of plots and ideas. They are made of words, words arranged with loving precision, rhythm, sound, shape, and even taste. The form words take is what makes literature literary. No summary can capture that.

True, some sense of the style of a story can be gained from quotations, and I have tied to give excerpts that capture a bit of the unique element of each novel's language. But copyright laws and space constraints limit books like the one you are reading to a small number of those. And while as I suggested, plot is often secondary in fiction, in some novels the unfolding of plot lines is very dependent upon a certain order of revelation, so in those cases I have tried to avoid "spoilers" as best I can. (This is not always a problem. As one wag quipped in reference to the classic modernist novel *Death in Venice*: "Spoiler alert: He dies in Venice.") The question of thematic summary is even more fraught, since such comments sound like nonfiction that miss entirely the literary qualities that provide the unique insights of the novels in question. It should also be noted that works I treat under one of my thematic chapter rubrics often fit as well under one or another of the rubrics. None of the novels I discuss can be adequately understood solely through the particular theme I focus on for this book. In sum, the issues I highlight in a particular novel never exhaust its range of concerns, and it is not possible to convey fully the unique literary qualities and pleasures that make a given book worth reading.

All of this simply means that there is absolutely no substitute for reading these novels. In addition to relatively brief presentations of key examples of each theme, at points I make even briefer mention of numerous other relevant examples, both works by the most well-known authors and excellent ones by less-known authors. In this way I hope to acknowledge the breadth of possibilities, and lead a wide range of readers to find other novels that might capture their imaginations. In order to address many different books, I have confined myself for the most part to descriptions rather than elaborated interpretations, and I have focused centrally on their cultural and political themes as related through postmodernist stylistic features. I try to point out some postmodern literary features of each of the books in question, but have done so just enough to encourage readers to apply ideas from the section of Chapter 2 on style in their own analyses. A final note of irony: this book itself is decidedly *un*postmodern in its linear structure. That's yet another reason to remember that this book exists only to point you toward the real books (and not the movies made from some of them, most of which are poor representations of the novels).

In the chapters that follow I examine ways in which postmodern realist texts can help to illuminate what it feels like to live life under postmodern conditions, and how we might best adapt to and thrive under those conditions. Chapter 2 outlines the two aspects of postmodernist realism: some of the major conditions of postmodernity and various elements of postmodernist style. Chapter 3 turns to the novels, looking at postmodern conceptions of the self, and questions of identity in the postmodern era. Chapter 4 examines the changing conceptions of the sexuality, the body and bodily pleasures as driven by both changing social thought and biotechnologies. Chapter 5 treats changing social and literary conceptions of the family and family life in the postmodern era. Chapter 6 treats postmodern reconceptualizations of the nature of history-writing as they shape and are shaped by literature. Chapter 7 deals with postmodern literary re-writes that reimagine the political and cultural meaning of certain novels from earlier eras. Chapter 8 looks at the literature of geographic and cultural dislocation and creative relocation made necessary by war, terrorism, migration, economic transformation, and other forces of postmodernity. Chapter 9 analyzes the fusing of nonfiction and fiction forms by postmodernists to challenge static notions of truth. And Chapter 10 looks into the future, tracing works that examine how the increasingly digitized nature of our lives will continue to reshape our experience, and how looming threats like neo-fascism and the climate crisis will be averted or come to pass depending on the nature of the stories we tell ourselves and each other.

2

Postmodern Conditions and Postmodernist Styles

Like everything else surrounding the term "postmodern," the factors and forces constituting a postmodern condition, or better, postmodern conditions, have been subject to much debate. However, this is hardly unique to postmodernity. The characteristic aspects of any historical period are subject to debate. There are, however, several areas that have been widely accepted as characterizing postmodernity or the postmodern era. In outlining some of these issues, I want to include both certain general, abstract conceptualizations arising from postmodern theory and some more specific, concrete sociopolitical, cultural, and economic developments. The first important caveat, one not always acknowledged in high-level theory, is that all postmodern conditions are experienced very differently depending upon one's geographic, economic, and social location. There are few, if any, postmodern conditions that equally impact all people on the planet. Even the planetary threat of climate change is already affecting different regions and classes of people differently. So, as I lay out these conditions, I will try to specify some of these differing impacts, but I will leave to the chapters that follow more detailed representations of how various postmodern forces and factors are embodied and embedded in particular lives.

Postmodern Economic, Political, and Social Conditions

As with every other aspect of the question, the starting date of postmodernity is contested. Some place it at the end of the Second World War; others see the beginning as the 1960s. My own sense is that the war makes an excellent marker in terms of historical breaks but that the 1960s was perhaps the moment when the era became conscious of itself as an era, if initially primarily among artists and certain segments of the intelligentsia.

While the term "postmodern" had been used on and off for several decades, the translation and publication in 1984 of French philosopher Jean-François Lyotard's short book, *The Postmodern Condition: A Report on Knowledge*, touched off extensive discussion of *postmodernity* as a descriptor for contemporary life in the English-speaking world.[1]

Originally published in French in 1979, Lyotard's book, subtitled "a report on knowledge," is a series of observations on the state of knowledge and belief. In particular, he claimed that the postmodern era is characterized by "incredulity" toward *gran recits*. *Gran recits* is generally translated as "metanarratives" but could be more colloquially translated as "big stories." This incredulity means unwillingness to believe in the big stories—religious, philosophical, political, and historical—that claim to explain the overarching character or meaning of history and human existence. Whether it be belief in historical progress, scientific truth, metaphysical essence or all-encompassing political systems, Lyotard claimed the postmodern era would challenge singular, totalizing belief systems, preferring instead the proliferation of *petit recits*, more modest stories, more partial or local truths. While this is clearly a partial truth, it is also apparent that the postmodern era is still filled with people who maintain or believe master narratives—religious, political, and every other kind. A more accurate claim would be that a significant sector of the intelligentsia and a swath of the wider public became skeptical of *gran recits*.

Lyotard suggests that two primary factors or forces have given rise to this skeptical stance, one from the recent past, the other from an emerging future. To posit a new era one must, of necessity, relate it to what has gone before. Many of those positing a postmodern condition, including Lyotard, argue that it was the Second World War that dealt a death blow to key intellectual components of modernity. In the wake of the horrors of that war, especially the Nazi holocaust, the dropping of atomic bombs on Hiroshima and Nagasaki, and the crimes of Soviet totalitarianism under Stalin, it was simply impossible to believe the story of an ever-upward trajectory of human progress toward greater and greater enlightenment. The modern exalting of faith in human reason that began in the humanist Renaissance of the sixteenth century, and grew more central in the seventeenth-century-European Enlightenment, came to a crashing end in the ever so rationally organized Nazi concentration camps that extinguished the lives of millions of Jewish, gay, communist, disabled, and otherwise "unfit" women, men, and children, the incineration of thousands of Japanese civilians by the "good side" of the war, and the transformation of a revolutionary political ideology into a barbaric cult of authoritarian personality in the USSR.

The second of Lyotard's causal factors, one looking not backward in time but presciently forward from 1979 when he offered his analysis, cites the then still relatively undeveloped world of computerized communication. Lyotard presciently argued that the future will be characterized by the increasing power of what we now call digital cultures with their tendency to generate competing, irreconcilably different narratives. He welcomed this pluralism of possibilities as a far healthier state of the world, but also acknowledged that it would generate a great deal of disruption.

Lyotard's analysis of this disruption remained rather abstract, but his analysis was welcomed by many in the intelligentsia who sensed wide shifts in the economic, social, political, and cultural spheres that had as yet no name. If postmodernity became something of a grab bag term, it touched on some fruitful discussion of the new, if not wholly novel, elements of the post–Second World War era. While that era is now more than half a century old, no alternative name or set of divisions of this time period has yet gained the currency of the term "postmodernity." But given this long time frame, each of the elements described as central to postmodernity has itself undergone significant transformation, such that the conditions of postmodernity have in some respects varied from decade to decade.

Decolonization and Revolutionary Movements

If the horrors of the Second World War produced a good deal of skepticism about human progress, the struggles to undo the horrors of European colonialism in the postwar years set in motion a more directed critique of who did and who decidedly did not benefit from Western notions of the "progress" and economic development. The critique of Western culture, that forms a key part of postmodern thought, stems to a great degree from a series of decolonization struggles in the aftermath of the Second World War. The decline and fall of the British and other European empires, including the Gandhi-led nonviolent revolution in India, and revolts across Africa, Asia, the Middle East and Latin America, profoundly reshaped both the Global South and the Global North. Postmodernity includes what came to be called *postcolonial* conditions in which previous colonial domination has been incompletely overthrown and morphed into *neocolonial* relationships, especially as driven by the United States, in which less direct forms of colonial rule have been imposed through economic and/or cultural means, intermittently backed by military intervention.

One key branch of postmodern theory, poststructuralism, is sometimes dismissed as the product of privileged white French males, but of the five most cited of these authors two (Barthes and Foucault) were gay in a still decidedly homophobic context, one (Derrida) was by origin not a native of France but rather an Algerian Jew, and one (Kristeva) was neither a male nor French but a woman and a Bulgarian immigrant. Only one (Lacan) more or less fits the straight white Paris-born label. While these writers often wrote at a high level of abstraction seemingly quite removed from the rough and tumble of political life, all of them were profoundly shaped by the social change movements of their time, including anti-colonialism (Algeria and Vietnam most directly), and the massive uprising in France known as *Mai '68*, a key moment that coalesced many of the rebellions of the 1960s.[2]

The anti-colonial struggles of the 1950s and 1960s also inspired numerous marginalized groups in all regions of the globe—women, people of color, those oppressed due to their sex/gender identities, Indigenous peoples, persecuted castes and classes, as well as ethnic and religious minorities—to decolonize their lives through cultural and political movements. The social movements of the 1960s and 1970s profoundly shaped both postmodern theory and postmodern literary expression. Indeed, social movements are in many respects the key impetus behind the new theories and the new literature. Millions of previously overlooked, oppressed, or underrepresented people achieved new forms of cultural power in the postmodern era.

Political Economy

Early discussions of postmodernity sometimes used the term "postindustrial" to describe socioeconomic shifts in the latter half of the twentieth century.

This has proven to be a highly problematic concept since it elides the fact that not only does traditional industrial production (of automobiles and all manner of material goods) persist, but the increasing centrality of symbolic production (mass media, digital culture, etc.) is still dependent upon an industrial base, as anyone visiting a cellphone factory can attest. While ever greater numbers of symbolic products are available to more and more people around the globe due to new electronic media, often quite exploitative material processes go into the production of the very devices that enable consumption of images—TV sets, computers, cell phones, video games, and so on. Thus the conception of the postindustrial (and related terms like "postmaterial" or "information economy") draws attention away from ongoing material production and the dependence of symbolic production on factories that often entail horrendous labor practices and serious environmental degradation through e-waste.[3]

Terms like "postindustrial" do point to significant economic changes that have profoundly impacted the lives of millions of people, both positive and negative. While the term is highly misleading as a general description, it accurately describes many locales. Many places have witnessed a decline in certain traditional industries and the higher-paying blue-collar jobs they provided. Two main forces, automation and outsourcing from "overdeveloped" to "underdeveloped" countries, account for much of this decline in the Global North. Cities like Detroit in the United States and Manchester in the United Kingdom were devastated by this economic shift. This has often occurred without shifting many of those workers into the newer information sector, instead relegating them to lower-paying jobs in the service sector. While many of the lost factory jobs in the overdeveloped world have not been replaced by equivalent ones in the new economy, in the Global South the new economic system has moved millions of people who were previously not part of industrial society, people whose lives were lived primarily as peasants or agricultural workers, into industrial production, sometimes in ways that have improved their lives, at other times through dangerous conditions that seem a throwback to what the poet William Blake called "dark satanic mills" of the 1800s. Since these global economies are deeply shaped not only by class stratification, but also by race, ethnicity, and gender, these shifts have brought about major changes in social life in and beyond the workplace all over the world.

Cultural theorist Fredric Jameson argues that postmodern fiction and the other arts bear in their very style the mark of these economic transformations and their attendant social dislocations. In *Postmodernism, or The Cultural*

Logic of Late Capitalism, Jameson develops the idea that a new stage of capitalist economic development, *multinational capitalism*, profoundly shapes the art produced under postmodernity. He posits that a new fractious, fragmented, and globally scattered production process, combined with the increasing importance of symbolic image production (mass media and digital culture), is mirrored in many postmodern aesthetic objects.[4] Jameson is making a complex causal analysis, but it is perhaps more convincing as a set of analogies between the economy and cultural production. In any event, it is clear that political economic decisions have played a key role in driving postmodern conditions into ever more fragmented and globally complicated directions that have shaped the production of fiction and other art forms, or been their underlying subject matter.

The political economic system of postmodernity has been conceived as passing through two major phases, a Cold War bilateral phase, followed by the multilateral, but capitalist, dominant later phase. The first phase led to a devastatingly wasteful and dangerous nuclear arms race that distorted the US economy and eventually helped bankrupt the Soviet Union. The fall of the iron curtain between the former Soviet empire and Western Europe greatly transformed the lives of millions of eastern Europeans, for better and for worse, and also eliminated the main alternative economic force.

Postmodern economic globalization was accelerated by the end of the Cold War and the consequent dominance of a period of capitalism known as *neoliberalism*. While putatively a new form of "free market" economy, neoliberalism has generally meant increasing concentrations of economic (and thereby often political) power in fewer large, multinational mega-corporations. This has in turn contributed to growing economic inequality in most countries around the globe, and set up various complicated relationships between nation states and transnational economic forces. Neoliberalism has coincided with the deepening of post- and neo*colonialism*, the economic rather than direct political domination of the Global North over the rest of the world. This includes *cultural imperialism*, the domination of other national traditions through cultural products (TV, film, video games, etc.) created and circulated by corporations in the overdeveloped nations, especially the United States, Japan, and certain European countries. While new networks, economic and technological, allow flows of culture from multiple locations around the globe, the overdeveloped world's culture industries continue to dominate this process due to greater economic resources.[5] The fall of communism in the Soviet Union and its accommodation to elements of capitalism in China have had profound impact around the globe, including the dissolution of the so-called social safety net in many democracies, increasing inequality within most nations on earth, and the contributing to the rise of new right-wing social movements.

Some degree of economic globalization has existed for at least the last 500 years (since Europeans set out on their colonial "adventures"). Because of this long history, critics disagree about the extent to which the most recent manifestation of postmodern neoliberal globalization is wholly new. But most agree that beginning sometime around the 1970s (just as postmodern fiction was becoming widely acknowledged), certain novel features of a transnational political, economic, and cultural system were emerging. Particularly when viewed in combination, these new features represent a significant change in global power relations that became much more acutely felt after the end of the Cold War. The key elements of globalization include the increased role played by transnational organizations like the World Bank, the International Monetary Fund (IMF), and the World Trade Organization (WTO); a weakened role for national governments and an increase in the power of multi- or transnational corporate power; new economic practices that greatly intensify the segmenting of the labor force by distributing various parts of the production process around the globe rather than centralizing it in one nation; and new digitized global communications network.

Critics of corporate globalization argue that these interlocking institutions and practices have intensified environmental degradation, undermined worker rights and human rights, exacerbated a worldwide health crisis, and facilitated cultural domination by the corporate media of the United States and other parts of the English-speaking world. They argue that transnational corporations, located primarily in the seven most developed nations (the United States, Canada, France, Germany, Japan, Italy, and Britain), have used organizations like the WTO, the World Bank, and the IMF to serve their profit interests at the expense of workers and the middle class, worldwide. By acting transnationally or globally, these corporations have been able to circumvent basic human rights once guaranteed by national governments, and sink standards of worker and environmental protection to the lowest level available.

The main mechanism through which a neoliberal corporate order has been imposed on the developing world has been *structural adjustment programs* (SAPs). In structural adjustment, a developing nation's government is obligated to transform its economy to better serve First World corporations if it wants to receive loans from the IMF, World Bank, or avoid trade sanctions from the WTO. Corporate globalizers call this a necessary transition. Critics call it multinational blackmail. This process of imposed structural adjustment has included devaluing national currencies, turning government-run industries over to private corporations, lowering environmental standards, limiting or eliminating workers' right to unionize or strike for better conditions, and cutting social services, such as child care, public education, health care, or unemployment insurance. While the worst impact of these processes has been vastly increased poverty in the southern hemisphere, globalization has also rebounded back on the industrialized Global North, hurting workers and virtually all other citizens who are not corporate executives, and increasing income inequality there as well.

The collapse of communism after 1989 brought with it the collapse of much of the welfare state system in the overdeveloped world and virtually all other ameliorating social mechanisms in the rest of the world. The presence of an alternative economic system in the Soviet model, however deeply problematic it was, as well as the demands of the new social movements, forced the capitalist world to provide services, basic rights, and a social safety net (especially in the social democratic countries) that have now been rolled back. In the Global South, various nationalist and socialist efforts to lessen the impact of unrestrained markets were eliminated through structural adjustment. In the overdeveloped world, similar benefits were eliminated through the deregulation of industry and the shrinking of government services. According to neoliberal theory, "freer markets" should increase market power and eventually raise everyone's level of income. According to critics of corporate globalization, including those who formed a massive *anti-globalization protest movement*,[6] what has happened instead is a "global race to the bottom," in which countries competing for the most exploitable, least expensive labor force have progressively degraded the environment, undercut local self-sufficiency, lowered the quality of life for most workers, and left more than one billion people without any work at all. Whatever gains have been made in lowering the overall level of poverty have been overshadowed by an exponential growth in the amount of economic inequality between the 1 percenters of the world that Occupy Wall Street called out and the rest of humanity.

Globalization

Many of the ways in which economic dislocations have occurred are captured by the term "globalization," but globalization is about more than political economy. While certain degrees and kinds of globalization have existed throughout human history, the extent and nature of globalization as a feature of the postmodern era is unique. While, as noted, producing things like those glittering digital devices that delight wealthy North Americans and Europeans has been extraordinarily disruptive in the Global South, so too has the spread of mass media and digital culture across borders. Cultural theorist Arjun Appadurai posits five different arenas of global transformation in the postmodern era: *ethnoscapes*—disruption caused by the increased migration of people across cultures and national borders; *mediascapes*—the opening by mass media, especially TV, film, and the internet, of vast new perspectives on the world; *technoscapes*—the impact of computer technology on all aspects of work and personal life; *financescapes*—the increased domination of a single economic system, neoliberal multinational capitalism, in complicated relationship with the nation state; and *ideoscapes*—the increased circulation of ideas and ideologies from all realms, social, cultural, economic, and political.[7] Appadurai should have added that each of these "scapes" has had an impact on the *enviro*scape, on the natural world, including the rise of vital environmentalist discourses. The global flows in each of these arenas have been powerful in isolation, but they also overlap and combine in various ways that have brought an extraordinary degree of creative, cultural, and cross-cultural change, and both positive and negative disruptive challenges to traditions, values, and other settled social conditions.

Migration and Multiculturalization

Each of these aspects of postmodern political economy and globalization have contributed to a vast expansion of emigration and in migration (migration within a given nation). The percentage of the world's population living outside the nation of their birth has never been greater than in the postmodern era. By 2020, over 275 million people were classified as migrants. The massive economic dislocations discussed above have been a major factor, but in addition terrorism, war, ethnic cleansing, political repression, and climate change have driven unprecedented numbers of people from their homelands. This in turn has created many new *diasporas* (pockets of immigrant life outside of homelands), including new kinds of diasporas with a higher degree of contact with former homelands due to new communication technologies.

The massive migrations mean that increased multiculturalization is an undeniable fact of postmodern history. Over the last several decades, due to all the forces named above, virtually every country in the world has seen an increase in the number of residents of ethnic and cultural backgrounds that differ from their historically dominant populations. This has transformed all layers of society, bringing both highly positive forms of diversity and deep ethno-racial tensions. Multiculturalism as a political concept has a range of ideological variations, from reactionary to conservative to liberal to left radical versions, each with very different notions of how multiethnic societies should function. But in recent decades, conservative resistance to the fact of cultural diversity has countered the longer trend since the Second World War of accepting or celebrating the positive contributions of such diversity. Literature has reflected profoundly upon the dislocations and creative relocations these cultural migrations have entailed.

Identity Fluidity

Decolonization, migration, and new movements for ethno-racial, gender, and sexual equality challenged the centrality of a *liberal humanist self* that claimed to be universal, but was in fact marked by the particularities of whiteness, maleness, and middle-classness that did not represent the actual range of humanity. In response to this critique and the social movements of the era, identities of all kinds have been challenged and new definitions of human rights have been put in place in key institutions. At the level of postmodernist theory, this has been characterized as a general psycho-social "decentering," "fragmenting," and otherwise undermining of the singular, coherent self. Some postmodernists have translated this decentering into a wholesale notion of liberation from stable identities and a call for a positive profusion of possibilities. Other theorists have been careful to argue that social and linguistic constraints on identity are extremely difficult to overcome. Critics have also noted that a generalized theoretical claim for a "decentered" identity fails to consider how this might be impacting folks whose identities have never been centered, who have been pushed to the margins of cultures structured by dominating racial, ethnic, class, and sex/gender hierarchies.

The fear here is that because political change is often based in collective identities, the critique of all *essential identities*—identities based in some unchangeable essence of gender or race or LGBTQIA2S+ identities—undermines the basis of social change. In response to this problem, notions like *strategic essentialism*, a kind of necessary fiction of commonality, have been theorized as a basis of collective action that does not permanently lock people into identities initially imposed upon them by oppressive notions of racial, gender, or sexual stereotyping. The notion of different "races," for example, has been thoroughly debunked as a largely meaningless concept by contemporary biological science, and replaced by historical analyses of how such social categories have been constructed in particular ways under particular (and changeable) social conditions over time.[8] Postmodern realists have used many of the techniques elaborated in the second part of this chapter to represent this complex understanding of identity.

Identity issues were increasingly seen to be complexly *intersectional*, to involve multiple categories like race, gender, sex, class, region, and ideology interweaving in particular communities.[9] This led to more nuanced analyses beyond the general critique of a dominant Western self, ones adopted and adapted to the needs of a variety of specific forms of decolonization and political resistance. Identities have become fiercely contested formations, and the work of postmodern realist fiction writers from previously marginalized communities has been crucial in redefining socially constructed identities, and in rewriting literary and cultural histories that ignored or misrepresented them. This has led to powerful new perspectives on life under postmodern conditions for those outside dominant cultural formations, as well as for those who have previously been unaware of the impact of their more privileged social positionings.

These processes have entailed immense amounts of instability at all levels of society, among not only those whose power has been challenged but also among the challengers as well. The liberations entailed by the loosening of identity formations have, however, been experienced in very different ways by people in both previously marginal and historically dominant positions. Multiplicity, diversity, open-endedness, and freedom of possibility can be exhilarating, liberating. But for others mutability of identity has not been liberating but frightening, a fact that has played a role in the *rise of religious and political fundamentalisms*, and other reactionary formations that seek to turn back the clock to some age with allegedly firmer social foundations.

Terrorism

Terrorism, like globalization, has a long history that has taken on new forms in postmodernity. Another contested term, it is often pointed out that one group's terrorism is another group's liberation struggle. Due especially to new communication technologies, the ideas and deeds of terrorists have an unprecedented degree of circulation beyond their point of origin. And the most pervasive forms of terrorism are clearly linked to other postmodern conditions, especially economic and cultural imperialism from the West, and accompanying dislocations of political and religious identity. While the number of people killed and harmed by terrorism has been small compared to war, and the threat of terrorism has been greatly exaggerated by Western media, the psychological impact has been widespread and politically impactful.

Where in previous eras, knowledge of terrorist acts could often be contained, TV and the internet have allowed massive dissemination of terrorist propaganda, while its dramatic value has led to constant coverage by both mainstream and alternative social media. These new modes of representation have enabled politicians in the US and European countries to use exaggerated fear of terror to dangerously curtail the civil liberties not just of terrorists, but all citizens. The psychological, social, and ideological roots of terrorism, the role of media, and the impact on the targets of terrorism have been widely explored by postmodern realist authors.

Digitization, Information Proliferation, and Virtualization

Virtually all aspects of postmodernity are being shaped by the existence and increasing centrality of new modes of communication. A major impact of the growth in the information sector of the economy is an explosion in the amount of information—social, economic, political, and cultural—available to the billions of people who have access to the new communication technologies that circulate this information. Far more people know about sociocultural variations, about the range of possible ideas, values, experiences, and lifestyles than ever before in human history.

These technologies have also entailed an increasing sense that our reality is virtual, the sense of coming unhinged from material reality to live in a virtual one of images on screens of various sorts. Jean Baudrillard calls this *hyperreality*, a reality in which images of images of images of images circulate with no reference to the external world. The emergent technology of *virtual reality* devices when widely available will no doubt intensify this set of processes that have increasingly replaced things with images of things. This has led some fiction writers, as well as some ideologues who call themselves *posthumanists* and *transhumanists*, even to fantasize a transcendence of the body, a downloading of our brains into computers. Both science fiction writers and scientists have also warned that the increasing development of *artificial intelligence* (AI) may lead to a different kind of posthuman reality, the Singularity, or more colloquially the Robot Apocalypse, in which humans are enslaved to, or fully replaced by, intelligent machines. Cultural texts treating this very real possibility have ranged from the humorous to the tragic, presaging a range of outcomes from war (as in the *Terminator* films) to creative cooperation between humans and AIs (as in Iain Banks's "Culture" series of novels).

Virtualization processes that have shaped the sense of self of many people have been termed by one critic, *avatar fetishism*, the creation of imaginary selves inhabiting virtual spaces that increasingly inform, if not displace, other ways of imaging and experiencing reality.[10] While these processes obviously differ in degree and intensity depending on the extent of an individual's immersion in various kinds of electronically delivered cultural experiences, these phenomena shape thought and behavior in difficult-to-predict ways around much of the globe in the postmodern era. A sense of the virtuality and malleability of the self has been intensified also by the proliferation of surgical and biotechnological interventions into the human body through transplants, plastic surgery, gender reassignment surgery, technological implants and prostheses, and so on. All of these phenomena have found literary expression. Both the joys and the dangers of our increasingly digitized lives have been richly explored in fiction.

Surveillance Culture

Alongside and entangled with the creation of an increasingly virtual reality, digital technology has greatly facilitated the move toward a total *surveillance society*. The internet is proving to be the most perfect tool for surveillance ever available to the state. The interplay of corporate social media and the state has made possible the almost total elimination of personal and political privacy. The paranoia that has been pointed to as a feature of some early postmodern fiction is looking increasingly prophetic, like an intimation of a digitized reality where the state and corporations have ever greater power to surveil and manipulate the lives of citizens. What is perhaps most ominous about the possible rise of what might be called digital totalitarianism is that it is likely to arrive not through military takeover, but through our addiction to the pleasures of our technological playgrounds.[11]

Nuclear Proliferation and Climate Crises

As with the economy, there is a twofold structure to what might be called the threat of *postmodern apocalypse*. While all the factors above have transformed the world in radical ways, there are two forces that threaten not just transformation but annihilation. Since 1945, the world has known about the existence of nuclear weapons with the capability to destroy huge swaths of the world, if not all life on earth. Over the intervening decades, the proliferation of those weapons into the hands of more and more state actors, and now possibly nonstate terrorists, has increased the likelihood of their use. An initial panic over these weapons in the 1950s gradually gave way to a kind of domestication of this reality that only periodically erupts into a general fear, yet exists as a kind of background noise to postmodern experience, one frequently audible in postmodern fiction.

In a kind of reversal of this process, extreme climate change has grown from a background concern to become a central one around the globe. It has also grown from being a future possibility to become a present reality, through species extinction on an unprecedented scale, devastating new storms, fires and floods, and with *climate refugees* forming a significant subset of global migrants. The end of the world has been prophesied in virtually every period of human history but never before with such a rational basis. Humanity has arguably never faced such a high likelihood of devastation on a global scale as will occur if significant political action on climate change is not taken. This is a postmodern condition that, like wide-scale nuclear warfare, threatens to make all others irrelevant, since, if not forestalled, there could very well be no humans on earth to experience those conditions. Postmodern fiction writers have recently begun to tackle this threat in works focusing on both current and likely future impacts of the climate crisis through a body of work labeled climate fiction or *CliFi* for short.

This brief catalog certainly does not exhaust the range of factors and forces making up the experience of postmodernity, and hence some additional ones are treated in the chapters that follow. But this list should give some sense of the most commonly cited aspects of the postmodern condition, both liberatory and dangerous ones, that have shaped the literary imagination from the 1960s to the present.

Postmodernist Aesthetic Approaches, Styles, and Techniques

There is no plain sense of the word,
   nothing is straightforward,

description a lie behind a lie:
but truths can still be told.
—Charles Bernstein, "The Lives of Toll Takers"

Postmodern fiction has the reputation of being difficult, inaccessible. Certainly some of it is, but so are some works from every other era and in every other style of writing. Much of what makes postmodern writing seem difficult can be overcome if we make a couple of simple adjustments to our expectations and relax our grip on certain habits of reading. Most importantly, postmodernists want to free us from slavish devotion to literary techniques and assumptions that have for long (perhaps too long) been seen as essential to fiction. They challenge pretty much each and every entrenched idea about characterization, setting, plot, theme, style, and meaning. They don't do it to be difficult or perverse but to liberate us. Moreover, those writers I call postmodern realists especially want us to see the link between certain traditional ideas about fiction and repressive societal formations within postmodern conditions.

In this section I lay out the most commonly cited elements of postmodernist literary style in order to make clear both their nature and the rationale behind the choice to challenge certain traditional narrative styles. Postmodern authors draw from an entire panoply of techniques for breaking free from the verbal tricks that master narratives are built upon. At the core of postmodern aesthetics is the rather traditional idea that form and content are inseparable. The postmodern twist on this truism is that content and form are also deeply political because *literary conventions* not only reflect but *shape social conventions*. Literature is one among many modes of persuasion reality constructors use, one among many rhetorical forms that teach us how to be and how to think. Social conventions are inseparable from linguistic conventions. That means that not only in fiction but also in daily life we are taught—"know your place"—by narratives that tell us who we are and what our social role(s) should be. Even the most innocuous of these linguistic conventions can play a role in keeping people from resisting disadvantageous social conditions that might otherwise be changed. Conversely, alternative stories can empower transformation of those conditions. Any standard literary *trope* (figure of speech, theme, image, character, or plot element) can play a role in locking us into dominant story lines of our lives and our society. To paraphrase poet and cultural critic Audre Lorde, postmodernists believe that "the master's tropes will never dismantle the master's narratives."[12]

While modernism used most, if not all, of the techniques elaborated below, modernist authors often believed that form alone, art alone, could provide social redemption, that art alone could compensate for the dehumanizing forces of the modern world. But the incorporation by capitalism of so much modernist art into just another thing to be consumed as object has left postmodern authors skeptical that art can maintain some pure, oppositional stance against dominant cultures. Much modernist literature, works of the Harlem Renaissance, for example, was extremely politically rich and important.[13] And while modernist techniques were probably never as liberatory as they hoped they would be, they no doubt did, especially in such actively avant-gardist moments as Dada and surrealism, have some power to disrupt oppressive social norms. And they greatly influenced postmodern realist writers. But in the postmodern era, a proliferation of avant-garde, self-reflexive techniques have been used to sell all manner of consumer goods, consumerist images, and patriarchal/ capitalist ideological positions. These once avant-garde techniques have not lost all their disruptive power, but they have become useful to capitalism as elements of a strategy in which a disorienting proliferation of discourses, rather than a single, realist one, is a prime agency of domination. Likewise, fields like postmodern marketing and postmodern management have trivialized and sought to incorporate critique into the system.

Contrary to the image of postmodernists as faddishly embracing the ever new, postmodernists acknowledge that mostly every technique or strategy they use has been used before, by modernists or even earlier writers. One way some of those writing about postmodern fiction talk about this recycling of techniques is that in many postmodernist works there is an intensification or proliferation of these earlier approaches (more modernist technique per square inch than among modernists). Brian McHale proffers this claim in his influential book, *Postmodern Fiction*, arguing that certain experimental forms that were a less central part of modernist fiction become *dominant* in postmodernism, that is, these techniques are used more often and used as a more pervasive organizational feature. This is certainly true of many texts labeled "postmodernist," though it is possible to find exceptions.[14]

Disrupting the "Reality Effect"

Given this history of appropriation, postmodernists in general, and postmodern realist authors even more so, offer more direct critiques of particular story lines that contribute to inequality and other injustices, and often include more direct political statements in an effort to limit appropriative misreadings by dominant cultural forces. These gestures represent a flaunting of the alleged stylistic "error" that novelist Henry James, a key transitional figure between the realist and modernist eras, called "the platitude of statement," a mere *telling* rather than the *showing* he thought proper to fiction.[15] Postmodern realists recognize that artistic resistance is largely meaningless if not turned into political praxis. Many postmodern works draw attention to the *act of reading*, to reading as more than passive consumption. Postmodern realistic works often underscore the analogy between the passive reading of fiction and political passivity. They know that any given novel can be read in a variety of different ways, and that political contexts largely determine how texts are interpreted. Postmodern authors put numerous roadblocks in front of the passive reader, challenging them to actively co-construct the text, to take responsibility for the meaning-making process. In that sense, all of the techniques discussed below are designed to engage readers in interpreting the world inside and outside the text with active skepticism and skeptical activism.

Postmodern authors seek to reveal how conventional ways of narrating our lives shape the underlying *structures of feeling*[16] and thought that determine political belief and action. Beyond the pleasures of play with conventions, many postmodern realist authors feel the wider ethical obligation to show that these same techniques for making up the real, for inculcating belief, are used in the wider world by politicians, advertisers, and authorities of all kinds. As the Italian social theorist Antonio Gramsci argued, it is "common sense," the daily things we take for granted as simply true, that solidify oppressive power. It is far more difficult to resist something labeled as "natural," "normal," or "just the way things are." Note that for centuries it was simple "common sense" that women were intellectually inferior and cut out only for domestic activities; it was Western colonialism's "common sense" that all non-white people were inferior, including millions whose alleged inferiority justified their enslavement. Postmodern theorists like Michel Foucault argue that larger oppressive systems are built up and kept in place by dozens of micro-powers, dozens of seemingly small discourses that add up to acceptance of a "reality" that profoundly restricts our freedom to even imagine alterative realities. This includes challenging the reading habits by which we often consume literature as thoughtlessly as we consume a can of soda.

In literary terms, much of this ideology resides in a set of techniques that go under the term "realism." This includes the period in the latter half of the nineteenth century known as the era of *realism* and its cousin, *naturalism*, but entails a longer history. Over the course of the several centuries in which novels have been written in the Western world, certain conventions for writing character, setting, plot, and so on, have been used often enough that they have created a kind of literary common sense that passes for the real. In point of fact, looked at more closely, as the critic Erich Auerbach was among the first to carefully analyze, the nature of "the real" in fiction, the nature of *mimesis* (mirroring the real) and *verisimilitude* (the semblance of truth) has changed greatly from era to era.[17] As novelist-critic David Shields notes, "Every artistic movement from the beginning of time is an attempt to figure out a way to smuggle more of what the artist thinks is reality into the work of art."[18] The fact that just prior to the rise of modernism, a body of fiction specifically labeled itself "realist," made modernists even more adamant about challenging naïve claims of straightforward realism. Supposedly realistic representation became a key target for modernists in all the arts in the late nineteenth and early twentieth centuries. Think, for example, of the move away from representational painting, one that seemed close to photographic in quality, that gave way to dozens of experiments in form through movements like impressionism, cubism, expressionism, surrealism, and so on.

Modernist writers likewise carried on this assault on certain clichéd forms of realism such that, as Vladimir Nabokov, one of the key novelists in the transition from modernism to postmodernism, could assert, "'reality' is one of the few words which mean nothing without quotes."[19] Postmodernists continue that assault on naïve realism in the arts, but given the ways in which modernists became assimilated to the very forces of social conformity they sought to disrupt, many raise additional questions about the limits of art alone as a force under current conditions. Putting "realism" in quotes is not, as some uncareful critics of postmodernism have suggested, a denial of reality, and certainly not a claim that nothing is real. Rather, it is a way to call attention to certain forms that claim to be realistic, and thereby to open questions about how we come to know what is real and what is not, what is realistically possible and what is not. Putting quotes around "realism" is designed to call attention to what critic Roland Barthes called the "reality effect,"[20] the linguistic rules by which things come to be considered real, become common sense.

This particular critique of the reality effect is decidedly a response to the new conditions of postmodernity. As the postmodern novelist J. G. Ballard put it,

> the balance of reality and fiction has changed [under postmodern conditions]. We live in a world ruled by fictions of every kind—mass merchandising,

advertising, politics conducted as a branch of advertising, the instant translation of science and technology into popular imagery, the increasing blurring of identities within the realm of consumer goods, the pre-empting of any free or original imaginative response to experience by [electronic media]. We live inside an enormous novel.[21]

Metafiction. Many of the techniques used by postmodernists to disrupt reality effects can be grouped under the term "metafiction."[22] Metafiction is fiction about fiction, fiction reflecting on its own means of construction. Most of the elements addressed below are metafictional to one degree or another, and postmodernism should be given credit (or blame?) for the fact that the slang term "meta" has become widely used by media-savvy cultural consumers. But whether or not such meta gestures become merely smug self-awareness or lead to greater awareness of the political meaning of a given technique depends upon the context and use to which the device is put.

One way that metafiction works is through a technique called "double coding." Double coding aims to literarily disprove the metaphorical adage that "you can't have your cake and eat it too." Postmodern authors offer up lovely literary cakes, let readers eat them, then show them that the cake was never really there. That is, postmodernists use the same techniques that were used by fiction writers of the realist and modernist eras, but then undermine them through one or another realism-questioning gesture. Postmodernists are like magicians who do their tricks, but then show you how the trick was done.

In the traditional fiction contract between author and reader, the reader is asked to engage in the "a willful suspension of disbelief" in order to embrace the story as true. Now the "willful" part might suggest an active decision, but everything about traditional realisms feel more like a drawing of attention away from the unreal, constructed nature of the fiction. Postmodernists, in general, and postmodern realists even more so, want readers instead to "willfully suspend *belief.*"

The idea that we now "live inside an enormous novel," or an increasingly virtual reality, is a large part of what has driven postmodernists to reveal more explicitly how novels, and by extension other linguistic systems, generate the illusion of reality. One classic early postmodernist fiction that presents a veritable compendium of these gestures is John Barth's story, "Lost in the Funhouse."[23] The story never really goes anywhere, in a traditional sense, in part because it is constantly interrupted by the narrator/author with comments like, "Description of physical appearance and mannerisms is one of several standard methods of characterization used by writers of fiction. It is also important to 'keep the senses operating'; when a detail from one of the five senses, say visual, is 'crossed' with a detail from another, say auditory, the reader's imagination is oriented to the scene, perhaps unconsciously." "Narrative ordinarily consists of alternating dramatization and summarization." "The diving would make a suitable literary symbol," and so on. As the narrator remarks less than half-way through the story, "There's no point in going farther; this isn't getting anybody anywhere; they haven't even come to the funhouse yet." Any normal enjoyment of a "good story" is disrupted at every turn by explaining how a "good story" is constructed (and then largely ignoring these rules, or making only half-hearted gestures toward doing so).

Barth's story has been a target of a common critique of postmodernist fiction, that it is full of cynical *black humor*. This strikes me as doubly mistaken. It confuses skepticism, a very healthy social attitude, with cynicism, an admittedly often unhealthy one. Dark humor can be quite apt in dark times, while aesthetic play is one of the great joys of the world, one which can give solace in such dark moments. And, as a character in one story by an exquisite master of the playful style, Donald Barthelme, shouts: in postmodern texts there is "enough aesthetic excitement here to satisfy anyone but a damned fool."[24] Humor, dark or otherwise, can not only give respite in tough times, but can also be deployed in the service of significant social analysis. Indeed, humor can be one of the most potent political forces in the world, as illustrated over the last couple of decades by satiric talk shows broadcast worldwide from the United States like *The Daily Show*, *Colbert Report*, *Last Week Tonight*, and *Full Frontal*, and similar ones in the United Kingdom, Canada, and Australia.

In Barth's literary funhouse, it was enough to expose playfully, and rather abstractly, the techniques by which the illusions of realism are created in fiction. But in the postmodern realist fiction this book focuses on, these rhetorical gestures usually take more explicitly political form. In "How to Tell a True War Story," Vietnam War vet Tim O'Brien, for example, tries again and again to use conventional war story techniques, but each time is frustrated by the inability of these techniques to fully capture the senselessness of the war in which he participated. His text refuses to turn the war into a mere "story," suggesting that the perpetuation of certain kinds of war stories encourages the perpetuation of war. The story begins with the words, "This is true," and lays out what seems to be a straightforward account of one of

O'Brien's experiences in Vietnam. But soon the story takes a twist with this comment.

> A true war story is never moral. It does not instruct, nor encourage virtue, nor suggest models of proper human behavior, nor restrain men from doing the things they have always done. If a story seems moral, do not believe it. If at the end of a war story you feel uplifted, or if you feel some small bit of rectitude has been salvaged from the larger waste, then you have been made the victim of a very old and terrible lie.[25]

This observation does not stop the story from continuing, but it exists to challenge every subsequent version of this war story the author offers.

Disrupting the Liberal Humanist Character

The identity fluidity characteristic of much of the postmodern world is manifest in postmodern fiction in a variety of ways, perhaps most obviously in the treatment of character. Postmodernist realists argue that we can only achieve a degree of freedom to the extent to which we can come to understand the limits of our freedom, to understand the larger forces—psychological, social, ideological, linguistic—that have shaped us and given us the illusion of total freedom. Given the ways in which literature helped create and generally reinforces the idea of the liberal humanist self, much postmodern fiction seeks to deconstruct fictional characters as an embodiment of that sense of self. As literary critic Mary Holland summarizes, this fiction challenges a kind of "humanism that assumes an unchanging, wholly self-aware [individual] subject unaffected by exterior forces, a universal human nature, and fully knowable truth we all agree upon; sees form as subordinate to content and therefore tends to be formally anti-innovation; detaches the [literary] text from historical, social and political contexts; and keeps its values, and its ways of inculcating them, invisible."[26] Clearly, not all literature historically has embodied these concepts or embodied them at all, but much fiction has been far better at exploring individual psychology than larger cultural forces.

Postmodern fictionists, in general, and postmodern realists, especially by contrast, celebrate a diverse array of historically and socially constructed identities and undermine the standard claim that fiction should provide "consistent," "well-rounded," "three-dimensional" characters.[27] Postmodern metafictionists remind us that characters are in fact *one-dimensional*. They only exist on that flat page of text, or now a flat digital screen. Sometimes this technique is also used to suggest that under postmodern conditions we readers are becoming more and more one-dimensional ourselves, more absorbed into a world of images and products that brand us. If consistent character represents the trap of mainstream identity, then how might that trap be avoided? Discussion of a host of ways this occurs is taken up in Chapter 3, where the most explicit version noted is embodied in the works of Kathy Acker. Acker approached the issue of challenging the traditional literary conception of the self by creating characters who, far from being consistent, changed things like their age, name, gender, race, and nationality in the course of a novel. While others seldom went this far, the notion of the individual as an unchanging, or autonomously self-motivated, entity has undergone constant challenge by postmodern writers.

A less individualistic function of character, but one still problematic from the point of view of some postmodernists, is as representative or symbolic agents. This has often been signaled in traditional literature by giving characters names that seem to reveal something essential about their character. Think of Sir Toby Belch (one of Shakespeare's party boys) or Holly Golightly (Truman Capote's frivolous devotee of Tiffany's jewelry store). Postmodernists may evoke this type of character-naming, raise the expectation that it may reveal character, but twist off away from such a revelation. A number of writers use this technique but none more often or more amusingly than Thomas Pynchon. His short novel, *The Crying of Lot 49*, for example, includes these names: Oedipa Maas (the sort-of heroine), Stanley Koteks, Manni DiPresso, and Genghis Cohen. Some of these names might seem laden with revelatory, symbolic meaning, but ultimately they don't map neatly onto character traits. Are they meaningful in a way the reader can't see, are they just there for comic effect, or are they both? Given the increasing numbers of students and others who have been given an academic literary education, that doubt also aims to tease readers to break the cycle of doing the lit crit bit, of applying traditional approaches of literary analysis.

Here's another doubly playful little example from Samuel Beckett, who has named one character after a spice (clove) often used to enhance the namesake of the other character (ham):

Clov: What is there to keep me here?
Hamm: The dialogue.

This bit is, of course, dialogue in the literary sense, but the double joke is the fact that Beckett's dialogues seldom go anywhere and that Hamm's response is a metafictional one, reminding us that "dialogue" is also just a literary device, one that fakes real communication.

Disrupting Plots: Fragmentation, Minimalism, and Maximalism

Modernists like T. S. Eliot and James Joyce often experienced and represented modern life as fragmented and chaotic, but through works like Eliot's epic poem "The Waste Land" and Joyce's novel *Ulysses* they sought to aesthetically reclaim these fragments through a new mythology. In contrast, most postmodernists seem more comfortable living with fragmentation, rather than aesthetically wishing it away. Indeed, one key postmodern author, Donald Barthelme, has a character in one of his stories proclaim that "fragments are the only things I trust." Barthelme was quick to point out in an interview that this was a character, not the author speaking. But methinks he doth protest too much, and in any event the phrase is a mantra that many postmodern texts might use as an epigraph. Some postmodern authors, and perhaps most famously William Burroughs, do place greater trust in fragments. Burroughs for a time used a "cut up method" in which he literally cut his novels into pieces and randomly rearranged them, and many other postmodernists create works that seem deeply fragmented.

Fragmentation is experienced under postmodern conditions both externally and internally, both sociologically and psychologically. Given that a "plot" names both the story arc of a novel and some nefarious political intrigue, it can be highly useful in revealing ideological traps. A number of influential postmodern writers, like Don DeLillo and Pynchon, seem to suggest that the alternative to embracing fragments is to embrace conspiracies. In fact, Pynchon often suggests that literary plotting, like the plotting that goes on in a conspiracy, is a kind of paranoid delusion that denies the reality of chaos or the chaos of reality. The rise of conspiracy theories in the politics of the first two decades of the twenty-first century has made this kind of work more relevant than ever in uncovering the techniques through which plots and conspiracies are made believable, made to seem real when they are not.

An approach related to fragmentation is one that postmodernist critics have called *maximalism*. Novels like Pynchon's *Gravity's Rainbow* (1973) is an early example, David Foster Wallace's *Infinite Jest* (1996) is a later example, and in the twenty-first century this strategy has returned in works like Mark

Z. Danielewski's multilayered *House of Leaves* (2000) (see Chapter 10), and Lucy Ellman's *Ducks, Newburyport* (2019) built out of no doubt, carefully arranged, but seemingly random, fragments that make up a 1,000 page run-on sentence monologue.

In such works, the plot lines grow so complex, so loaded to the max with multiple, forking story lines, reversals, and intricacies that there is simply no way to sort them out into a typical story arc with a beginning, middle, and a resolution at the end. These writers create labyrinths, but with no reachable center, and no way out the other side. While this kind of tale would seem to violate the literary goal of making sense of the world, it could be claimed that these labyrinthine tales are in one sense a *more realistic* mode of storytelling, since few things in life resolve themselves as neatly as most fictional plot lines, especially under postmodern conditions of information overload.

An opposite approach that nevertheless achieves a similar undermining of the notion of coherent plot has been called *minimalism*. Minimalism is most famously deployed in a postmodern way by Samuel Beckett, whose works refuse the traditional story arc by not providing enough of a story to arc. Beckett worked as a kind of secretary to the great modernist James Joyce on the author's last work, *Finnegans Wake*. Written as an amalgam of some seventeen languages, and including among its mythic understructure stories from all the major and several minor religious and literary traditions, *Wake* sought to be the book of all books, the novel to end all novels. It was in a sense a wake for literature as such. At least it must have felt that way to some writers who followed in its wake. It left Beckett, for example, with seemingly little choice but to work in the opposite direction from his mentor. His novels are famous for how little happens in them, how little they seem to have to say about the world. As in Beckett's most famous play, *Waiting for Godot*, readers wait for something to happen, for someone (Godot?) to appear, but it appears that no one appears and that nothing happens. Indeed, as one critic put it regarding *Godot*, "nothing happens, twice" (once in each act of the two-act play). Beckett's novels, like *The Unnamable*, likewise strip away not only plot but virtually all other traditional aspects of the novel like developed characters or meaningful settings. Their minimalism seems to refuse all the normal ways that novels offer the solace of coherent meaning.

Disrupting History

Another type of "realist" plotting that postmodern authors have put into question is historiography, writing by professional historians. As two of the chapters of this book (Chapters 6 and 7), as well as some texts discussed in other chapters, make clear, postmodern realists believe history writing is too important to be left to historians alone. Their concerns about the limits of plots extend to those who claim to plot the real past. Just as they argue that traditional techniques of fiction can be inherently conservative, so too can historians tell stories of the past in ways that fall into the trap of naïve realism. As historical theorist Hayden White noted, all historians use fictional techniques to turn the inchoate mass of historical data into plots (White calls this process *emplotment*). And by claiming to tell the past as it really happened, they make up stories with even less self-consciousness about how language determines ideological meaning than do fiction writers (since the very term "fiction" puts a little distance between the world and writing about the world, even to some extent for authors who call themselves realists).

Literary theorist Linda Hutcheon claims that a self-conscious play with notions of historical causality is actually the most central form of postmodern writing. She calls such works "historiographic metafiction."[28] This approach suggests that all metafictional techniques undermine the kind of storytelling we call history. Breaking the historical reality effect can also take such specific form in postmodern fiction as conflating historical eras, reversing chronology or using nonlinear, jumbled timelines, using deliberate anachronisms (such as a character supposedly living in the nineteenth century using a cellphone), mixing real historical figures with fictional characters or combining real events with ones that never happened, and in its most elaborated form writing full *counterfactual histories* (in which, for example, Germany and Japan won the Second World War). All of these gestures seek to remind us that historical knowledge is always partly a trick of language that invariably works from particular ideological perspectives. But where some postmodern novels engage in this work at an abstract, general level, postmodern realists provide more directed attacks on particular, oppressive versions of the past, as is the case with the retelling of the stories of the conquest of Indigenous lands, African American slavery, and Nazi holocaust discussed in Chapter 6.

Questioning Author(ity)

Unreliable narrators have long been an element in fiction, often in somewhat subtle ways. But postmodernists up the ante on unreliability, sometimes by making the narrator clearly, absurdly, unreliable, at other times by giving the narrator the same name as the author. This latter move creates a kind of distorted mirror in which confessions by the author-narrator, often confessions of their unreliability, reflect back on the "real" author in a kind of infinite loop of doubt. Can I believe an author who tells me s/he is unreliable? Is that confession also unreliable? Sometimes the author (or at least someone with that same name as the author) is also a character in the story. And it is not always clear that the author as character is the same as the author as narrator, or that either of them are the same as the real person who has written and published the fiction. This technique has in more recent years been augmented with the invention of electronic literary *hypertexts* like Shelley Jackson's *Patchwork Girl* (see Chapter 4), where the reader/user is invited to choose among differing possible directions the story might take. Like many of the other techniques, these authorial intrusions are intended to distance the reader from immersion in the story being told, drawing attention not only to its fictiveness, its literary conventions, but also suggesting that these conventions are a kind of manipulation that readers can resist in their everyday lives.

This play with the author role also draws attention to what in postmodern theory has been rather too dramatically called "the death of the author." What this phrase means is that authorial omnipotence, pure originality, is challenged by recognition of how writers are caught in webs of language they only partly control. Postmodern theorists downplay the notion of complete authorial originality in favor of recognizing all fictional works are part of a continuum of language and literature that is a social, not a personal, construction. Thus a more accurate term, something less than the death of the author, might be *deauthorization*: authors are no longer authorized to lay personal claim to their creations, or to be perfect interpreters of their own works. This is recognition that at the end of the writing process, authors become readers, readers who obviously have certain intimate insights into the texts but for whom the reading process is nevertheless one of always imperfect interpretation, one that changes in each reading an author might give to their own work just as it does for any reader. Writer Doug Dorst, working from a concept proposed by film and TV director/producer J. J. Abrams, plays with the death of the author trope in *S* (2013), a packet of boxed materials that includes a novel, *The Ship of Theseus* (in the form of a mock library copy complete with a checkout form), as well as postcards, handwritten letters, a map hand drawn on a napkin, typed letters, a telegram, scribblings on notepads, photocopies and photographs, yellowed newspaper clippings, a possible secret text decoding device, and more. Allegedly written by one V. M. Straka, who may or may not be dead, the novel is covered in marginal notes by two young student decipherers whose comments highlight how each reading rewrites the text and ultimately makes authorial intent irrelevant.

Metafictional self-reference can also be used to draw attention to *authorial complicity* in many postmodern texts. These gestures note that making the truth claim that truth claims should always be approached with a degree of incredulity must include the truth claims of postmodernism itself. This embodies one of the key tenets of postmodernism: that we can never get fully outside the ideological forces that simultaneously enable and constrain our sense of what is real. This is not cynicism but rather humility amid a healthy skepticism that any one of us can have the whole truth, nothing but the truth. Neither is this a pure relativism, but rather a call to more deeply understand all knowledge as situated, to understand that various personal angles of vision on the world are rooted in particular historical and social locations.

Situated Knowledges

Interwoven with and often linking together many of these techniques is an approach to culture that refuses omniscient, god-like knowledge in favor of what postmodern feminist theorist Donna Haraway calls *situated knowledges*.[29] Knowledge is situated in the sense that it is rooted in particular perspectives shaped by history and by key interwoven structuring social factors like nation, age, gender, ethnicity/race, and class. This is not, as it is often misread, some totally open, anything goes, relativism because the relative social positions each embody particular limited, perspectives on the social totality. And these perspectives can be put in dialogue with one another to constitute something more closely resembling an accurate picture of a given social world. No position can see all of reality but what one can see from a particular position is not random, nor is it permanently structured. Rather, it is historically and socially shaped by the relative amounts of power individuals and groups have to control a given society's narrative. For these writers, exposing the situated nature of knowledge is aimed at challenging inequities in the distribution of cultural, economic, and political power with regard to class, gender, sexual identity, nationality, race/ethnicity, educational attainment, and other key social factors.

Intertextuality

In recognition that pure originality, pure novel(ty), is impossible, postmodern fiction tends to have more than the typical number of allusions, quotations, and other types of reference to other texts, fiction and nonfiction ones. That is, they draw attention to the *intertextuality* of their writing, its entanglement with other previous writings. Biblical allusions, allusions to other fictions and so on, have been common in novels from the beginning. But, again, postmodernists take this process further than most. Indeed, one of the first postmodernists, or proto-postmodernists, Jorge Luis Borges, takes the process about as far as it can go. The Borges story "Pierre Menard, Author of the *Quixote*" tells of the ambition of the eponymous author to write *Don Quixote*. Not a revised *Don Quixote*, but the original word for word. And he succeeds, at least for some pages, which leads the narrator to exclaim how it is superior to the original!

Perhaps because *Don Quixote* has been called by some the first novel,[30] and by others even the first postmodern novel, the book has figured quite prominently in the intertextual references of a number of postmodern texts, though in very different ways, including most recently Salman Rushdie's *Quichotte* (2019). Acker, for example, a postmodernist whose sensibility and style has often been compared to punk rock, goes so far as to title one of her novels *Don Quixote*. But unlike Menard's search for a letter perfect rewrite, Acker's text veers wildly away from Cervantes (her Don Quixote is a woman and the opening scene is of her having an abortion), while nevertheless, stealing a good deal from the sixteenth-century version. Acker also works in both allusions to and actual chunks of dozens of other literary texts from the whole history of literature. She writes at times like a lit major gone mad during her essay exams, cramming in everything she knows, regardless of its apparent relevance. Her technique of mixing broad chunks of other authors' works into her novel is an example of a kind of intertextuality sometimes known as *pla(y)giarism*, a kind of plagiarism that openly acknowledges its theft.

Two related forms of intertextuality that are more extensive kinds of allusive playfulness and intermixings are versions of *parody* and *pastiche*. Parody mimics but exaggerates the style of a genre or a "serious" form like tragedy, with the goal of revealing these forms to be manipulators of emotion. *Pastiche*, less well known than parody, comes from the Latin word for paste (*pasta*) and can be thought of as pasting other works, styles, or genres into the body of postmodern texts. Where parody aims to make fun of its object, pastiche can sometimes take a more ambiguous form in which homage and critique are simultaneously present in the same gesture. These pastings and mixings often mimic the wild intertwining of discourses that daily life offers under postmodern conditions. Postmodernists seldom seek to bring order out of this chaos, but instead offer readers some better ways to live with the effects and affects of the chaos of words and images that bombard us through advertising, television shows, and the internet. They can give both pleasure through the aesthetic rearranging of these messy mixes, and knowledge of how readers might creatively re-mix their own lives.

A related kind of postmodern intertextuality takes the form of the *revisionary novel*. The many varieties of this type of novel are the subject of Chapter 7. These are generally less radical departures from the original than what Acker did. Sometimes they seek to imitate the style of the earlier novels they retell or recontextualize. Often they are written as a prequel or postscript to a famous novel. They may be from the perspective of a minor character or from one excluded completely from the earlier work, as when the novelist Chinua Achebe points out the limits of Joseph Conrad's ostensibly anti-imperialist novella *Heart of Darkness* by including African villagers who were almost wholly absent from the earlier text. These works seek to demonstrate to readers that new lenses provided by new time frames and new social conditions call us to rewrite the literary past, allow us to see new things in older works.

Disrupting Genres, Levels, and Emotional Tones

One of the forms of serious play among postmodern texts is a *mixing of genres*. Genres are in effect literary rulebooks, and postmodernists have been very fond of the notion that rules are made to be broken, or at least seriously bent. In the case of genre bending and breaking, this can include quite wild mixes of tragedy and farce. Of particular importance in many of these novels is a mixing of discourses in order to critique the distinction between putatively *high culture*, and *mass* or *pop culture*. These distinctions have long been used as class distinctions, as ways to separate the wealthy and well-educated from the allegedly less sophisticated masses who know only popular culture not high art. To disrupt this, postmodernists incorporated genres that are generally looked down upon by supposedly serious writers: romance novels, comic books, mysteries, westerns, pulp sci-fi, fairy tales, tabloid newspapers, advertising copy, and so on. These mixes are aimed not so much to devalue "high" literature per se, but to show the ways in which various kinds of writing contain ideological prescriptions which uphold social divisions, constraining lessons on how to live or how to feel. Close cousin to genre bending, or sometimes an effect of it, are incongruous *shifts of mood* or *atmosphere* or *emotional registers*, a tragic story that suddenly turns absurd or vice versa. The effect here again is to remind us of fiction as emotional manipulation, and to break the conventions of affect used in fiction as they connect to the reality effects of daily life.

Sometimes these gestures may be trying to make a more specific point about the politics of culture. For example, Dominican-American author Junot Diaz's novel *The Brief Wondrous Life of Oscar Wao* (2007) (see Chapter 5) shows how the fascination with s/f, video games, and comics of a nerdy lead character allows him to counter certain masculinist stereotypes of Latinos. Diaz also shows how these other-worldly pop culture genres provided imaginative relief to characters suffering from both external racism and bullying within their immigrant community for failing to meet certain standards of male behavior.

Magic Realisms

Another key school or element in recent fiction, that is sometimes seen as part of postmodernism and at other times as a related parallel school, goes by the names *lo real maravilloso* or *realismo magico*, and is most often referred to in English as *magical realism*. Arising first in Latin America, magical realism, like my broader term, "postmodern realism," puts emphasis equally on both terms. Much of this work pits a suppressed folk culture against the dominant ideas of contemporary Western rationalist culture. It offers alternative epistemologies in which what is unbelievable to the dominant is real to the dominated. This is a paradoxical strategy in which placing seemingly logically impossible occurrences side by side in a story alongside perfectly reasonable, everyday occurrences, the reality of the real is undermined. The most famous and influential early magical realist text, Gabriel García Marquez's novel *One Hundred Years of Solitude* (1967), for example, tells the history of seven generations of recurring political betrayal in Macondo (a thinly veiled version of Marquez's native Columbia) through the use of constantly shifting time frames not unlike s/f time travel. The novel shows again and again politicians bowing to forces of Spanish and later US imperialism, while other magical elements suggest the possibility of a different future, one that escapes the same old story of political ideals used as a cover for greed and corruption. The story is filled with ghosts and apparitions who exist on the same plane as the other "characters" and reinforce a sense of the weight of history, the presence of the past. Meanwhile, other marvelous elements acknowledge everyday miracles of love and beauty that exist even amid repeated political and personal betrayals, and may provide the basis for an alternative future politics that may break this cycle.

Magical realism moved from Latin America all around the globe, including into the UK (Salman Rushdie, for example), Japan (Haruki Murakami, for example), and all over North America. I have followed a precedent in using the term as a general one to discuss many different texts. But it is important that local variations be noted. African Americans like Toni Cade Bambara (Chapter 3), Ishmael Reed, and Toni Morrison (Chapter 6) draw upon specifically African American folk forms, African novelists like Akwaeki Emezi (Chapter 3) and Nnedi Okorafor (Chapter 10) use specifically Nigerian folk traditions, Indigenous writers like Thomas King and Sherman Alexie (Chapter 7) draw on Native trickster motifs, and so on. Likewise Latina Ana Castillo's novel *So Far from God* (Chapter 5) draws from regionally specific Southwest US folk traditions that differ somewhat from those of Latin America. Often these folk traditions are offered not as fantasy but as an alternative metaphysics, an alternative reality that challenges Western rationalist versions of realism. Other texts invent forms that go beyond or mix folkloric counter-knowledges with other forms of magical thinking as, for example, when one of her character is resurrected after "immaculately contracting" HIV/AIDS. The manner of contracting and the rebirth are meant to challenge the repressive political idea that some AIDS patients were guilty (homosexuals and drug addicts), while some were innocent (like the boy who famously contracted the disease through a blood transfusion), while also offering alternatives to some patriarchal versions of Christianity.[31]

S/F: Speculative Fiction, Science Fiction, and Fantasy

This mixing of the normally real with the normally unreal, again, aims to draw attention to the processes by which the "real" is invented through narrative, through storytelling. That is one reason that, as critic Brian

McHale argued, science fiction/speculative fiction/fantasy (henceforth indicated by "s/f") is the archetype for postmodernist fiction.[32] McHale notes that while the detective story offers a useful analogy for modernism, with its emphasis on epistemology, on differing angles of vision on the same subject matter, postmodernists, like some s/f writers (and including postmodern s/f writers), often raise questions of *ontology*, as they posit not different angles on the same world but multiple, incompatible worlds. They ask questions like: "Which world is this? What is to be done in it? Which of my selves is to do it?" (10).

SF authors have been deeply interested in shifting time scales, changing bodies, multiple genders and sexualities, AIs, and oppressive political regimes. Much non-postmodern s/f deals with these issues, and in figures like Samuel R. Delany, s/f directly engages with postmodern theory as well as postmodern condition. The astrophysical and favorite science fiction hypothesis of a *multiverse* is a kind of postmodern principle writ large in which multiple realities cannot be resolved into a single, coherent universe of discourse, and/or into a single coherent self. This is one concept that blurs the genre line around s/f. Paul Auster, for example, an influence on multiple generations of postmodern authors, uses this notion in his 2017 novel *4321*. The protagonist(s) of that novel is/are a character(s) named Ferguson whose life stories are told in four quite different versions in which certain circumstances and character traits remain the same while others change, often drastically, due to sometimes random, sometime seemingly determined, sequences of events. These four Fergusons live in parallel universes, but not in a science fiction sense so much as in an historical sense, a sense of the multiverse as here and now, not somewhere off in another dimension. While postmodern fictions don't often make this notion of a multiverse quite so apparent, their story lines often suggest realities that are not simply viewed from different angles, but that are utterly incompatible with one another.

When we say that someone is "telling stories" to mean that they are making up untrue things we are close to the postmodernist claim that all storytelling is telling stories, that therefore readers should analyze political storytelling, or the nightly news, with the same degree of care they put into interpreting novels. Authors who weave the "fantastical" into the "realistic" may get the reader to wonder how it is that the same technique can be used to describe them both. If that is so, how can we be sure that what we take for granted as the ordinary real, the daily real, is, well, really real?

Sometimes the play with texts considered fantasy or fable works in the opposite direction. That is, an author may take fantasy stories and imbue them with "real-world" elements. This has taken the form, for example, of a different kind of revisionary writing—postmodern retellings of fairy tales to generate morals and messages far different from the original. This has included many feminist retellings of tales like "Beauty and the Beast" or "Little Red Riding Hood," transforming passive female victims into empowered actors against male dominance in stories by writers like Angela Carter.[33] These kinds of revisionist tales have subsequently made their way out into mass culture in children's books, young adult fiction and film.

There are additional techniques used by postmodernists, but this sketch should provide some sense of many of the most typical ones. But how many of these techniques have to be in a text before it can be called postmodernist? I don't know. Quantification is not my strong suit, and ultimately is not the issue. Given the instability of the category I've discussed, people will no doubt quibble about whether this or that particular text I include in this book is truly postmodern. I would simply reply that in my use of the term it takes very little for a text to go from realist or modernist to postmodernist. Indeed, I would argue, for example, that Nobel Prize–winning author Toni Morrison's novel *Jazz* is modernist all the way to its last couple of pages where it turns, through a brilliant surprise, postmodern.

What all these techniques and approaches are ultimately struggling against is the massive machinery of contemporary consumerist culture that turns everything and everyone into something to be sold and passively consumed. Writers have seen the ways in which even the most radical modernist works of art, works utterly opposed to the mad pursuit of material things, have been drawn into the deadening morass of the capitalist market which, to paraphrase Oscar Wilde, knows the price of everything, but the value of nothing. Postmodernists realize that they cannot fully control how their works are going to be presented and consumed in the so-called literary marketplace. Thus, it is up to us as readers to work with these texts, to create contexts of reception that release their power to help bring about much needed changes in the world. Keep that task in mind as we turn to this selection of postmodern realist novels. My readings are only one of many ways to approach each of these texts. I assume that if you have read them or read them in the future you will argue at times with my approach and will find your own, perhaps better, ways to use these novels and other examples of postmodernist realism you encounter to challenge internalized and external powers that are shaping your future in dangerous ways.

3

Identities

Mysteries of the Self

The subject of the subject has been subject to much debate in recent decades. If that sentence seems confusing to you, then welcome to the world of the postmodern self. The depiction of selfhood or subjectivity in postmodern fiction can be understood through two, sometimes interrelated, elements of analysis that might be called philosophical and sociological, respectively. When postmodern theorists talk about the "subject," they are talking about something that is related to an idea of the "self" or "the individual," but they are suspicious that the terms "self" and "the individual" cover up more complex psycho-social and linguistic processes. Key to a shift to postmodern understandings of the self is an awareness of split between two concepts, "identity" and "subject." If "identity" is how we view and name ourselves, the "subject" is how we are shaped by larger social forces beyond our individual capacity to control. The latter means that all identity can be a kind of subjection, a kind of imposition by power.

Postmodern theory includes positing a subject made up of many selves, each linguistically and socially constructed through ideological systems (the church, the state, educational institutions, mass media, family dynamics, etc.), that suture over the contradictions between or among these many selves. Ideology is a kind of cosmetic surgery that erases these suture markings. These processes begin even before birth, as things like gender expectations (is it a boy or a girl, needing a blue or pink wardrobe), and become solidified with the acquisition of language, a system shot through with ideological assumptions about what is normal, realistic, rational, and/ or appropriate. Subjection continues with the imposition of that other subject, the subject of grammar, the "I" that gains a sense of power through manipulation of an object through a verb.

Since the beginning of the modern period, the self in the West has primarily taken the form of the *liberal humanist subject*, an individual who claimed to represent universal human essence. That self has increasing been revealed to be a culture- and history-bound version, only one among many other possible conceptualizations. This concept, sometimes also referred to as the Cartesian self (after the philosopher René Descartes), emerged during the sixteenth-century Renaissance and came into full bloom during seventeenth-century European Enlightenment. The key features of this self were rationality, independent will, and the superiority of the mind over our bodily nature, including the superiority of the public sphere over the domestic sphere and human society over the natural world. Liberal humanist subjects were said to possess individual will and an essence apart from the impact of societal forces—a nearly absolute ability to define themselves, their needs, their beliefs, and their desires apart from the influence of others. Many challenges to this idea of an autonomous, rationally controlled self have occurred over a long historical process, but in the postmodern era these critiques have been extended and have penetrated further into the popular imagination, and into literary expression.

The novel as a social form has long been viewed as one of the forces that popularized this notion of the self as part of the rise of the middle classes or "bourgeois" individual.[1] But beginning in the middle of the nineteenth century, this view of the self was dealt a series of destabilizing blows. First, Charles Darwin put us back in nature, arguing that humans are not uniquely created beings, but rather beings evolved from "lower" animals. This notion of evolution also suggested a changing rather than an essential human nature. In the same era, Karl Marx challenged the sovereign individual by declaring this notion of the self to be a construct of ideology, one designed to hide the power of an economically dominant class of people to control less privileged classes for their own profit. Soon after, Sigmund Freud dealt a blow to the idea of the autonomous ego and the rational mind by elaborating ways in which human un- and subconscious impulses shape much of our behavior in ways beyond our control. A fourth blow, occurring at the beginning of the twentieth century, one that would play a crucial role in poststructuralist and postmodern thought, took the form of various theories that saw language not as a neutral lens on reality but rather as a determining and limiting constructor of "reality," including our sense of self.

Both theoretical and empirical social science in the postmodern era elaborated this critique, noting that the liberal humanist self is not a universal, neutral category but was instead implicitly a middle-class self that was also the colonizer self, the white self, the male self, the heterosexual self. Every arena of life was shown to be biased toward this limited self, from medical focus on the male body as a norm to the underrepresentation of women and persons of color in politics, the arts, and most other spheres of human endeavor. Postcolonial and decolonial theorists have challenged this white-male European subject as the sole marker of "humanity," noting that purely race-based cultural identities are a myth, that the world's various cultures have deeply influenced each other in ways that shape every being into a mostly unacknowledged hybrid identity. At the same time, environmentalists have pointed to the devastating consequences of an individualist, consumption-centered self that ignores its impact on the natural world. Ever-deepening social movement–bred political challenges to a human subject understood solely through a white, male, European lens have been proffered over the six decades of the postmodern era, and each has been accompanied by a backlash from the groups whose dominance is being challenged, a fact that has become the central focus of much of the era's political contestation.

In addition to the theoretical challenges to classic conceptualizations of the self, twentieth- and twenty-first-century anthropology, psychology, and sociology have deeply challenged this naïve notion of personal autonomy, showing the myriad ways in which even the most iron-willed of us is shaped by highly structured and standardized societal forces. The myth of individualism is still alive in the postmodern era, especially because it remains a cornerstone of consumerism reinforced by the advertising industry in dozens of ways, and shapes politics as a kind of consumerist enterprise. But an ever-increasing awareness of the forces—economic, political, social, and cultural—that drive us to conform to certain governmental and corporate ideas of the self has been a key part of this historical period.[2]

On the sociological level, many postmodern social conditions—geographic dislocations, multiculturalism, information overload, and technological enhancements—have transformed subjective experience and ideas of selfhood in profound ways. Long-standing stability in the realm of class and caste status has been deeply undermined, while virtually all the major supposedly "natural" categories of identity formation, especially ethnicity/race and sex/gender, have been profoundly challenged and changed since the middle of the twentieth century. No longer seen as biological givens, race and gender have been revealed to be socially constructed fictions.[3] There is no gene or cluster of genes common to all blacks or all whites, for example. Were race "real" in the biological sense, racial classifications for individuals would remain constant across national boundaries and across time. Instead, racial categories in the United States and the United Kingdom have shifted over time, and in the present a person who could be categorized as black in America might be considered white in Brazil, colored in South Africa, and aboriginal in Australia.

In addition to these challenges to the liberal humanist subject, new developments in technology over the last half century have led to radically new conceptions of what it means to be human, of what human essence is, and the degree to which it has been, and can be, reshaped by a variety of biotechnical interventions. The possibility of artificially intelligent beings matching or surpassing the human self, the fantasy of downloading our consciousness into computers, and a variety of related realities and fictions have led a number of theorists to posit a "posthuman" self. In most cases this might more accurately be described as posthumanist in that it too essentially means challenging the idea of an essential self, unchanged by history or the social order. Even the most allegedly stable site of identity location—the body—has proven to be extraordinarily mutable, not only via philosophical challenges to putatively natural categories that have marked bodies but also by surgical and biotechnological interventions into the human body (transplants, plastic surgery, gender reassignment surgery, technological implants and prostheses, etc.).

More recently, the fields of neuroscience and consciousness studies have also contributed significantly to reconceptualizations of the "self," a word that must now appear in scare quotes because many reject the idea completely, or see it as a kind of illusion of conscious control.[4] Brain science is still in its infancy, but a number of very interesting developments seem to reinforce previously posited ideas about the self as a kind of illusion created by neurochemical processes. As one prominent neuroscientist dramatically phrased it, consciousness is "a controlled hallucination." That sounds remarkably close to postmodern s/f novelist William Gibson's famous description of cyberspace as a "consensual hallucination," which leads me to the last element on the assault on the self, the growth and elaboration of digital culture as a space where a remarkable degree of elasticity of the self is often central to the experience.

The response to the multiple and varied challenges to the notion of a coherent, socially or religiously grounded and fully self-aware essential identity runs the gamut from utter rejection to ardent embrace of the possibility of an open-ended postmodern self. On one extreme, fear of a losing a stable identity has been a major factor in the rise of religious and political fundamentalism. In stark reaction to such radical uncertainty, many have grabbed firmly onto certainty in the form of an extreme belief in a deity or a cause. In the face of incredulity toward certain big stories, some have chosen to deepen a rigidly defined identity that tolerates no alternative. On the other extreme, some people seem utterly content or exhilarated by the relatively open flow of identity made possible when cut free from traditional sociohistorical restraints. Most people on the planet who have been bombarded by postmodern challenges to identity stability, rather than fully embracing some notion of a constantly changing self or seeking to return to the certainties of an earlier era, no doubt negotiate a space somewhere between these extremes.

Throughout most of human history, the majority of people have led lives that have been profoundly shaped and limited by social factors like social class and caste, gender, religious and political affiliation, sexual orientation, geographical locations, and related social and cultural forces. There have been few, if any, times in the history of humanity when such a high percentage of the global population has faced the degree of identity fluidity we are currently dealing with. But that fluidity is also limited by linguistic conventions, social forces, and by ideology at every level.

Postmodern theorists like Judith Butler and Michel Foucault make clear that underlying instability or the illusion of coherence does not mean that transformation of the self is a task easily accomplished. Overcoming deeply set ideological boundaries to identity is an arduous task.[5]

The paradox of postmodern identity is that it is only by analyzing the limits imposed upon the self by institutions and ideologies that we can achieve some degree of real choice about who we are. As the nineteenth-century writer/philosopher Goethe expressed it, "None are more hopelessly enslaved than those who falsely believe they are free." Postmodernists argue that there is no complete escape from the prison of identity, from what Foucault calls the shaping force of *power/knowledge*, but self-fashioning is possible through sufficient attention to the social and linguistic limits inscribed on our bodies and minds. In richly nuanced work, postmodern realist novelists have explored every aspect of both the limits and the possibilities of identity construction and reconstruction under postmodern conditions. These novels, as well as the hybrid "autofiction" discussed in Chapter 8, have greatly expanded the variety of selves represented and richly interrogated the linguistic and sociopolitical bases of identity formation.

Deconstructing the Self: Kathy Acker's *Don Quixote* (1986)

Arguably, no writer more fully embraced the postmodern self as fragmented, fractious, and fictional than Kathy Acker. As the title of one of her novels, *In Memoriam to Identity* (1998), makes starkly clear, Acker's work has little interest in settled notions of the individual subject. A devotee of sex, drugs, and (punk) rock'n'roll, she was as famous for her life as her work, both of which luxuriated in chaos. Acker's real and fictional worlds were deeply embedded in the avant-garde artistic and intellectual scene of Manhattan at the 1980s and 1990s during the high point of poststructuralist theory. As much as any body of fiction, her writing attempts to translate those theories into literary form(lessness). Taking very seriously the poststructuralist notion of language as the cage of the self, her novels seek to shatter that cage, or at least bend its bars, through denial of all stable characterization. Her characters can change their gender, race, nationality, age, or virtually any other characteristic during the story. Subjecthood is also disrupted by plots with no sequence of beginnings, middles, and ends, no continuity in time or place, and through discursive disruptions with little or no obvious connection to the action.

In an interview with cultural theorist Sylvere Lotringer, Acker remarks that "At a certain point I realized that the 'I' doesn't exist. So I said to myself: If the 'I' doesn't exist, I have to construct one, or maybe even more than one."[6] Her texts undermine the "I" as author(ity) by openly stealing passages, characters, and themes from other novels, which she then twists into a unrecognizable form in hers. Along the way her novels reject not only realist literary devices, but also rules of grammar, syntax, logic, and semantics as well. In terms of content, if such a word makes sense in her work, she uses graphic depictions of sex, violence, sexual violence, and other extreme experiences to shock readers out of complacent embrace of the so-called real and the stable self that supports it. Her aim is to break open the violent subjection that creates a stable, politically pliant self. She also frequently draws upon the disorientations occasioned by psycho-active drugs, a "derangement in the senses," in the words of one of her literary heroes, French poet Arthur Rimbaud. But these experiences are not presented as unreal or abnormal, but rather as a different reality, one as real or more real than what normally and normatively passes for everyday life and literary coherence.

Typically, Acker's fictional self is a phantasmagoria, with all the creative and horrifying elements that term implies. As she explains in her interview with Lotringer, "You create identity, you're not given identity per se. What became more interesting to me wasn't the I, it was text because it's texts that create the identity. That's how I got interested in plagiarism" (8). Her intentionally obvious intertextual incorporation of other novels, her pla(y) giarism, is a playful derangement of other texts within hers. Some titles of her novels, like *Great Expectations* and *Don Quixote*,[7] flaunt this approach, but her play with plagiarism is present in a host of ways in all of her works.

Like Jacques Derrida, she insists that every text contains within itself elements of other texts it tries to repress. Given the sexism of much of the literary world, including the avant-garde literary world, Acker sought especially to challenge the gender norms in fiction through protagonists who radically shift not only their sexual preferences but their embodiment as exclusively male or female (Acker was "gender fluid" decades before the term arose). Hence, a typical Acker novel is a carefully crafted mélange of plagiarized texts penned by classic male writers subverted by juxtaposition with bits of autobiographical material, cultural theory, political polemic, pornography, and other disruptions all aimed to undermine the romantic, misogynistic, and sexist elements of the original. Acker is unafraid to mix her story lines with theory. *Don Quixote* (1986), for instance, includes sections of dialogue, more or less randomly placed, in which characters debate the merits and limits of Derrida, Foucault, Gilles Deleuze, Jean Baudrillard, and other figures (54–5). The theoretical elements are transformed by being placed in the context of the ongoing action, most of it sexual, violent, or both. Her point is that identity construction in a society structured by race, class, and gender hierarchies is inherently violent.

Acker also mixes in other essay-like philosophical and political commentaries, as when she reveals the hidden agenda beneath the liberal humanist version of rationality: "For reason, on the one hand, signifies the idea of a free, human social life. On the other hand, reason is the court of judgment of calculation, the instrument of domination, and the means for the greatest exploitation of nature" (72). As the epigraph to the second section of *Quixote* shouts, the virus carrying this unreasonable notion of reason is language: "BEING DEAD DON QUIXOTE COULD NO LONGER SPEAK. BEING BORN INTO AND PART OF A MALE WORLD, SHE HAD NO SPEECH OF HER OWN. ALL SHE COULD DO WAS READ MALE TEXTS WHICH WEREN'T HERS" (39; capitalization in the original). Her *Quixote* rewrite begins with Don's abortion, an act that is the symbolic counterpoint to rebirth. This female Quixote's quest is to become a knight who can take on the dark forces of a land shadowed by the then current "leader of the free world," Richard "I am not a crook" Nixon. Acker uses sado-masochistic violence, pornography, and every kind of rage she can muster to bury forever any image of passive or submissive femininity, and in the process reveals the sadistic violence of sexism, racism, and economic exploitation hidden beneath the surface of the "American dream," which is sutured into the language of everyday life. For Acker, identity is the enemy, a prison house that can be broken out of only through literary explosives hurled at the walls from inside and outside the socially constructed "self."

Detecting the Self: Jonathan Lethem's *Motherless Brooklyn* (1999)

There are a number of rich postmodern novels, including Thomas Pynchon's *The Crying of Lot 49* (1966), Paul Auster's *New York Trilogy* (1990), Clarence Major's *Reflex and Bone Structure* (1996), and Robert Coover's *Noir* (2010), that rework the classic mystery genre as a kind of metaphysical search for identity. Pynchon's suburban housewife, Oedipa Mass, becomes a kind of unlicensed detective by accident, or perhaps by destiny, and may be chasing a paranoid fantasy rather than solving a mystery. Auster's detective, who seems to be named Paul Auster, may be shadowing himself. Major's unreliable narrator is not even sure where he is. And Coover's hilariously confused version of Philip Marlowe, aptly named Philip Noir, mostly just discovers more and more of the genre's hackneyed attempts at realism ("The smoke in here is thick enough to slice and sell as sandwich meat"), and as the story progresses clues lead not to more and more clarity, but to more and more confusion about the crime.

An equally funny, genre-bending, richly imagined and revelatory postmodern detective is the (sort-of) hero of Jonathan Lethem's *Motherless Brooklyn* (1999).[8] The novel is, in good postmodern fashion, a loving tribute to the detective novel genre, and a rousing parody of it. In the classic detective novel, especially its literary and cinematic "noir" form, the detective is a cool character of few words who keeps his ideas and emotions close to his chest. The narrator of *Motherless Brooklyn* could not be much further from that type. He is one Lionel Essrog, a young man with Tourette's syndrome—a disease that leaves him largely unable to filter his words or control tics of his body. That means he is constantly broadcasting the inner workings of his mind, revealing not only secrets but all his intentions and true feelings. It is a loving portrait of a neurodiverse individual such that by the end of the novel it is the other characters, not Lionel, who seem abnormal. Though wonderfully strange and bizarrely funny, the novel is dramatic enough to be a true mystery. Lionel, while hardly a conventional Sam Spade-like detective, in fact turns out to be pretty effective in searching for the killer of his friend and mentor, Frank Minna.

As a bonus, *Motherless Brooklyn* seems to humorously embody (and parody) poststructuralist language theory. You don't need to know that to enjoy the novel, but it is even more fun when you do. Poststructuralist theory argues that associations between a word ("signifier") and the thing it names ("signified") are arbitrary, conventional. There is no natural connection between the word "cat" and the small furry feline we use that word to point toward. And the entire meaning system is a kind of arbitrary substitution game in which "cat" means something only because it is similar in sound to words like "rat," "hat," or "bat." Meaning is always oppositional. We know cat not only because it is not these other three letter rhymes, but also because it is not dog, lion, or pig. Meanwhile, if you use a dictionary to find out what a cat is, you end up running in word circles without ever reaching some base in an actuality beyond words. A cat is a feline. And what is a feline, but a category for cats, and so on. You end up like a cat chasing its own tail, or like Paul Auster's sleuth chasing his own trail.

In addition, because word concepts only make sense by being contrasted to other word concepts, Derrida argues that they call up *traces* of other words. It is impossible, for example, to think of the word "male" without conjuring up its supposed opposite, "female," and it is impossible to use the word "nature" without calling up its supposed opposite, "culture." These little slippages and binary oppositions may not be much of an issue at the level of telling a cat from a dog, but as language builds up to larger structures of self and society, considerable complexities emerge. Lethem plays with this, with opposites collapsing into one another, as when Essrog notes: "I'm tightly wound. I'm a loose cannon. Both—I'm a tightly wound loose cannon, a tight loose" (261). Derrida says that there is play in language, like the play in a steering wheel, a device that must be both tight and loose.

Lionel's condition causes him to emit long strands of seeming nonsense, and in doing so he reveals the extent to which all speech is dependent upon the imperfect suppression of the nonsensical and alternative meaning always on the edge of the sense you intend. Following a line of clues that leads to a Zen temple, for example, Essrog disrupts the meditators by shouting "Zengeance! . . . Ziggedy zendoodah . . . Pierogi Monster Zen master zealous neighbor. Zazen zaftig Zsa-Zsa go-bare" (201). And, of course, it is not Zsa Zsa who goes bare, but Lionel whose hidden thought-associations are revealed to his audience through moves reminiscent of deconstruction.

Part of the reader-as-detective experience is decoding Lionel's outbursts, looking there for clues while also following more traditional parts of a whodunnit trail. Even his own name is impossible for him to give without free association riffing: "*Liable Guesscog, Final Escrow, Ironic Pissclam,*" (7) and "*Lyrical Eggdog! Logical Assnog!*" (104) Of course, as psychiatrists, or at least the ones on TV, have taught us, such associations are seldom free of meaning. And apart from the hilarity of these riffs, part of the fun is detecting when these improvisations reveal something about Lionel, or even provide clues to the murder mystery at play.

The slippage in meaning in these word plays also suggests the poststructuralist observation that language is a structure with no center, it is *decentered* from any core of grounded meaning. Essrog says, "We were all four of us an arrangement around a missing centerpiece, as incoherent as a verb-less sentence" (91). There is a poetry to Lionel's speech, and like much poetry, meanings are often allusive, as well as elusive. Elusive allusion and illusion is the way all meaning works. Language is constantly deconstructing itself, and in doing so it is deconstructing the self. We are all made of words, but Lionel's eccentric behavior makes us aware of just how strange and arbitrary that making and remaking is. At one point Lionel's mind skips from "I'm afraid not" to "I'm *afrayedknot*" (32–3). He is, but so are we all, "afrayed." He may be an eccentric, but we are all eccentric, ex-centric to ourselves. We stand outside ourselves looking at our self, yet who is the self looking? We think we are in control and yet are driven by the compulsive tics of language embedded in unconscious drives and ideological impulses we cannot see.

Lionel's Tourettic self creates a kind of doppelgänger. When the expectation of a sexual tryst arises, he muses that "I want to slow it down to a crawl, . . . get to meet my stilled self, give him a little time to look around" (104). But this doubleness is also his gift, his awareness. Lionel refuses to "narcotize" his self with drugs, refuses to give up the insights his linguistic eccentricities have built: "The chemicals slowed my brain to a morose crawl, were a boot on my wheel of self." He refuses any "dimming of the world (or my brain—same thing)" (83).

The novel also uses Lionel's verbal ticcing and compulsive touching disorder to comment pointedly and poignantly on a phenomenon that has become increasingly prevalent in recent years:

> Conspiracies are a version of Tourette's syndrome, the making and tracing of unexpected connections a kind of touchiness, an expression of the yearning to touch the world, kiss it all over with theories, pull it close. Like Tourette's, all conspiracies are ultimately solipsistic, sufferer or conspirator or theorist overrating his centrality and forever rehearsing a traumatic delight in reaction, attachment and causality, in roads leading out from the Rome of self. (178)

Lethem is clueing us into an element of paranoia unleashed by postmodernity's fragmenting forces and now amplified a hundred fold by social media's Tourettic tics on a touchpad's send buttons.

What is amazing about *Motherless Brooklyn* is that all of this use and parody of language theory, and all this speculation on the nature of the self, is seamlessly embedded in an unusual but still quite recognizable tragic-comic detective story. Part of the pleasure is figuring out if the exact opposite of the cool, taciturn private eye can nevertheless succeed in catching the bad guys. Again, you need to know nothing of language theory to enjoy the book, and Lethem's humanizing of a person marginalized by a complicated medical syndrome can work on you without thinking about how his disorder reveals the way language works for all of us. But knowing something about this theory can add another lovely layer of appreciation. Part of what Lionel is detecting is that we are all Tourettic now. "New York is a Tourettic city," (113) and by extension the whole postmodern world is becoming more Tourettic, more filled with compulsive tics, extreme self-consciousness, and struggling to say what we mean or mean what we say.

Hybrid Selves: Gloria Anzaldúa's *Borderlands/La Frontera* (1987)

Gloria Anzaldúa's uncategorizable hybrid text, *Borderlands/La Frontera* (1987), offers a journey into the mystery of the self that is every bit as complex, contradictory, and culturally challenging as Acker's or Lethem's, but with a very different set of interests and concerns.[9] Where Acker's gender-bending tales are told from a position of racial and class privilege (she was a refugee from an upper-middle-class upbringing), and Lethem was dealing with a character marginalized due to a medical condition, Anzaldúa's marginal status as a poor, *indio*, Chicanx, queer, Nahuatl-descended and Spanish-speaking *tejana* provided her with a different set of insights. The "borderlands" of her title are only superficially a geographic space. It is better understood as psycho-geographic, as a set of cultural spaces where identities imposed and identities forged align, conflict, turn, and return to questions of power. The search for the power to define and redefine the self in the face of external forces bearing down on one's being is at the heart of this book. *Borderlands/La Frontera*'s mix of genres (novel, poetry, memoir, history, and theory) is not just a play with form but another way of embodying multiple selves. Form reveals and conceals certain truths that are at once personal and cultural, historical and of the moment. *La frontera* is not an easy place; it is a place of pain and trauma, where identities rub against one another to form open wounds. But it is also a place of immense creativity. Anzaldúa speaks of the multiple linguistic/cultural "lands" that make up her geography, making clear that it is the existence of this multitude of selves that has moved her toward freedom, toward the possibility of creating herself. The trap of fixed identity is opened up at the borderlands as cultures crash into one another and reveal their partialness, their limits.

If there is any single quality that distinguishes the postmodern, it is rejection of singleness. Postmodernists favor multiplicity in virtually everything—politics, religion, aesthetics, sexualities, and so on. For Anzaldúa, it is a multiplicity of languages and dialects that she credits for allowing her to form a more complex (postmodern) notion of self. She identifies seven linguistic communities she had to negotiate as she grew to maturity: (1) standard English (2) working-class and slang English; (3) standard Spanish; (4) standard Mexican Spanish; (5) north Mexican Spanish dialect; (6) Chicano Spanish (with regional variations from her native Texas to her travels in New Mexico, Arizona, and California); (7) Tex-Mex; and (8) *Pachuco* (called *caló*) street Spanglish (77). Each of these languages is deeply embedded in cultural assumptions, values, possibilities, and limits. Apart from the so-called standard English and the so-called standard Spanish, each of these languages was devalued, looked down upon by those of higher social and economic status. Moreover, within these broader languages, she had to negotiate with many additional communities created around her sexual, political, religious, and ethnic/racial identities, each with their own unique idiolects or jargons, and each with an internal hierarchy. Anzaldúa translates some of the Spanish and Native words in her text, but strategically leaves others untranslated to underscore the limits of monolingual English speakers and to embody the rootedness of language in the particulars of experience.

The book begins with a key history lesson about how the most controversial US border was formed. She reminds or introduces readers to the fact that, as some Mexican Americans point out, they did not cross the border, the border crossed them. This refers to the Mexican American War (1846–8) or, as it is known in Mexico, *Intervención Estadounidense en México* (The United States Intervention in Mexico). The latter term is arguably more accurate, as it was in fact the United States that goaded Mexico into hostilities with the clear goal of expanding US territories. The victorious United States forced the remnants of the Mexican government to sign the Treaty of Guadalupe-Hidalgo, a move that added Texas and large parts of the Southwest to the slave-holding portions of the United States. These lands were inhabited primarily by Spanish-speaking and Indigenous language–speaking peoples, who soon found their languages denigrated, their citizenship called into question, much of their land and property stolen, and their very being transformed into a borderland battleground. Entering the world more than 100 years after these events, Anzaldúa saw constantly that her identities continued to be shaped by lines drawn by that treaty, a situation that has again and again been politicized through the often purposeful conflation of subsequent legal and illegal migration with people whose ancestors lived on the land for hundreds of years before "Americans" arrived across that violently imposed 1848 border.

Anzaldúa calls herself a *mestiza*, a word originally coined to describe a person of mixed Indigenous (*indio*) and European ethnic identity (originally Spanish conquerors), but given these linguistic/cultural complexities, she expands the term to mean any identity that crosses the neat lines of race, gender, class, sexual, and other identities—identities viewed as incompatible with each other and unequally valued by the dominant culture(s) around her. As much as any writer of the postmodern era, Anzaldúa richly lays out the ways in which borderlands of identity, while often fraught with the pain of oppression, open up new vistas, new possibilities for escaping traps for the self that limit life on all sides of socially constructed borders.

The Abstract Self: Don DeLillo's *Cosmopolis* (2003)

Don DeLillo is perhaps the postmodern novelist who has best captured a kind of self lacking all human empathy, a self utterly abstracted from any kind of community or common reality. Other postmodern novelists like Brett Easton Ellis in his *American Psycho* (2003) diagnose a similarly hollowed-out kind of narcissistic identity. These authors detail how all the social forces of family or community or the wider social order that might contain or constrain such a person slide off of them like so much rainwater on a slicker. This is a self that has lost all interiority, has become fully absorbed into an abstract idea of the self. Ellis's character becomes a serial killer, but DeLillo creates an even more pervasive character, the kind who uses "killer apps" to make a "killing" on the stock market.

In *Cosmopolis* (2003), DeLillo captures the chilling, senseless drift of a fabulously wealthy young man unmoored by belief in anything but his own pleasure. The central character is Eric Packer, an utterly amoral, vacuous young Wall Street billionaire who rides through the streets of Manhattan in a limo as blankly white as his soul. As he travels about, he is being stalked by a terrorist with an equally empty sense of self. Packer is what used to be called a "self-made man," but his money no longer brings him any pleasure—nor do sexual trysts, spa treatments, or much of anything else. The one thing that became something of a purpose in life, the making of more and more money, now seems so burdensome that he seems bent on losing it all as he recklessly gambles it away on investments that make no sense to his advisors. "Money has lost its narrative quality the way painting did once upon a time. Money is talking to itself" (77).[10] DeLillo shows the maniacal single-purposed terrorist self and the power-mad capitalist self to be mirror images of one another.

The white limo Packer rides around in has been, as he phrases it, "Prousted," lined with cork like the room in which Marcel Proust wrote his sumptuous, voluminous study of *fin de siècle* Paris, *A la Recherche du Temps Perdu* (*A Search for Lost Time*). This Prousting announces DeLillo's postmodern questioning of the role of art under multinational capitalism. It is as if the richness of a novelistic narrative that had sought to contain the whole world has been reduced to a technique for keeping the world out. The floor of his limo is lined with Carrara marble, the material out of which many of the great sculptured artworks of the Renaissance were carved. The twenty-eight-year-old Packer buys now fantastically expensive works of abstract expressionist art, not out of either aesthetic joy or as an investment, but just because he can. Robbed of their role in the liberation of art from certain historically imposed limits, these once powerful expressionist canvases stand in for a life that is abstract in its expressionlessness: a life abstracted from all of the social forces—family life, community connection, political belief—that have traditionally anchored the self.

> He liked paintings that his guests did not know how to look at. The white paintings were unknowable to many, knife-applied slabs of mucoid color. The work was all the more dangerous for not being new. There's no more danger in the new. (8)

"No more danger in the new," the plaint of modernism's death. DeLillo's postmodern artistry demonstrates the once subversive power of modernist art incorporated into the empty games of a man living in a pale, pure, privileged narcissistic bubble.

DeLillo conveys this all through a flattened prose whose surface never varies regardless of the action being portrayed (a rectal exam, the funeral of a "Sufi rap artist," an anti-capitalist protest, two assassination attempts—one by pastry). All life is reduced to the smooth surface of a laptop screen. Packer casually muses, "Do people still shoot at presidents? I thought there were more stimulating targets" (20). He is more unmoored from any kind of social fabric outside his self than is the delusional terrorist assassin who stalks him.

The ordinary people outside his limo fail to understand that reality is whatever he projects onto the several monitors mounted inside. Packer wants to live on a disc, to become data. His life is a simulation, something he performs as if it were someone else's: "This is good," he says to his rich young wife of twenty-two days when they are having an intense conversation about infidelity. "We're like people talking. Isn't this how they talk?" "How would I know?" she replies (119). This is not merely the cluelessness of the hyper-wealthy. It reflects the deeper structure of a world in which everything has become a tradeable commodity, a digitized world reduced to 0s and 1s, to abstractions having no connection to other human beings. His wife, his partners, those who work for him, are images on a screen he projects, or they appear and disappear in his limo as he is driven around. In a world that worships the wealthy and celebrities as gods whose every tweeted thought is a revelation, the self ends up performing an empty march toward a death that also cannot be believed in. Packer thinks that "When he died he would not end. The world would end" (6). Packer may be an extreme case driven by extreme wealth, but, DeLillo suggests, his is a disease that has to varying degrees infected all of us caught up in the dizzying digital whirl of the world today.

The Terrorized Self: Mohsin Hamid's *The Reluctant Fundamentalist* (2007)

Terrorisms of various kinds have occurred for hundreds of years. In the postmodern era there are both continuities and new elements in the nature of the phenomenon, and therefore also among literary depictions of those labeled terrorists. Terrorist acts in the context of the Irish "troubles," for example, have been interrogated in a number of novels that explore the ambiguities of political identity in the postmodern era. Eoin McNamee's *Resurrection Man* (1994) captures the all-too-real, yet hallucinatory, experience of terrorism, while Patrick McCabe's *Breakfast on Pluto* (1998) uses a gender fluid main character to obliquely examine the complexly mixed motives of characters drawn into the orbit of terrorist violence. And Anna Burns in *Milkman* (2018) removes all character names and place names to trace the mutual terrorization of two warring communities that emerges through a process of linguistic entrapment in which every word is given a polarized political meaning, while also showing deep masculinist connections between sexual predation and terrorism.

During more recent decades, it is terrorism from groups ostensibly based in radically conservative strands of Islam, that has dominated the popular imagination and literary representation. There are at least four main trends in these depictions. The first, and perhaps, most common is the fanatical religious extremist trope, often depicted as a kind of madness. Second, has been the "disintegration of self" trope, one especially closely tied to postmodern cultural transformations. A third views terrorists as personally flawed individuals, troubled by deep conflicts, frequently sexual in nature. And finally, a fourth approach actually examines the roots of terrorism in international and transnational political factors and forces. While often one of these tropes or emphases will dominate the representation, in the best novels these differing motives work in some combination, in recognition that individual reasons for support of terrorism vary immensely.

In a series of novels including, in addition to *Cosmopolis*, *The Names* (1982), *Mao II* (1992), *Falling Man* (2007), and *Point Omega* (2010), Don DeLillo has captured chillingly the process of terrorists becoming unhinged from any reality not existing at the surface level of mass-mediated images. Through a process that might be called de-realization, the transformation of life into simulated images on televisual and digital screens can distance certain consumers of these images from stabilizing social contexts. DeLillo is widely regarded as the foremost novelistic analysist of this process, and he has linked it to the rise of terrorism. He offers harrowingly intimate glimpses of terrorists driven to pathological levels of detachment from human connection that lead them to embrace fundamentalist religious or political ideologies. Importantly, over time these portraits have increasingly deepened the political contexts to counterbalance an overemphasis on personal pathology in DeLillo's early novels. In contrast, Salman Rushdie, himself a target of an incitement to assassination by Islamist fundamentalists, in works such as *Shalimar the Clown* (2005), still largely confines his exploration of terrorism to pathology driven by personal vengeance. Disintegration of self and personal pathology may indeed be among the factors in the rise of terrorism in the postmodern era, but novels that center on these factors underplay the roots of terrorism in international and transnational political realities.

In contrast, Mohsin Hamid, in his novel *The Reluctant Fundamentalist* (2007), captures the fluidity of the self in the postmodern era as more organically linked to geopolitical realities by tracing one man's path from Ivy league–educated corporate raider to potential terrorist.[11] At once a realistic story and postmodern allegory, the novel explores the relationship of dominance between the United States and less powerful nations around the globe, by giving each character a name symbolic of their role in global politics. The novel is narrated as an extended monologue in a café in Lahore, Pakistan. The symbolically named narrator, Changez, speaks to an unnamed, silent interlocutor who may or may not be a CIA agent. This structure suggests a kind of payback for the fact that for too long the United States has spoken without hearing the voices of those others of the world who have had their lives deeply, often catastrophically, shaped by its foreign policy. Crucially, the narrator is a young Pakistani émigré to the United States who has enjoyed a privileged life there. Changez obtains a degree from the prestigious Princeton University, gets a good job in a New York financial institution, and enters into a relationship with a very wealthy and attractive young white woman named Erica. In the allegory, the financial firm is

Underwood Sampson, suggesting both the United States and Uncle Sam, Erica is seemingly short for AmErica, and her boyfriend Chris may stand in for a certain strain of Christianity.

The main catalyst for change in the life of Changez is the terrorist attack of 9/11. As the narrator experiences a new, deeper form of discrimination (before he was an exotic foreigner, now he is viewed as a possible terrorist), he also begins to question his role in the US empire. He gradually comes to realize he is on the wrong side of a global divide. In another important allegorical moment, a key part of Changez's awakening comes while he is on assignment in Chile, a country where a CIA–backed coup in 1976 ousted a democratically elected socialist leader and put in place a vicious, murderous authoritarian regime. There he meets a man, Juan-Batista, who tells him he is acting like a reverse Janissary (Janissaries were Christian children who were kidnapped and raised to fight for the Muslim Ottoman empire during the medieval Crusades). In this scene, an awakened Changez recites the long litany of US military and financial interventions into sovereign nations around the world over decades: "Vietnam, Korea, the Straits of Taiwan, the Middle East and now Afghanistan: in each of the major conflicts and standoffs that ringed my mother continent of Asia, America played a central role. Moreover, I knew from my experience as a Pakistani that finance was the major means by which the American empire exercised its power" (156).

In contrast to the many nonfiction and fictional treatments of contemporary terrorists that treat them as pathological, as personally damaged by trauma, or as turned into automatons by religious brainwashing, this novel suggests something different. Changez admits that he had "no stable core" of beliefs at one time, that his "own identity is fragile," but it is not a particularly deep fragility (148). To the extent that Erica represents AmErica, she is the most deeply psychologically troubled of the characters. She is obsessed with the past, with her idealized dead lover, Chris, himself a symbol of a problematic white Christian identity threatened by the nation's increasing diversity. Is Hamid suggesting that it is (am)Erica that exhibits pathological behavior, an obsession with an idealized past that is blind to what it truly embodies in the present?

The novel is purposely ambivalent in its double-coded form in terms of the position of the narrator and of his silent counterpart. Changez claims to want only nonviolent change but may possibly be a terrorist. The title, for example, changes meaning as the novel progresses. Given the subject matter, it might at first suggest a fanatical Islamist fundamentalism, but there is another kind of fundamentalism to which the narrator is subjected. As he travels the world for his rapacious multinational corporation that specializes in destroying and rebuilding other financial institutions, he is told by his boss to "focus on the fundamentals" (98), and it is clear that the philosophy of Underwood Sampson is free-market fundamentalism, postmodern neoliberalism's dominant ideology.

It is also the case that the response to terrorism in the United States, the United Kingdom, and elsewhere in the overdeveloped world has been fundamentally flawed. Terrorism has often found its mirror image in counter-terrorism. As Richard Jackson, one of the foremost scholars of terrorism and author of an excellent novel on the topic, writes:

> The dehumanization and demonization of the "terrorist" to which much literature contributes is directly implicated in a range of ethically questionable and mostly ineffective security practices, including military invasion, torture, extra-judicial drone killings, extraordinary rendition, preventive detention, mass surveillance, the denial of *habeas corpus*, and the broader securitization of social life. Ironically, such practices, in a self-fulfilling manner create the very conditions that encourage more acts of terrorism.[12]

The "terrorists win," Jackson suggests, not when the targets of terrorism negotiate with them, but rather when state-sanctioned counter-terrorism actions become indistinguishable from terrorism, and when once democratic societies use terrorism as an excuse to drastically curtail the privacy and civil liberties of their own citizens. This is made possible in larger measure by the refusal to acknowledge the political contexts of terrorism in favor of treating it as only a pathology.

These other fundamental perspectives are embodied in the silent partner to the protagonist of *The Reluctant Fundamentalist*. The ambiguous status of the silent stranger at whom Changez directs his book-long monologue is a crucial part of the action. The listener to this one-sided conversation is never clearly identified. In an act that might be called counter-profiling, he may have been picked up on the street because he "looks American." The possible identities of this man range from a spy sent to assassinate the narrator to a businessman to an "innocent" tourist. And that is precisely the point. Readers are left to ask whether US foreign policy and global economic dominance is as much the responsibility of the tourist who remains blind to the operations of the government as it is of the one actively working to assure American dominance over the rest of the globe no matter what the cost to the citizens of other countries?

Self as Community: Toni Cade Bambara's *The Salt Eaters* (1980)

No postmodern novel better illustrates the opposite of the abstract or the alienated terrorist self than the embeddedness of the self in community in Toni Cade Bambara's novel *The Salt Eaters* (1980).[13] Stylistically, Bambara turned from the traditional realism of her two highly regarded short story collections, *Gorilla, My Love* (1972) and *The Sea Birds are Still Alive* (1977), to the postmodern realist form required by her new theme, the fragmentation of self. The main character has her consciousness shattered, her sanity shaken, by the excessive demands of her concurrent roles as a worker, spouse, mother, and community activist amid the deeply conflicted forces of postmodernity. But the fragmenting of her mind, as embodied in the fragmentation of the novel's story lines, also clearly mimics the dissolution of the wider community during the reactionary aftermath of the Civil Rights, Black Power, and other progressive social movements of the 1960s and early 1970s. The central character is the community, and in the novel each member struggles to turn fragments into something that can sustain resistance in the face of powerful centrifugal forces.

The novel is set in the fictional predominantly African American town of Claybourne, Georgia. The "self" at the center of the novel is Velma Henry. A full-time wife, full-time mother, full-time worker at a chemical plant, and full-time activist in several of the protest movements of the era, Velma has so stretched herself that as the novel opens, she breaks, and attempts suicide. The key figure helping Velma rebuild her self is the community's elder folk healer, Minnie Ransom.

The action of the novel takes place on at least three planes of reality that Bambara seamlessly blurs together: the mundane level of everyday life around the town; life inside the mind of Velma; and a spiritual plane where Minnie goes in search of ancient folk wisdom. In the eye of the hurricane that is the novel's action, Velma and Minnie stand together in a room in Claybourne's hospital. Modern medicine having played its role in patching up Velma's slashed wrists, the lead doctor allows Minnie to ply her ancient trade of psyche healer. The elder and the burnt-out younger woman engage in a kind of battle of wills in which Minnie must convince Velma to help with the restoration process.

While Minnie works on Velma's mind/spirit, readers are presented with a variety of scenes that seem to be a mix of memories from the two central protagonists, along with events in the present in the wider world of the town. Several of the scenes take place at the Seven Arts, a local community activist center where the aesthetic arts, spiritual arts, and the political arts seek a balance. But it is clear that there is a major imbalance in how the work at the center is done, with the women doing virtually all of the real work while the male members argue endlessly about abstract fine points of ideology. A related scene of a prominent impeccably dressed, sunglasses sporting black politician emerging from an air-conditioned limo to orate to a crowd of people sweltering in summer heat evokes the decline of the idea of black power into the hands of a few opportunistic black politicians.

In addition to analyzing the gender relations within black movements and the co-optation of social movements, the novel was among the first to raise issues of environmental justice. The late 1970s and the early 1980s saw the emergence of a branch of the environmental movement that was documenting the fact that working-class white communities and communities of color were subject to far more ecological devastation and pollution-related illness than wealthier areas.[14] This includes radioactive uranium mining waste left behind on Native reservations, carcinogenic toxic dumps and incinerators in black and Latino/a/x neighborhoods, and a host of other well-documented examples of what came to be known as environmental racism. Bambara highlights these issues via Velma's discovery that Transchemical Corporation, where she works, has been secretly transporting radioactive waste through downtown Claybourne.

In contrast to the forces of fragmentation, the novel poses a kind of utopian allegory in the form of the theatrical-activist group, the Seven Sisters. Each sister represents a continent that has been exploited by the 500-year cycle of European imperialism, symbolized by a key food crop (i.e., the Sister of the yam for Africa, Sister of maize for Latin America, and so on). The troupe embodies a nonbiological but nature-based kinship, a collective resistance to colonialism, and a creative transformation to a possible future order of sustainable energy and equitable distribution of life's necessities, including the arts. Isolated from such a sisterhood, Velma struggles to find herself.

Throughout the various scenes, Minnie is trying telepathically and directly to convey to Velma that she is desperately needed by the community, and that she can serve that role only to the degree that she can keep her own mind, body, and spirit healthy. The novel makes clear throughout that significant political change can only occur when there is a balance between the inner lives of activists and their outward actions in the world. Minnie's rootedness in a long-standing folk tradition allows her to see that the heavy burdens of life under the fragmenting, materialistic conditions of postmodernity pale beside the conditions of slavery and Jim Crow segregation out of which the community was born. Nevertheless, she recognizes that the relative freedom available to some in the wake of a certain amount of Civil Rights progress poses new challenges. She sees that an excess of freedom in some areas of life can be as dangerous as its absence, that a version of the American individualist disease is infecting the community. Minnie is a lifeline between generations and between the spiritual world and the political one. But she can only go so far. She can offer a lifeline, but Velma, and the community she embodies, need to grab that lifeline after listening attentively to voices almost drowned out by the noise of postmodern culture. The search is not for some timeless essential self locked in the past, but rather a search for the emotional resources for change, for the power to shift the self in ways that play meaningfully through destabilizing conditions that can never be fully controlled.[15]

The Selfless Self: Ruth Ozeki's *A Tale for the Time Being* (2013)

Postmodernists and Buddhists have in common the belief that the "self" is an illusion, a false fixing of the random flow of experiences. It is perhaps fitting then to end this chapter with a book that is both postmodern and Buddhist. Examining the chaos of the self under postmodern conditions by bringing ancient Japanese ideas into struggle with contemporary North American and Japanese experience, a novel of Canadian-American-Japanese author and Zen priest Ruth Ozeki, *A Tale for the Time Being* (2013), offers profound meditations on identity.[16] Like other metafictionists, Ozeki invents a character who is and is not her self. The character's name (Ruth) and certain key details (her profession—writer; her home—British Columbia) clearly mirror the author's own. But as she makes clear in an interview, not only is she not the character but that "every act of representation is also an act of misrepresentation, so there is no way to represent without fictionalizing."[17] Where in the hands of others this kind of observation might generate a near nihilistic disregard for truth, in Ozeki's hands it is a call to a greater responsibility to make the best true fictions we can carefully carve out of the materials our lives offer us. This includes recognition that there is no such thing as an isolated self, no self-made man or woman. Such myths narcissistically suppress recognition of the many threads of connection to others that made us and continue to make us throughout our lives. This interconnectedness is not some vague humanistic notion, but a sociological, historical, psychological, and linguistic fact underlying the characters offered in this multilayered, multicultural tale.

The premise of the novel is that Ruth discovers a diary inside a Hello Kitty lunchbox wrapped up in a plastic bag that washed up on a beach near her home on a remote island in British Columbia (the diary amusingly has a false cover of Proust's *A Search for Lost Time*). Ruth and her spouse speculate that the diary may have been sent her way by the tsunami that led to the devastating Fukushima nuclear plant meltdown in 2011. Playing detective, the Ruth character begins reading the diary and trying to track down its author via internet searches and her local library. While the narrator wonders if the diary is real or possibly a work of fiction, readers are brought to wonder about *A Tale for the Time Being*. How much, if any, of the story is based on fact? As the novel progresses, we become less interested in that dichotomy than in the ways in which all of us are fictional creations.

The act of reading is thematized as the character with the same name as the author reads the writings of another character, a young Japanese girl named Nao. The skepticism Ruth brings to Nao's diary is one that readers of Ozeki's novel come to share. In addition to this metafictional narration by Ruth/Ozeki, we are given direct access to the diary of Nao (pronounced Now), who seems to be a sixteen-year-old girl caught between cultures. Born in Japan to Japanese parents, as a young child her family moves to Sunnyvale, California, in the heart of the Silicon Valley digital electronic industry, where her father has found employment. Nao is raised as an English speaker with only a rudimentary knowledge of Japanese. When her father is fired for raising ethical objections to the potential military uses being built into a video game he is designing, the now sixteen-year-old must accompany her parents back to Tokyo. In a lovely ironic play on what has become the center of the world's unreality, Nao laments "life is unreal [in Japan], and Sunnyvale, which was real, was a jillion miles away in time and space, like the beautiful Earth from outer space" (79). Her inability to fit into her new Japanese homeland leads to bullying and cyberbullying, driving Nao to become suicidal. In turn, the bullying prompts her father to try to protect her by inventing two apps that can erase all evidence of a person from the web. This is a sweet, welcomed gesture, though, in another twist, Nao's erasure from the internet was one of the things fueling Ruth's doubt that she actually existed. Is this comment on what happens when our online identities threaten to take on a reality of their own?

While the erasure of self in the form of 1's and 0's is superficial, the erasure can be read as one element in the undoing of Nao's illusory self, one part of a transformation of the young woman into something more. The next key phase of this transformation occurs when Nao is rescued from a suicidal end partly by becoming involved in some of her own detective work, locating a long lost relative. In that process, she becomes closer to her great-grandmother, a Buddhist nun, and a figure whose melding of ancient wisdom and contemporary savvy provides her a lifeline, at least for the now of the tale, at least for the time being.

This multilayered novel reflects profoundly on the relation between self and other, present and past (are not they the same thing in the mind's eye?), and on the space between cultures. It is especially attuned to the ways in which the empty world of selfies and self-aggrandizement can be erased and replaced by a selflessness that is full of joy and beauty. In the case of Nao, a cleansing of the multi-mediated consumerist self frees her to better pursue the common work of fighting the forces of social injustice and environmental degradation. While most postmodernists diagnose the problem of the self, they rarely offer solutions; Ozeki's work suggests at least some paths. She believes in the possibility of working upon the self through disciplined, meditative exploration. The recent attention in the West to mindfulness often faddishly trivializes what that exploration means, at times turning it into just another form of narcissistic practice. For Ozeki mindfulness becomes meaningful only if accompanied by compassion for others, and by political action based not on absolute truth but on an ethical foundation. Calming the flow of excessive representation, cleaning the clutter from the self, can leave us seeing more clearly the paths that lead away from our current drive toward social and ecological disaster.

4

Bodies

Reflective Surfaces and Fluid Borders

Few areas of human experience have undergone more significant transformation during the postmodern era than the interwoven terrains of gender, sexuality, race, and the body. Bodies betray us, all the time, every day. Our bodies are texts read by others in ways that do not match how we feel inside. Our bodies betray ethno-racial, gendered, and sexualized conceptions that mark us as different and in which we may or may not recognize ourselves. Beautiful bodies are taken either too seriously or not seriously at all. The body speaks for us before we speak and in ways we cannot control. Body politics constantly shape the body politic.

Transformations have occurred not only in the ways in which bodies are psycho-socially sexed, raced, and gendered, but also at the level of material bodily alteration through increasingly available forms of surgery and technological interventions.[1] The conservative sexual and body politics of the 1950s have been utterly exploded by social movements in the subsequent postmodern decades, beginning with the women's and gay liberation movements of the 1960s and 1970s, the disability rights movement in the 1980s and 1990s, and accelerating into the queer and trans rights movements in the first two decades of the twenty-first century. Within and beyond these movements, various kinds of body modifications and technological interventions into the body have further reshaped our ideas of the human and posthuman physical form. Postmodern fiction has played and continues to play a significant role in all these transformations.

The 1950s was a particularly bleak time for those not adhering to sexual norms labeled as traditional. Not only was homosexuality a criminal offense throughout most of the Western world, but in the United States (and elsewhere) it was actively persecuted and tied into a vicious anti-communist witch hunt led by figures like Senator Joseph McCarthy. In both the United Kingdom and the United States, "commies" and "queers" were linked in these attacks as alleged threats to national security. In the United States, one of the major forces of this repression was a congressional body calling itself the House Un-American Activities Committee (HUAC).[2] The complexities of the mapping of ideologies onto bodies is suggested by the fact that one of the lead lawyers in this shameful charade was a man named Roy Cohn, himself a closeted homosexual, and a man who would later become lawyer for and mentor to a then-young would-be real estate tycoon named Donald Trump. Cohn is brilliantly played by Al Pacino in the film version of the postmodern, magical realist play "Angels in America," by Tony Kushner (absolutely no relation to Trump's son-in-law, Jared). Like the novel *Koolaids* (see Chapter 9), "Angels" explores the insidious initial mapping of HIV/AIDS exclusively onto gay male bodies in the 1980s.

Postmodern theorist Michel Foucault (perhaps riffing on Franz Kafka's image of a machine etching the body) describes ideology as etched onto the body at a level far deeper than any tattoo. Allied postmodern theorists Deleuze and Guatarri address these oppressive psychosocial ideological embodiments by positing the concept of a "body without organs," a kind of metaphor for a self open to virtually infinite possibilities of affect and action. What these theories have in common is a notion of the body as a site where meaning is created and recreated, where the seemingly most material part of ourselves can be rewritten. They posit the difficult, but possible, task of creating a new draft of the fiction that is our embodied self.

The reconceptualization of the body has gone hand in hand with medical interventions into the reconstruction of the body.[3] Various biotechnological developments like in vitro fertilization, cloning, gender reassignment surgery, implantation of tech devices into human bodies, and related forms of *body hacking* or *bio-hacking* have challenged basic notions of the human body as a natural, bounded, unique entity. Postmodern realist Shelley Jackson has literalized this process as fiction writing through her "Skin," a story tattooed on the bodies of over 2,095 volunteers, each of whom are given one word.[4]

A large body of cultural analysis, especially *cyborg theory*, and various shades of *posthumanism*, has arisen around questions of the body's entwinement with technologies.[5] In terms of our examination of postmodern fiction as a source of social change, a key political and literary development is the rise of various forms of *cyberfeminism*. Coined in the 1990s, the term is shorthand for a set of arguments that women should embrace and use technology in the service of gender equity. Cyberfeminisms of various stripes urged women to make their presence known in every type of digital space, and to use digital spaces to advocate for greater economic, political, social, and cultural equality among sexes and genders by challenging the allegedly natural limits of the body.

Another area with an apparent affinity between postmodern gender theory and postmodern fiction emerges, is through the idea of performance or *performativity*. Given the ways in which so many women's bodies have been objectified, raped, beaten, and otherwise denied dignity, freedom, and interiority, it is no wonder that a major body of feminist theory and fiction has sought to rewrite the body. Critics like Judith Butler argue that gender is a kind of performance, something that exists not naturally, but through repeated daily bodily and affective enactments and reenactments.[6] In this context, she argues that while drag shows can be used to reveal the gendering process, they are not always inherently subversive because they can be framed as "mere performances." Instead, Butler is talking about the way in which each of us all the time is performing gender, through our clothes, our hairstyles, our use or avoidance of make-up, our gestures and bodily movements, our tone of voice, and through it all the language we use to sex and gender ourselves and others.

Moving sex and gender out of the category of the natural and into the cultural frightens many conservatives, and can also seem to undermine certain kinds of progressive political solidarity. Thus, as feminist theorist Donna Haraway notes,

> Many feminists have resisted moves like those Butler recommends, for fear of losing a concept of agency for women as the concept of the subject withers under the attack on core identities and their constitutive fictions. Butler,

however, argued that agency is an instituted practice in a field of enabling constraints. A concept of a coherent inner self, achieved (cultural) or innate (biological), is a regulatory fiction that is unnecessary—indeed, inhibitory— for feminist projects of producing and affirming complex agency and responsibility.[7]

In other words, political identities can be formed without a base in some biological essence, and solidarity can be based on temporary, strategic alliances understood as real fictions. Given that postmodern fiction often celebrates literature as an ongoing performative text rather than a static, essential work, the literary fictions of embodying, gendering, and sexing have played and continue to play one key role in reimagining categories once thought to be immutable biological facts.[8]

Two of the most famously sexual taboo and norm-challenging books of the early postmodern era, *Lolita* by Vladimir Nabokov, and *Naked Lunch* by William Burroughs, mark a transition to a new frankness about the body's needs and desires. As fictions, the two could not be more different. They remind us that postmodern fiction has from the beginning been not one thing, but many things. Despite its salacious and offensive theme (an older man lusting after and statutorily raping a prepubescent teen), *Lolita* is a beautifully restrained, impeccably crafted novel. In stark contrast to *Lolita*, *Naked Lunch* is a vicious, excessive, seemingly structureless screed about indulgence, debauchery, and near madness. On the surface, about the only things the two novels have in common is their love of language (though Burroughs claimed "language is a virus from outer space"), and the fact that they were censored. But for our purposes they have a third similarity: they both offer a postmodern critique of hypocritical sexual morals. While in some readings *Lolita* uses sexual perversity primarily as an allegory for other kinds of deviance, it nevertheless offers a quite devastating critique of US suburban sex lives. The novel can be read as a critique of sexual objectification, in that it is relayed from the male gaze point of view of one Humbert Humbert, a decidedly unreliable narrator with absolutely no interest in the interiority of his twelve-year-old object of desire, Dolores Haze (who becomes Lolita in his fantasy life). To the degree that the reader buys into the narrator's version of Dolores/Lolita, we are the ones who are seduced, seduced by a slick wordsmith into coming close to violating our own presumed moral abhorrence of pedophiles. The focus on language has led some critics to argue that ultimately the novel is more about lust for the American (not the English) language than lust for what we would now call a tween. While surely open to reactionary readings in its 1950s context, *Lolita* helped open up the domain of bodily and sexual representation in contemporary literature.

Naked Lunch attacks the hypocrisy of sexual morality in the Western world far more directly, while celebrating the joys and pains of queer sexual practices socially constructed as unnatural and deviant. Burroughs exposes, among other things, a vicious kind of sadomasochism in American life that dare not speak its name, one that gets a kind of sexual pleasure out of persecuting sexual minorities. Legally prosecuted for his sexual practices and for his literary representation of those practices, he understood better than most the impact of a system that uses sexuality as a power tool, as it were, to suppress other dimensions of dissent from mainstream ideologies. Conversely, the novel suggests that cracking open the sexual system may be one key entry point into cracking open the wider system of oppression under consumer capitalism. For Burroughs, a heroin addict for much of his life, drug addiction is at once itself and a metaphor for various other kinds of addiction—to sex, to power, to consumer goods, to controlling the bodies of others. *Naked Lunch* is a kind of primer for understanding Foucault's concept of power/knowledge as an intricately entwined system that builds not just from the top down, but from the bottom up through discourses of sexuality and embodiment.

Scripted Sex: Jeannette Winterson's *Writing the Body* (1993)

However subversive these early postmodern novels may have been in context, they are nevertheless limited by a deep immersion in masculinist perspectives. The limits of that perspective were subsequently revealed by the rise of the women's movements in the 1960s and 1970s, and by feminist novelists who have been in the forefront of postmodern fiction that explores the sex/gender system. This includes a large body of imaginatively rich feminist science fiction/speculative fiction. The archetype of these is Joanna Russ's *Female Man* (1975) in which the central character is seemingly four clones or parallel universe versions of the same woman that develop into four wholly different characters because they grow up in utterly different social environments. A classic example of the postmodern use of the multiverse concept, the novel was remarkably prescient in that in addition to illustrating richly the far greater importance of nurture over nature with regard to both gender and sex, it also presents sex transition surgery and even robot sex, as ways to comment on bodily pleasures and social construction of the self. The novel demonstrates again and again how we are taught socially to read bodies in ways that privilege only certain ones as normal, acceptable, and reducible to two binary labels, "female" or "male." An equally rich treatment of these issues is offered in Marge Piercy's *Woman on the Edge of Time* (1976), in which the central character time travels to a future world in which transcendence of the sex-gender system has been made possible by new reproductive technologies that relieve women of exclusive roles in childbirth, and where children are raised by multiparent family units in which "mothering" is not solely a female activity.

Likewise, British postmodern novelist Jeanette Winterson has approached these issues over several decades in a powerful series of novels set in historical and contemporary times that underscore the parallel between the way we read novels and the way we read bodies. This theme is developed with exquisite nuance, for example, in Winterson's aptly titled, *Written on the Body* (1993).[9] A dreamlike, yet realistic, novel that is as lyrically lovely as it is psychologically acute, its special brilliance lies in the fact that the gender of the narrator is never revealed despite it being almost solely a story about physical love. The gender mystery rises and falls in such a way that what starts out as a riddle to be solved has by the end come to seem irrelevant.

As Winterson herself describes the novel:

> All my work is experimental in that it plays with form, refuses a traditional narrative line, and includes the reader as a player. By that I mean that the reader has to work with the book. In the case of *Written on the Body*, the narrator has no name, is assigned no gender, is age unspecified, and highly unreliable. I wanted to see how much information I could leave out— especially the kind of character information that is routine—and still hold a story together.[10]

All through the novel it is impossible to tell the narrator's gender or the other attributes Winterson mentions. Thus his/her/their erotic attachment to a female character is exquisitely poised with near-clues that would seem to be about to let us know whether the narrator is male or female. But we never learn the answer. Instead we are forced to confront along the way again and again the strength of our desire to know, our desire to impose a gender. It seems that as readers we are meant to feel our discomfort at our inability to do so. At the same time, by illustrating a rich love of a body, as well as a deep love of the person possessing the body, readers can learn that the gendering of desire is not necessary. It is one thing to claim, as the pseudo-tolerant cliché has it, that "love knows no gender," but quite another to read a verbally sensuous, erotic, winding story that embodies that truth on every page.

Beauty and the Beastly Gaze: Jeffrey Eugenides's *The Virgin Suicides* (1993)

In *The Virgin Suicides* (1993), Jeffery Eugenides builds a novel around the mysterious lives and deaths of postmodern suburban girls whose outward bodily beauty consumes their inner lives.[11] It details the problem that Winterson sought to solve, the problem of an oppressive, obsessive gendering process. The novel is set in Grosse Point, Michigan, an upper-middle-class, middle-sized, largely European-American town. The family at the center of the novel consists of a math teacher father, homemaker mom, and five "beautiful" daughters: Celia aged thirteen, Lux fourteen, Bonnie fifteen, Mary sixteen, and the eldest, Therese seventeen. The apparent mystery at the core of the novel is given in the title: Why do all five of these girls commit suicide?

The novel is narrated in a rare second-person plural voice "We" as the recollections, twenty years later, of several neighborhood boys who had witnessed the extraordinary pageant of the five girls' lives and deaths. These well-meaning attempts to understand the girls, drawing upon two additional decades of experience, subtly reveal key aspects of gender dynamics particular to male and female adolescence in the postmodern North America. For all their attempts, the boys-become-men are ultimately at a loss to understand, and that lack of understanding is built into the structure of the novel. It is not that the narrators are unreliable; it is that what they reliably show is the inadequacy of a point of view locked into what film critics were the first to name "the male gaze." Continuing a tradition that goes back centuries but is finally being challenged in the postmodern world, that formula is captured in the phrase: "women are to be looked at and men do the looking." Every museum in the Western world offers examples of this process, those thousands of nudes all painted, photographed, or sculpted, to be looked at from the point of view of men.[12]

It is vitally important that the narrators are not bad men, and were not bad boys. They held no ill-will toward the girls. In fact their gaze fell upon the sisters with love at least as often as lust, and they did nothing overtly terrible to them. (Though in the creepiest moment, the boys spy on the girls via telescope.) Ultimately, they too were caught up in the limits of a gender system that has long trapped everyone into two neat boxes, a fact perhaps made clearer to readers in more recent decades in which many boys and men are increasingly caught up in a gym-body obsessed construction of masculinity and a host of insecurities and misinformation driven by the proliferation of porn culture.

The Lisbon girls are torn between repressive social and religious norms and a hypersexualized pop culture. Part of the problem for the girls is that the male gaze somehow intensifies the unreal nature of their family lives. The perceived boring emptiness of suburban life, alongside the ineffectual authoritarianism of the father, the repressive religious dogmatism of the mother, and the infantilizing hyperfeminine frilly pinkness of their habitats, leaves the girls without a purpose other than to be looked at and admired. No one around them, not parents, priest, boyfriends, or the psychologist to whom they are directed after the first failed suicide attempt, have any clue what their lives feel like. As Celia replies to the male psychologist who patronizingly asks her "What are you doing here, honey? You're not even old enough to know how bad life gets." "Obviously, doctor, you have never been a thirteen year-old girl" (7). Indeed. Caught between parental expectations, the sexualized male gaze, and aimlessness of postmodern society, the girls have nothing but each other. The family matrix has been turned into an unbearable prison with no mechanisms for matching bodily beauty to equally beautiful internal lives or socially effective external action. Given no meaningful outlets, the loving sororal solidarity among the girls and their power can only express itself through the ultimate erasure of their bodies through serial suicide.

Winged Delights: Angela Carter's *Nights at the Circus* (1984)

Another quite different set of devices used to question the rigid gendering of bodies is indebted to Latin American magical realism. In Angela Carter's *Nights at the Circus* (1984), for example, the protagonist is a winged woman named Sophie Fevvers.[13] A world-touring Cockney trapeze artist, Sophie's body is the subject of constant attention and constant speculation. Are her wings "real," a freakish fact of birth? Or are they fake, merely put on for show? The novel scrupulously avoids answering that question by turning it back on the reader: What exactly is the line between fact and fiction and why do we worry that line so much? Can't Sophie be, as the narrative asks at one point, "neither one thing nor the other"? (76) The initial asker of these questions is a journalist, a just-the-facts-ma'am kind of guy out to prove fraud. But soon he finds himself asking new questions:

> She neither attempted nor achieved anything a wingless biped could not have performed, although she did it in a different way, and as the Valkyries at last approached Valhalla [her act was done to the music of Wagner], he was astonished that it was the limitations of her act that made him briefly contemplate the unimaginable—that is the absolute suspension of disbelief.
>
> For in order to earn a living, might a genuine bird-woman—in the implausible event that such a thing existed—have pretended she was an artificial one? (17)

Away from her performance, in the putatively real world, Fevvers's wings are reduced to a deformity; she is viewed as a hunchback that mars her otherwise "Rubenesque" beauty. By contrast, on the stage her beautiful wings unfurl. But what of the *theatrum mundi*, the world as a stage? The reporter scoffs when recalling a conversation with an "old charlatan" Indian fakir who asks, "is not this whole world an illusion? And yet it fools everybody" (16). Before the novel ends, the reporter and the reader will be asking the same question. The novel approaches these questions from a host of philosophical and scientific positions, none of which provides a glib answer. But as the questions multiply, the imagination opens toward the real in new ways.

As with the anxiety created by the refusal of gendering in *Written on the Body*, Carter wants to challenge readers to think beyond binaries, the either/ors and fact/fictions, that trap us into deeply limited choices. Why is the first question we ever ask an expectant or new mother, is it a girl or boy? In *Nights at the Circus*, readers are led to ask if this makes any more sense than asking winged or not-winged. The novel multiplies this logic through other stories of a whole host of women who live double lives on the margins of society—a street urchin with the voice of an angel, a circus performer called the Abyssinian Princess who tames tigers with her music, a prisoner who becomes a guard and then reforms the prison, a brothel cleaner who secretly heads an international anarchist network. Each of these characters thrives because they are underestimated solely because they were born into bodies and conditions deemed beyond the norm and gendered as the "lesser" sex.

Life Is a Freakshow: Katherine Dunn's *Geek Love* (1989)

One of the most comprehensive, complicated, and cogent fictional treatments of the nonnormative body in the postmodern era is Katherine Dunn's *Geek Love* (1989).[14] Narrated by Olympia, the daughter of parents who created the Fabulon, a traveling carnival freakshow, it deeply interrogates ideas about what is normal and abnormal about any given or altered body. The novel contrasts "natural"-born nonnormative bodies (freaks) with "culturally" created bodies altered by surgery, suggesting each has a role to play in challenging notions of what a body is supposed to be like in order to qualify as normal. The psychic damage of being labeled "abnormal" is explored, but not used to justify certain hateful behaviors of some of the novel's freaks. At the same time that it seeks to normalize bodies coded as freakish by the dominant culture, it shows how "freaks" can fall victim to a kind of reverse normalization in which freakhood itself becomes an oppressive norm. The family becomes a kind of cult, and the novel has much to say about the dangers of marginalization contributing to the creation of dangerously self-destructive collectives.

In another twist, a classically beautiful young woman, product of an illegal, taboo, and magical insemination, considers disfiguring herself under the influence of a woman who claims to want to rescue her from objectification, but may in fact be acting out of jealousy. (Is this a warning about the limits of literary disfiguring as well?) The introduction of a beautiful individual solidifies the text's many efforts to dissociate beautiful and ugly personhood from particular bodies. This includes exploring the apparent contradiction that altering the body to either challenge *or* achieve normative standards of beauty can equally distract from a focus on subjecthood that is more than a physical body.

The Cyborg Body: Shelley Jackson's *Patchwork Girl* (1995)

Much discussion of the limits of the liberal humanist subject, and possible routes beyond the limits of this concept, draws inspiration from the multifaceted arguments of Donna Haraway in her "A Manifesto for

Cyborgs" (Haraway 2003 [1984]).[15] In particular they draw upon Haraway's claim that the breaking down of the human-machine boundary can be used to undermine historically oppressive claims that gender inequality is a "natural," biological thing. Haraway argued at the dawn of the digital era that the human-computer interface can serve to challenge assumptions about naturalized female and male roles and identities, and advocated embracing the "cyborg" as a symbol of this boundary-crossing work. The cyborg was a metaphor for the social construction of sex/gender, rather than an actual call for human-machine beings. She argued that because in patriarchal cultures men have long been identified with the mind and women with body, the cyborg—a creature part-human, part-electronic machine—can disrupt our imagination in relation to the notion of the "natural" body, and therefore can be utilized to challenge the assumption that there are natural roles into which women and men must fit. This argument was later taken up by transgender and transsexual activists, and others seeking to get beyond oppressive biological determinist notions of a natural binary of sexes and genders.

Haraway not only offered a highly nuanced analysis of the positive possibilities of cyborg identities in liberating women from historical forms of sexism, but also pointed out the many material dangers facing women, especially women from the Global South, who do much of the most painstaking and toxic labor in constructing digital products. Their "integration into the printed circuits of capitalism" exemplifies one of the many downsides to the cyborg. Haraway also reminds readers that cyborgs were in origin the "illegitimate offspring" of militaristic science and corporate exploitation, and that the prime popular culture examples of cyborgs were mindless killing machines like those in the *Terminator* movie series (while a tough female protagonist with a "natural" body, Sarah Conner, is the Terminator's nemesis). Unfortunately, some less astute cyberfeminists hyped the plus side of the cyborg metaphor, without equally attending to Haraway's warning that technocultures can perpetuate and even deepen some dimensions of sexism. It is thus necessary to talk of cyberfeminisms in the plural, to acknowledge several strands of this work, with varying degrees of complexity and effectiveness in using the cyborg metaphor and actual cyberspaces to further the cause of gender equity, sexuality, and the rights of persons with dis/abilities.[16]

Haraway acknowledges feminist science fiction novels, like those of Joanna Russ and Octavia Butler, as an influence on both the ideas and the form of her writing, so it is no surprise that fiction writers have in turn drawn upon her concepts. For example, in both form and subject matter, Shelley Jackson's hypertext "novel" *Patchwork Girl* (1995) offers rich explorations of the postmodern cyborg-like self.[17] The publisher's promotional teaser for *Patchwork Girl* asks "What if Mary Shelley's *Frankenstein* were true? What if Mary Shelley herself made the monster . . .? And what if the monster is a woman, and fell in love with Mary Shelley and travelled to America? This is their story."

The opening image of the hypertext shows a grotesquely stitched body whose various parts can be clicked upon to enter the novel in one of several different ways. The image is a kind of literalization of the poststructuralist notion that the self is "sutured" from often contradictory, ideological narratives that create an illusion of wholeness and free will. Both sewing and quilting (one of the five main entry points of the hypertext is called "Quilt") ironically evoke a traditionally female-coded craft seldom treated as an art form. Thus having Mary Shelley, rather than the (not so) good Doctor Frankenstein, do the sewing, signals that this is an artful female and feminist revision of that earlier story (which, not incidentally, was written by the daughter of one of the world's first advocates in print of what we now call feminism).[18] The Frankenstein story has been the subject of numerous novels in the postmodern era, often with a feminist twist (as, for example, another Winterson novel, *Frankissstein* (2018), discussed in Chapter 10).

Haraway, beginning in the "Manifesto for Cyborgs" and further developed in later work such as *The Companion Species Manifesto* (2003),[19] also depicted the absolute boundary between humans and other animal species as one constantly being breached. Thus, it is partly in homage to Haraway (who is specifically referenced in the "novel") that Jackson embodies a creature that is part-male, part-female, and part-animal, yet all "girl." As in the original novel, this monster is animated via electricity, as, quite literally, *Patchwork Girl* is as electronic literature. As a hypertext, the novel is also a cyborg— digitally delivered, yet deeply marked by analog books like the famous one by the Jackson's half namesake, Mary *Shelley*.

Questions of self and authorship begin with the title page where the byline is "Mary/Shelley and Herself." This at once acknowledges the intertextuality of the project, the author, and the text by referencing "Mary Shelley," while acknowledging the role of "Shelley" Jackson, and the semi-autonomy of the text "Herself." "Herself" also points to the reader who must patch together the text, must patch together the creature. The conceptualization of subjectivity in the text, and its relation to the reading process, is evoked directly by this line of text: "If you want to see the whole, you will have to piece me together yourself." And how does the reader do that? By creating a narrative. The process suggests by analogy that to become the author of your "self" you too are required to do some active narrating. You must engage in creative storytelling about yourself, starting perhaps by analyzing the versions of your story told via questionable social and cultural discourses. In doing so, you will imitate Jackson who rewrites Mary Shelley's story for a new era, with the help of the "critifiction" parts of the hypertext (including quotes from a variety of postmodern theorists like Haraway).

Patchwork Girl acknowledges that this kind of revision of the body/self is not an easy task, with the digital era offering both confusion and new opportunities. The act of reading a hypertext, as opposed to an analog book, troubles the character called "Mary Shelley." And her anxiety can stand in for our own as readers, for us as folks trying to make sense of postmodern conditions:

> Assembling these patched words in an electronic space, I feel half-blind, as if the entire text is within reach, but because of some myopic condition I am only familiar with in dreams, I can see only that part most immediately before me, and have no sense of how that part relates to all the rest. When I open a book I know where I am, which is restful. My reading is spatial and even volumetric. I tell myself, I am a third of the way down through a rectangular solid, I am a quarter of the way down the page, I am here on the page, here on this line, here, here, here. But where am I now? I am in a here and a present moment that has no history and no expectations for the future.
>
> Patchwork Girl

Patriarchal denial of narrative coherence, and with it a denial of social power, has long been a part of women's lives. The digitized world provides both new versions of disempowerment and also new resources for becoming empowered. This new world seemingly without "history" or "expectations" has created new perils and new possibilities for all those of us who are caught up in it, regardless of how we have been sexed or gendered. We may be with Mary in asking why our lives and our bodies, turned into hypertext by new communication devices, lack continuity or coherence. We may be asking why it is so hard to build an empowering narrative out of our digitized lives. We may be asking how to become more than random fragments. We may be asking how we can be at once boundaryless bodies and active agents for political change. *Patchwork Girl r*eminds us that the struggle to change the word is part of the struggle to change the world, and that this requires us to think and rethink the forms and media through which we communicate and are embodied. The process of reading a novel like Jackson's may offer crucial clues as to how we can reshape the memories, hopes, dreams, and fears that shape our mind-bodies in order to become different, more powerful creatures.

Oedipus Trans*: Daisy Johnson's *Everything Under* (2017)

Daisy Johnson's novel, *Everything Under* (2017), is a darkly beautiful mix of stark realism, fairy tale, and classical myth.[20] It deals ostensibly with a group of figures on the margins of British society, poor people living on the canals and streams of Oxfordshire. The world Johnson creates seems utterly unaware of and separate from the goings on in so-called mainstream society. "What comes back from that long trailing river—a spine against the backbone of the country? What did we summon up there? A wildish girl and a wilder mother living like animals or demons out where no one could get to them" (159). Two of the main characters would be classified as transgender by current social understandings, but they live in a world that, while seemingly contemporary, has little means to understand the forces that make them feel they live in bodies whose outward appearance does not match their sense of self. The novel's world seems at once dreamlike and filled with real, gritty, sensuous, and tactile detail.

The novel embodies a location in which the conscious and the subconscious lives of its characters seem almost inverted, as if the everyday world were written over by primal forces embodied in the weeds, reeds, vines, thickets, drifting snaglines, and debris of the waterways. And rewritten is the operative word, since the novel is also very much about the role of language in creating consciousness, especially its role in the formation of memory. One of the key narrating characters, Gretel, works as a lexicographer in the city of Oxford; though that city is present in the novel only through brief glimpses of her office. Her job is to pin down the meaning of words, but the words that seem to matter most in her life—dukduk, sheesh time, harpiedoodle, and above all the monstrous Bonak—exist in no dictionary. The plot of the novel involves Gretel trying to track down the mother who gave her these words then abandoned her as a teenager, and to also find a young man who briefly, but deeply, shaped their lives on the derelict canal boat that was their home.

The novel reenacts the tragic ancient Greek story of Oedipus, the myth made famous in modern times by its centrality to Sigmund Freud's psychoanalytic theory. The forces at play in the novel, while certainly psychosocial, do not play out in any neat Freudian schema. The novel is too darkly mysterious for that. But to the degree that the work makes sense of the complexly intertwined lives of its marginalized characters, it seems that language is in many ways the operative force. This might lead critics to examine the novel through the lens of Freud's postmodern re-interpreter, Jacques Lacan, who rewrote psychoanalytic categories through linguistic theory. But the novel also contains a social dimension that goes beyond the psychoanalytic. While much happens in the novel because the characters in effect do not have the language to understand their bodies, their minds, or their world, this failure does not fall neatly into Lacanian schemas. On the one hand, Gretel, also called by her mother Hansel, El, and most nastily, Regretel, is haunted by those made-up words given her by her mother. In contrast, another key character, Margot/Marcus, has their life profoundly shaped by not having the words to name and understand who they are.

Gretel's adult life is spent trying to get out from under those words deeply seeded in her unconscious by Sarah, her "awful, wonderful, terrifying mother": "Whatever it was that pressed through the calm, cold waters that winter, that wrapped itself around our dreams and left its clawed fingerprints on our heads. I want to tell you that it might never have been there if we had not thought it up" (159). Gretel seeks out her mother so that she can undo these memories, rewrite her life, by extracting true confessions from Sarah about her distortive use of words. But when she finally tracks down the woman who abandoned her to these twisted, murky memories, she finds that her mother's own memory has become deeply compromised. These breadcrumbs of memory may lead astray, rather than to the house of revelation, because "You do not remember the language that made you" (255).

Margot/Marcus's life, on the other hand, takes on a mythic turn because they do not have the words to understand themselves, and because prophetic words, uttered by a second character whose empathy for a fellow sexual misfit, are tragically misinterpreted. The genius of the novel is to play this out in incandescently beautiful, yet opaque prose that somehow leaves its psychosocial revelations both clear and as muddy as the waters of the Isis River upon which the houseboat homes of its characters float. As one reviewer summarizes, "Johnson's waterways—muddy, unpredictable, treacherous, full of half-submerged souvenirs and elusive creatures—evoke the fluidity of memory, as well as of language, gender, and sexuality."[21] The body of water is not merely a metaphor for the fluid bodies of the protagonists but something somehow utterly fused with those bodies.

Much has been made, understandably, of the role of fate or determinism in the novel. But both in the rewriting of Grimm's "Hansel and Gretel" tale and in the rewriting of the Oedipus story, the novel offers twists on the question of fate. In the version of the fable in *Everything Under*, the wicked witch, Sarah, put her own hands into the oven, unbidden by daughter Gretel. This suggests at some level a recognition by this mother of her guilt in imposing her own demons (in a variety of literal and figurative forms) onto her daughter. And the two transgender characters may well have been fated to be born in bodies that do not match their sense of self, but the tragic dimensions of their lives can be read as the result of social isolation and oppressive normativity, not blind determinism. Under the "everything" of its story, the novel offers a glimmer of redemption, a sense that things could have been otherwise had the right language and community of understanding been available. The thicket of prose that is the text, makes clear this is not an easy task, but is a possible achievement. The fault, it seems, was not in the stars but in ourselves.

Body as Multitude: Akwaeki Emezi's *Freshwater* (2018)

Every time a demographic group emerges into greater literary or cultural prominence—Jewish Americans, black British, lesbians of color, and so on, a similar set of reception processes is called into play. Initially, each artist stemming from the group or community is burdened with the impossible task of representing the entire community. Then, eventually, enough different texts exist that the burden on individual artists is lessened, if not lifted. Authors identifying as transsexual, transgender, genderqueer, and related categories (a list sometimes shortened as trans*) beyond cisgender and binary maleness/femaleness have in the twenty-first century emerged out of stage one into stage two.

We are living in a time of unprecedented sex/gender fluidity, and postmodern fiction has proven itself to be a particularly apt set of devices for conveying the diverse embodiments, theories, and psychologies of this fluidity. Some members of the trans* community have argued that even the most sympathetic fictions by cisgendered writers fall short of capturing their experience. For that reason alone, it is important to note that a significant new body of literature by transsexual, transgender, and genderqueer-identified folks has emerged over the last couple of decades, and that earlier writings about or by sex/gender fluid persons has been recovered, reinterpreted, and otherwise made more visible and available.

The recent wave of trans* work includes novels as different as the magical realist *Salt Fish Girl* (2002) by Larissa Lai, the punk surrealism of Sybil Lamb's *I've Got a Time Bomb* (2014), the cyberpunk/fantasy world of Rem Woram's *Escapology* (2016), the quiet lyricism of Jia Qing Wilson-Yang's *Small Beauty* (2016), and Jordy Rosenberg's queer-theory-heavy rewriting of the legendary Mack-the-Knife as a transsexual in *Confessions of the Fox* (2018), among many others. This body of work has perhaps crossed an important threshold where trans*ness itself can be both embodied and questioned, and in some other cases be a taken-for-granted aspect of a character rather than the central subject matter of the novel (or film or graphic novel or video game or TV series).[22]

In Akwaeki Emezi's novel, *Freshwater* (2018), the search for a viable, vibrant embodiment is a transcontinental, transcultural journey to bring a host of selves/bodies into a workable unity.[23] To say the novel is a struggle between the physical and the metaphysical is true only to the extent that both the physical and the metaphysical are totally reimagined. Identity in the novel is indistinguishable from cosmological drama. A luminously real and surreal work, the novel has three main narrators, We, AsỤghara, and Ada. Each voice tells stories of selves, of more than one entity, inhabiting one limited body. Terms like multiple personality disorder or similar psychological explanations seem shallow beside the articulation of the contradictions the novel explores, contradictions perhaps each of us seeks to deny in our own selves, however identified.

The novel interweaves a magical realism that might be called Igbo spiritual realism, a sociopolitical allegory, and traditional realist factual accounts, embodying and questioning all of them. Certain facts about a character whom her parents call Ada, but whom We would name otherwise, can be gleaned. She is the daughter of a Nigerian Catholic father, Saul, a doctor, and a Malaysian mother, a nurse. When the daughter is a child, her mother is away much of the time in Saudi Arabia and then in the UK. As a teenager, she, who may be called Ada, leaves Nigeria for the United States where she attends a college in Virginia. One of narrators believes there may be a kind of curse on their head "for crossing the ocean sifted with death" (the place where so many Africans died during the Middle Passage to slavery), though the traumas she experiences in her new country are also explicable in purely sociological race-gender dynamics. These traumas unchain a series of latent selves that may be manifestations of *ogbanje*, spirits who in Igbo metaphysics come to trouble and teach the one whose body they inhabit for a time.

It takes many selves to express some truth about who she/he/they is/are. At the beginning of the novel, We exists inside the mother's womb, and upon being birthed into the physical world remarks that

> By the time she (our body) struggled out into the world, slick and louder than a village of storms, the gates were left open. We should have been anchored in her by then, asleep inside her membranes and synched with her mind. That would have been the safest way. But since the gates were open, not closed against remembrance, we became confused. We were at once old and newborn. We were her and yet not. We were not conscious but we were alive—in fact, the main problem was that we were a distinct *we* instead of being fully and just *her*. (5)

Because the "gates were left open," the various components of this We each narrate parts of the novel, as it swings back and forth in time and geography. Each voice is in one sense a classic unreliable narrator since each tells only part of the truth of the being that can be known as Ada. Another of these narrating voices, AsŲghara, slowly reveals herself to be an insatiable seeker after sensual and sexual pleasure, an entity seemingly hell-bent on leading the body into great danger. Perhaps in response to the pain this entity brings, a new, gentler but masculine self emerges, Saint Vincent. This process of multiplication of self goes on through several more iterations. There are many different discourses that readers might use to categorize what is going on. Should they think of it as one or another form of long dormant mental illness? Is it a sign of posttraumatic stress disorder due to devastating events? Should it be read through the contemporary concept of nonbinary gender identities? Or should readers believe that *ogbanje* are in fact possessing the central character? In a sense, all and none of these explanations matter; it is the struggle to survive and thrive, that is in play, and the novel exquisitely chronicles those efforts that, however particular, are also akin to experiences all of us, to some degree, experience under postmodern conditions.

The beautifully lyrical mystery plot at the heart of the novel spins around finding out to what extent these selves can be brought into coexistence, can recognize what legitimate, if limited, claims each may have on her/him/them. Can the Ada come to love each of them? Can they embrace them all, come to see them as "a village full of faces and a compound full of bones, translucent thousands," each speaking some truth? The novel resists easy answers and the author has made clear the wish to keep alive a tension between modern Western discourses about the body and identity, and pre-colonization beliefs about the metaphysics of self: "Before colonialism, Igbo ontology was real for centuries . . . . Now the concept of *ogbanje* isn't considered real by Nigerians—and in general the idea of trans people isn't considered real either."[24] *Freshwater* offers a postcolonial reimaging of gender fluidity that eludes some of the traps that labels like trans*, however necessary in some contexts, bring with them.

5

Postmodern Families
Reimagining Kinship

Well into the postmodern era, most people in the contemporary West probably assumed that the "normal," "traditional" family consists of two parents (of different genders) and a couple of kids, with the father as the "breadwinner" and the mother the (unpaid) "housewife." In fact this notion of what was dubbed the "nuclear family" is of rather recent vintage, historically speaking, and limited to Western cultural contexts. The nuclear family is largely an idea solidified in the 1950s, and far from the only, or even the typical, family unit across the range of time and cultures. A more common pattern historically has been the extended family, including grandparents, aunts and uncles, and other cross-generational units that go beyond the mythical two parent/two children unit.

The ideal of the nuclear family was constructed in the wake of the Second World War and its construction had everything to do with postwar conditions and ideologies. In the UK, the devastation of much of the country by war fueled a massive rebuilding process, and an effort to return to normalcy that sought to reshape many decimated families into nuclear units. In the United States, a more deeply transformative process was underway. There, three main factors led to the promulgation of this new model household as the "normal" family. The first factor is economic. An immense manufacturing effort was required to win the war, and when the war ended, fear of a major economic downturn was widespread. One solution to this problem was the creation of a "permanent war economy," something built around the excessive weapons manufacturing rationalized by the start of the Cold War "arms race" with the Soviet Union, one that gave an ironic new meaning to a nuclear family.

A second key component was a related push for a culture of intense consumption, especially of goods such as large appliances and cars that could take up the increased industrial capacity created by the defense industry. Economists knew that a major uptick in the personal consumption of manufactured goods would also be needed. For this they needed a perfect unit of consumption, and that is when they hit upon the idea of the suburban nuclear family. The key to making this family work as a place of maximum consumption was the creation of a new kind of "housewife" to service men using giant shiny new cars to travel from suburbia to their breadwinning work downtown. During the war effort, women had been encouraged into taking many kinds of jobs that had previously only been available to men. The famous symbol of this effort to recruit women, created and pushed by the government, was "Rosie the Riveter," a woman capable of doing strenuous manufacturing work. But a great deal of concern arose after the war when men returning from combat would be forced to compete with newly empowered women who had worked in higher paying and often more interesting jobs in economic sectors that were previously almost exclusively male domains. Sexism and economic anxiety combined to create the new model family as a unit of excessive consumption.

The third factor in the creation of the nuclear family was suburbanization. A number of economic factors contributed to this process, including a massive housing loan program for war vets (the GI Bill in the United States), and the benefits of a new housing sector. But a crucial role was played by a decade-long demographic shift in which cities were becoming increasingly populated by persons of color, Asian, Indigenous, black, and Latino. In response driven largely by racism, there was a massive retreat of European Americans to these rapidly created suburbs, a shift known as "white flight." Similar patterns led to new forms of ethno-racial segregation in the UK, Canada, and Australia.

The creation of a new model of family was entwined with all these forces. The shifts were reflected in popular culture as well, with the white, suburban middle-class family unit idealized in 1950s sitcom TV like "Leave it to Beaver," "Father Knows Best," "The Donna Reed Show" in the United States, and similar ones in the United Kingdom, Canada, and Australia. But by the 1960s, the nuclear family model was showing deep signs of stress, represented as a "generation gap" between parents and children, and by the rebellion of middle-class women as embodied in books like Betty Friedan's *The Feminine Mystique* with its strong challenge to the housewife as the sole exemplar of female virtue. Never able to live up to the ideal (divorce rates, for example, skyrocketed in suburbia), a long process of unravelling the nuclear family model continued through the next several decades, despite conservative efforts to return to "family values" based on very narrow patriarchal criteria and a mythic natural status belied by its short historical existence.

In discussing fictional representations of postmodern families, it is crucial to note that some communities and some income levels never had the possibility of a single breadwinner middle-class family life. For example, as a number of postmodern novels treating American slavery remind us, black Americans were long denied the very possibility of the biological family unit, and for generations after the legal end of slavery, race-biased economic conditions often meant that black families required two incomes just to get by. Low-income white communities have likewise seldom fit the middle-class model of a single breadwinner and a stay-at-home mom. Many communities of color have featured a different family structure, at times more cross-generational and extended, but also often made up of two-income or single parent structures. In the twenty-first century, these family forms have become more common across all ethnicities, in an era of increasing economic disparity between the fabulously wealthy and the rest of us. Waves of immigration have also brought additional family models into play in new homelands, and in recent decades poverty, climate change, and political violence have brought increasing numbers of people to North America and Europe with non-nuclear models of family.

In myth, the home has historically been considered a sanctuary away from the rough winds of the larger world. I say myth because that supposed sanctuary has long been subject to spousal abuse, sexual abuse, and most every form of dysfunction. And every other problem of the outside world eventually finds its way home. But to the degree that there is some truth in the sanctuary notion, that degree has lessened in the era of postmodernity. The postmodern family home has become increasingly penetrated by the outside world. First television, then far more fully and complexly, digital media have breached the walls of the familial citadel, sending thousands of cross-currents spinning like a tornado through the household unit.

By the early twenty-first century, the 1950s family sitcom was but a distant memory, and a TV show like "Modern Family" was presenting a very different model that might be more accurately entitled Postmodern Family. The mythical isolated nuclear family with a working dad, stay-at-home mom, and 2.5 children (who were these half children, anyway?) had been replaced televisually by three interrelated families that stray far from that model. The three families are mixed race, have mixed biological and adopted children, include a woman as the primary income earner, cross the lines of normative sexuality as well as lines of "appropriate" age balance, include divorced members and blended siblings, and deal, however comically and superficially, with many of the conditions of postmodern life, including fluid identities, immigration, racism, homophobia, and the impact of digital technologies on personal lives. Certainly, this fictional family does not face many other issues due to the insulation of their upper-middle-class lives. The style of the show also employs the postmodern cinematic form known as the mockumentary, the satirically structured pretend documentary.

The inclusion of a married gay couple in the show highlights the ironic fact that in an era of declining marriage rates, high divorce rates, a rise in cohabitation outside marriage, a rise in single parent households, and increasing numbers of people who never marry, the surge in gay marriages before and after legalization has done much to shore up the institution in numerical terms, albeit in a way still viewed as illegitimate by conservative definitions of traditional marriage. And looked at from the point of view of literary fiction, rather than old or new sitcoms, the story appears to have always been more complicated.

If we look through the more nuanced lens of novels, the real 1950s family is revealed to have been far from what was portrayed in TV-land. Mainstream white male suburban writers like John Updike and John Cheever portrayed those families as riddled with infidelity, alcoholism, and all manner of other dysfunctions. But compared to the madly dysfunctional postmodern family of Don DeLillo's *White Noise*, Amy M. Homes's self-immolating family in *Music for Torching* (1999), or the digitally dazed family in Mark Z. Danielewski's haunted *House of Leaves* (2000) (see Chapter 10), Cheever's suburbia seems downright somnambulant.

Consuming Families: Don DeLillo's *White Noise* (1985)

Don DeLillo's *White Noise* (1985) offers a wildly amusing take on the powerful impact of postmodern mass-mediated consumer culture on academic and family life.[1] Set in a small New England college town, DeLillo explores the myriad ways that life in the overdeveloped world of North America has been turned into an image-world that consumes families whole. The novel randomly injects eerily poetic words from the world of product marketing throughout, seemingly to serve as a kind of Greek chorus echoing a tragic banality. Often the words come in triads or quartets: "Waffelos . . . Kabooms . . . Dum Dum pops . . . Mystic Mints" (3). Sometimes, as with the last term in this series, "Mystic Mints," they suggest a religious or spiritual quality. Others seem like consumerist mantras, "Kleenex Softique, Kleenex Softique" (39). A quartet of synthetic fabrics—"Dacron, Orlon, Lyrca, Spandex" (52)—hints at the synthetic fabric of the family's life. Terms like these are like pop song earworms that enter your brain even when you do not want them to, and shape your consciousness. And above them all, repeated at several points in the novel, is the Holy Trinity, "Visa-Mastercard-American Express" (100). Clearly, this is the only Higher Power arch-consumers recognize.

The novel suggests that consumerism had by the turn of the twenty-first century become not a feature, but comprised the whole of family life for many. The world of *White Noise* is a world drowning in mass culture's reduction of everything to one seamless string of event-things, as in a news show that segues from a tragic death to a sunny weather prediction to news about a pop star's marriage. Moreover, each member of the family seems lost in their own mass-mediated reality, untouched by their kin. Everything in their lives is filtered through the lens of advertising, mass culture, and consumption such that even when a potentially deadly cloud of toxic gas begins to loom over the city, the family treats it as if it were a vaguely interesting disaster movie, amid complains that it didn't get proper TV coverage, coverage that alone would make it "real" (161–2).

"White noise" has many possible meanings in the context of the novel. It is a technical term for random signals that have equal intensity in different frequencies, suggesting a kind of flattening of the diverse communication frequencies of life, a reduction of them all to sameness. It is also a term for background noise, sounds barely perceptible but nevertheless shaping our experience. White noise machines are marketed to provide a soothing ambiance, but the soothing ambiance created by the white noise of consumerist culture in the novel is soothing to the point of pure emptiness, numbness even to the threat of death.

On another plane, the novel's white noise is the noise of a particular kind of whiteness, a bland cultural state as free of taste, substance, or nutrition as white bread. Whiteness is what linguists call an "unmarked category." It is the racial category that need not speak its name. To understand how race works look at this page. You could not read these black words if they were not set against a white page (or screen). The words at once divide as they create blackness and whiteness, seemingly setting them apart as opposites. Whiteness in racial terms was formed from a diverse set of ethnicities into a single category only by being contrasted with blackness, only by the simultaneous invention of race and racism. In the North American and European West, whiteness remains the default identity against which other colors are set. In a US context, as Toni Morrison explains, "American means white." And everyone not white must "struggle to make the term [American] applicable to themselves with ethnic . . . hyphen after hyphen after hyphen."[2] The Gladney family in *White Noise* has the luxury of not seeing themselves as having a racial identity, the kind of unwokeness the Black Lives Matter movement has begun to shatter. For each member of the family, the luxury of living in a kind of white-out blizzard of media comes at the cost of losing their grip on reality, living in ignorance of the real social conditions of their lives.

The lead character of the novel, Jack Gladney, is a professor of "Hitler studies," who is nonetheless oblivious to the ways in which the specter of a new, postmodern "brand" of fascism haunts his world. What is most disturbing about DeLillo's take on contemporary culture is, to invert Hannah Arendt's famous words about the bureaucrats who carried out Nazi atrocities, the "evil of banality." *White Noise* finds in the banal, increasingly empty rhetoric of consumerist culture and the worship of celebrities, a drift into unreality that opens toward fascism.[3] There is a kind of randomness to postmodern life in the overdeveloped Global North that leaves people vulnerable to stories that tie together disparate elements into simple political plot lines, that hold up idealized notions of naturalized families while living in willed ignorance of the suffering of others. While written long before the rise of a certain "reality TV" star to the US presidency, the novel predicts that a hollowed-out culture that cannot separate the real from the simulated has rendered much of America susceptible to cultic myths, insane conspiracies, and authoritarian solutions.

Family as Talk-Story: Maxine Hong Kingston's *The Woman Warrior* (1976)

As part of an era of massive suburbanization, commodification, and economic dislocation, the postmodern era has also been one of unprecedented migration globally (see Chapter 9). The United States has long been "a nation of immigrants" and the variety of immigrants has increased during postmodernity, while at the same time almost every other country on Earth has also become more multiethnic due to migration. With this process, multiple models of family life have likewise migrated into new contexts.

One of the most imaginative and powerful accounts of what immigration can mean to a family can be found in Maxine Hong Kingston's *The Woman Warrior: Memoirs of a Childhood Among Ghosts* (1976), a text that is paradigmatic for many subsequent novels.[4] Published in the year of the US bicentennial, the text uses revisions of Chinese folk tales, "talk-story" (informal narratives mixing everyday life, myth, and folklore), family history, and more traditional forms of novelistic and memoir-style narrative devices to create a multilayered sense of the challenges imposed on a family that moves from China to the United States after the Second World War. The novel centers especially on the women members of the family (Kingston focuses on the men in her family history in another book, see Chapter 8).[5] The work uses these varied modes of storytelling and retelling to foreground questions of language and narrative as key forces of continuity and change in familial and personal identity. The book is exquisitely sensitive to the generational tensions between those arriving from another country and the children born in the new country. As the subtitle suggests, the novel is also a ghost story, but of a different kind. The ghosts are both the narrator's Chinese ancestors who inhabit her reality through her mother's stories, and the name given to the ghostly white people who inhabit her new American homeland.

The nature of the book confounded critics and led to controversy among those who could not decide if it was better characterized as a memoir or fiction. Kingston preferred the latter, in part because a memoir has long been treated as a lesser form, one particularly suited to "minority" writers who had not yet achieved the status of "literary" creators. *The Woman Warrior*'s five chapters—"No-name Woman," "White Tigers," "Shaman," "At the Western Palace," and "Song for a Barbarian Reed Pipe"—hardly evoke the typical chapters of a memoir. They are something quite other. The form and style of the text changes in each of the five thematically interconnected chapters. Kingston offers lyrical reimaginings of all the different kinds of stories told to a child who is, in metafictional style, at once herself and a character. Each chapter includes everyday life occurrences (going to school, picking up a relative at the airport) woven seamlessly into a world alive with ancient Chinese myths and legends. The aunt met at the airport, for example, gives her niece a paper cutout of the legendary woman warrior, Fa Mu Lan (120). While her mother dismisses the silliness of playing with dolls, this may well be the moment Fa Mu Lan's story enters into Maxine's young mind where it was destined to change her forever (and incidentally give her the title of the book).

The novel was accused of inauthenticity because it retold Chinese folktales in ways that diverged from the original, but this utterly misses the point. The stories are told from memory by a mother deeply scarred by history, forced to transition from the role of a respected doctor/midwife in China to a laundry worker in the United States. Moreover, we encounter these stories as in part filtered through the mind of a young girl. The stories are misremembered, actively reinterpreted, or merged with dreams (as when the young Maxine falls asleep during one of the mother's bedtime talk-stories). Over time the stories become lifelines for someone caught between two worlds, a distant, often frightening Chinese one, and a hostile, bullying American one. Kingston's beautiful renditions of these stories find their truth not in slavish reproduction of their originals, but in creative reimaginings.

The novel evokes the process by which frightening tales of what goes wrong when the social order is disrupted can be turned into empowering tales of defiance against oppressive social expectations. In great part this means recognizing that no one story can be the whole truth. As the mother character, Brave Orchid, tells it, "The difference between mad people and sane people . . . is that sane people have variety when they talk story. Mad people have only one story that they talk over and over" (159). Brave Orchid's many different stories allowed her daughter to weave something else out of what she was given, picking and choosing among the possible lessons intended by her mother. In perhaps the deepest irony, the mother models for her daughter the strength of character through which the daughter comes to resist many of the constraints Brave Orchid would place upon her. Through beautiful lyrical stories, Kingston fuses, refuses, and confuses Chinese and American familial and personal myths, and in the process embodies the painfully creative process by which the dangers of both excessive communal scrutiny and excessive individualism can be negotiated. *The Woman Warrior* demonstrates how something beautifully new can arise from the clash of cultural traditions.

Kingston's method of repurposing homeland culture in a new land is one that has been used by dozens of subsequent writers depicting postmodern cultural transitions in particular immigrant communities. To mention just a few examples that stand out from this strand of postmodern realist writing, I'd cite Theresa Hak Kyung Cha's *Dictee* (1982), Wendy Law-Yone's *The Coffin Tree* (1983), Julia Alvarez's *How the García Girls Lost Their Accents* (1991), Cristina García's *Dreaming in Cuban* (1992), Edwidge Danticat's *Breath, Eyes, Memory* (1994), Sherman Alexie's *Reservation Blues* (1995), Chang-Rae Lee's *Native Speaker* (1995), Karen Tei Yamashita's *Tropic of Orange* (1997), and many others up to twenty-first-century works like Tommy Orange's *There There* (2018), with its postmodern reconceptualization of urban Native life (see Chapter 9).

These types of text represent an acculturation process that rejects both assimilation (the giving up of all traits from the previous home culture) and ethnic insularity (trying to maintain some pure version of the old culture in the new one). Rather, these novels model the complex interactive process that creates a hybrid cultural amalgam. In doing so, they illustrate the concept put forth by postcolonial theorist Homi Bhabha that all cultures are hybrid, mixed, however much they try to disguise that hybridity under the banner of an allegedly pure tradition.[6]

These works may also expose the fact that the cultures being hybridized were themselves hybrid at an earlier moment in history. Traditions are selectively made, not simply given. Traditions result from a political process that emphasizes some parts of a wider cultural system and de-emphasizes others, with the goal of empowering some people and lessening the power of others. Failure to acknowledge this impurity is one of the forces behind the kind of twenty-first-century ethnic nationalism that led to genocide in Rwanda, the destruction of the former Yugoslavia, and that is now on the rise around the globe in right-wing pseudo-populisms.

Postmodern Matriarchy: Ana Castillo's *So Far from God* (1993)

Like Kingston, Xicanax author Ana Castillo's novel, *So Far from God* (1993), depicts an equally complex matrix of cross-cultural pressures weighing upon a group of women attempting to resist the fragmenting forces facing a family in rural New Mexico.[7] Five women, a mother and four daughters, must navigate a context long-shaped by a variety of patriarchal forces—religious, social, pop cultural, and personal/familial. The title references a wistful remark made in 1848 by Porfirio Diaz about the country he was then leader of, Mexico: "So far from God—So near the United States." Both God and the United States have a highly problematic status for the five Latinas inhabiting this novel. This family is essentially a matriarchal unit, with what could aptly be called a "deadbeat dad" absent from the picture throughout most of the novel, while the mother works to hold together the household of four daughters. Elements of magical realism (one daughter levitates, another is miraculously healed from mutilation) and a playful use of a rhetoric drawn from *telenovelas* (the Latin American equivalent of soap operas) allow the novel to explore surrealistically, yet realistically, the various centrifugal postmodern pressures that constantly threaten to tear the matriarchal unit apart.

Something of the crazy, yet serious play of the novel's multiple storytelling genres can be gleaned from two reviewer descriptions of the book: "*Little Women* Meets *The Flintstones*" (Elisabeth Mermman-Jozwiak) and "*One Hundred Years of Solitude* Meets 'General Hospital'" (Barbara Kingsolver). But these only hint at the many kinds of stories and stories within stories that are paid homage to, invoked, satirized, and incorporated in the novel. In addition to the parodying of *telenovelas*, an incomplete list of story-types would include magical realist novels; Native folklore from North and South America; Judeo-Christian biblical stories; Apache, Aztec, and Pueblo myths; *cuentos* and *corridos* (Mexican oral folktales and songs); comic books; as well as virtually every genre of high "literature"—tragedy, comedy, satire, and romance.

Long chapter titles give a sense of the playful tone, like this one for chapter 15: "La Loca Santa Returns to the World via Albuquerque Before Her Transcendental Departure; and a Few Random Political Remarks from the Highly Opinionated Narrator" (238). The novel's mix of styles and emotional registers offers a brew of tragic-comic sensibilities that also embodies a relevant inventory of the hybrid identity-shaping voices the characters sometimes fail, sometimes succeed in integrating into functional lives. The novel also complicates representation through code-switching between English, Spanish, and Spanglish, as well as words from Indigenous languages. A sense of the only partial translatability of experience is reinforced by leaving some Spanish words untranslated and by using Spanish syntax while writing in English (the double negative, for example, is bad grammar in English but common and correct in Spanish).

Each of the daughters is given a heavily symbolic name that, in postmodern style, only imperfectly fits their characters—Fe (Faith), Esperanza (Hope), Caridad (Charity), and, breaking up that Holy Trinity of virtues, La Loca (The Crazy One). Each embodies one or more aspects of the struggle against the postmodern condition. One is drawn into the war on terror as a reporter, another becomes lost in an initially self-destructive pursuit of a degraded form of sexual liberation, a third puts faith in corporations that lead her to suffer the ravages of environmental racism, and all four feel a pull between tradition and change with regard to religion, social mores, and their roles in the wider multicultural life of the US Southwest. Survival for the matriarch and her sororal clan seems to depend on the degree to which they can resist what passes for normality in contemporary America.

The novel's deconstruction of the "feminized" genre of *telenovela* is especially relevant as representative of a world of empty consumerism, internalized misogyny, and serial infidelities (sexual and otherwise) driven by multinational capitalism's exploitation of racial and gendered divisions. The family survives to the extent that it draws upon, while updating, ancient wisdom, by resisting the lure of wealth bought at the cost of environmental exploitation, and by creating a solidarity, a sororal unity, that mediates these external forces and allows them the clarity to offer a different social vision in the form of Mama's rise to political prominence (as mayor) and her creation of new eco-friendly businesses.

The family members who live and thrive carve out a hybrid blend of tradition and innovation, finding the sacred in atypical places, and opting out of a mad consumer-driven economic system that destroys everything it touches. The hopeful conclusion sees the matriarch start a memorial to female semi-secular saints, and a thriving cooperative business tied to care for the land and the production of a renewable product (based on an actually existing wool cooperative)[8] whose quality reflects the loving community that goes into its making.

Family Curses and Geek Masculinity: Junot Diaz's *The Brief Wondrous Life of Oscar Wao* (2008)

The destructive forms of masculinity explored in *So Far from God* as they impact women are dealt with more centrally in their impact on men in Junot

Diaz's *The Brief Wondrous Life of Oscar Wao* (2008). The title character, Oscar, is part of a second-generation Dominican-American immigrant family living in Paterson, New Jersey. The story is narrated mostly by his friend, Yunior, with a couple of chapters narrated by other characters. Oscar is a young man who escapes into the fantastic world of comic books and video games in search of an identity not defined by a family and community whose expectations about masculinity clearly do not fit him. Immersed in the fantastical worlds of supervillains and superheroes from *Lord of the Rings*, Marvel comics, "Dungeons and Dragons," "Star Wars," "Dr. Who," and dozens of other multiverses apart from the Dominican version of New Jersey, Oscar finds ways to make a different sense of his life. He finds lifelines and resistance points to carve out an identity not wholly subsumed by the hurricane of history that continues to blow through his family. That hurricane stems from the horrific thirty-year-long dictatorship of Rafael Trujillo in the Dominican Republic, and it follows the family to its new home in the "land of the free" (the brutal Trujillo regime is also the subject of the novel *In the Time of the Butterflies* discussed in Chapter 6).

The metaphorical representation of this historical burden in the novel is "*fukú*," a curse on the "New World" carried to the heavens "in the screams" of the first African slaves torn from their homeland and forcibly brought to North and South America (pronounced, foo-*coo* in Spanish, it also looks suspiciously like a very common English-language curse). It is a curse that also seems like what the CIA calls a "blowback," the colonized world's reply to the hubris of US foreign policy:

> Who killed JFK? . . . It wasn't the mob or LBJ or the ghost of Marilyn Fucking Monroe. It wasn't aliens or the KGB or a lone gunman. . . . It was Trujillo, it was the *fukú*. . . . Why do you think the greatest power in the world lost its first war to a Third World country like Vietnam? I mean, Negro, *please*. It might interest you to know that just as the U.S. was ramping up its involvement in Vietnam, LBJ launched an illegal invasion of the Dominican Republic . . . (Santo Domingo was Iraq before there was Iraq.) . . . [M]any of these same units and intelligence teams that took part in the "democratization" of Santo Domingo were immediately shipped off to Saigon. And what do you think these soldiers, technicians and spooks carried with them, in their rucks, in their suitcases, in their shirt pockets, on the hair inside their nostrils, caked up around their shoes? Just a little gift from my people to America, a small repayment for an unjust war. That's right, folks. *Fukú*. (4)

Oscar's personal story brings this history down to ground level. The epigraph to the novel—"Of what import are the brief, nameless lives . . .

to Galactus?"—sets up the main theme and countertheme. This boast from this supervillain from *The Fantastic Four* comic, who devours whole planets, is set against the more everyday heroes who oppose and thwart his callous indifference to the ordinary "nameless" ones. Oscar—bullied, battered, and almost beaten by his differentness (he is "fat" and "uncool"), including his refusal to be a "player" who treats women like toys—finds personal power in these stories. Moving back and forth in time and place, between earlier decades of the twentieth century and the dawn of the digital era in the 1990s, between wider history (with footnoted sources) and family history, between the Dominican Republic and the United States, the narrators unfold a multigenerational family struggle to overcome a violent masculinity present at once on the largest field of international politics and the most intimate field of interpersonal relationships. In sparkling, humor-filled, rap-rapid prose, Diaz moves through five decades of the postmodern era, tracing history's repetitions and hinting at the possibility of escape.

Oscar's family curse is one thread in a historical curse in which greed, power-hunger, and lust have shaped every aspect of life. The novel shows that the authoritarian and heterosexist masculinities embodied by Trujillo carry over to the generation of men who fled his regime and now many of their sons. These forces likewise embody the colonialism, slavery, and neocolonialism that have shaped both the Dominican Republic and the United States. The novel's redemptive beauty lies in the title character's ability to identify with the women in his life, including his mother Beli, his domestically battered would-be girlfriend Ana, his sister Lola, and a prostitute named Ybón, who constitute his constructed family. Oscar finally finds love in the most unexpected of places, and that love casts its light back onto the violent end that *fukú*, history's heavy weight, has in store for him.

Kinship and Lost Time: Jennifer Egan's *A Visit from the Good Squad* (2010)

Jennifer Egan's novel, *A Visit from the Good Squad* (2010), underscores the centrifugal forces facing families in the postmodern era and the new kinship patterns that seek to mitigate those forces. Through a form that utilizes a whole host of writing styles, shifting time frames, and narrator perspectives (from first to third and even once to second person), and utilizing a range of modes from classic realism to a PowerPoint presentation, Egan lays out a panoply of wildly whirling forces that buffet what's left of the mythic nuclear family.[9] Egan has often said, with tongue only part way in her cheek, that her inspiration for the book came from Proust's epic series of novels, *In Search of Lost Time*, and the mafia-centered TV show "The Sopranos." This strange duo only hints at the comic and tragic web of styles and lives that comprise this novel-story collection.

I use that double form because novel and story collection are the only traditional designations for a work like this one. But Egan suggests that we get over the restrictions of these two categories, and compares *Goon Squad* to a "concept album" where the elements are linked into an overarching story, but the parts differ greatly in tone, style, tempo, theme, and overall sound. Various chapters of the book employ different forms, tones, textures, perspectives, and voices like an album whose various songs are in different musical genres. This notion is reinforced by its division into two main parts, A and B, suggesting the A and B sides of an vinyl record. The analogy is particularly apt since the music industry is at the center of this word album. In turn, the music industry stands in for the decades-long process of technological change, roughly from the 1970s to the near future. It is very much a story about the dispersal and re-creation of a family under postmodern conditions, especially the impact of rapidly evolving technologies. The impact of technology on the *Goon Squad's* families manifests in a number of ways, from job loss due to technical obsolescence, to the impact of social media on language and communication, to an overall speeding up of our sense of time.

The crazy plot of the novel has challenged reviewers, several of whom have resorted to breathless summaries such as this one from Will Blythe in the *New York Times*:

The book starts with Sasha, a kleptomaniac, who works for Bennie, a record executive, who is a protégé of Lou who seduced Jocelyn who was loved by Scotty who played guitar for the Flaming Dildos, a San Francisco punk band for which Bennie once played bass guitar (none too well), before marrying Stephanie who is charged with trying to resurrect the career of the bloated rock legend Bosco who grants the sole rights for covering his farewell "suicide tour" to Stephanie's brother, Jules Jones, a celebrity journalist who attempted to rape the starlet Kitty Jackson, who one day will be forced to take a job from Stephanie's publicity mentor, La Doll, who is trying to soften the image of a genocidal tyrant because her career collapsed in spectacular fashion around the same time that Sasha in the years before going to work for Bennie was perhaps working as a prostitute in Naples where she was discovered by her Uncle Ted who was on holiday from a bad marriage, and while not much more will be heard from him, Sasha will come to New York and attend N.Y.U. and work for Bennie before disappearing into the desert to . . . raise a family with her college boyfriend, Drew, while Bennie, assisted by Alex, a former date of Sasha's from whom she lifted a wallet, soldiers on in New York, producing musicians (including the rediscovered guitarist Scotty) as the artistic world changes around him with . . . vertiginous speed.[10]

As this summary suggests, the characters, moving along at "vertiginous speed," are in danger of finding themselves in a manic Roadrunner cartoon full of disaster after disaster. But while some characters come to disastrous ends, others find a way through the postmodern maze of experiences.

In an increasingly sped up world, as quiet reflective times become fewer and fewer, these kinds of mass-mediated meanings more and more often define or even replace personal experience. As one character remarks, revealing one meaning of the title: "Time's a goon, right? You gonna let that goon push you around?" (332) Time has always been a goon, but it may well be more so in the current era. This is a novel where time and space disconnect, and centripetal forces—economic, technological, and cultural—create obstacles to human connection. With varying degrees of success, each of the characters struggles to find ways to reconnect, ways to reestablish traditional kinship patterns, and/or establish new kinds of family-like links.

The novel, like much postmodern fiction, is also a story about stories, stories we tell others and stories we tell ourselves, stories we tell and stories that tell us. In the opening scene, for example, Sasha remarks of her struggle with kleptomania that she and her therapist are "writing a story of redemption, of second chances" (7). Often the stories are embedded in or told by technological devices. There are numerous references to other media in the text, and entanglements between "real life" and mass-mediated life, as when a narrating character notes that "Two security guards showed up. The same on TV and as in life: two beefy guys whose scrupulous politeness was somehow linked to their willingness to crack heads" (8–9). Life's meanings are reinforced or reinvented by pop culture, like a song that pops into your earbuds just as you were thinking of something its lyrics reflect upon. This includes the fact that identity in the novel is often keyed, as it were, to the music one consumed during the most formative years of one's life, usually teen years. Each of the characters has their differing "glory days," marked especially by an era and style of music, to which they can never return but that continues to deeply shape their lives. Because it is not told in the chronological order of the period covered, the 1970s to the 2020s, we see past and future simultaneously. There is a great poignancy when later in the book we meet an unattached, hopeful young person who is a character we have met earlier in the novel as a harried parent who has deeply compromised their youthful dreams. Music functions as a kind of time machine, marking the goon squad's relentless push even though the text moves back and forth through the decades. The novel suggests that the pulse, rhythm, tone, and lyrical themes of youth can set deep patterns of thought and emotion that carry on through later decades not only as nostalgia but also as markers of ideals that need not be lost. The process of remembering is also subject to pop culture coloring, as when a character refers to their recollections as time "loops," like a repeated flashback in a film.

The novel shows again and again that time is a very complex thing. While it is a goon that marches inexorably onward toward an inevitable stopping point for each of us, it is also an illusion, only a trick of verb tenses. We always exist in the past, present, and future all at once. Memory is a kind of fiction we all constantly rewrite, and the future is full of fictive imaginings that shape the present and rewrite the past.

Egan's chapter "Safari" plays with the interplay of standardized fiction stories and the life stories we tell ourselves and each other. Mindy, an anthropology graduate student, habitually distances herself from her own family situation and life choices by describing them in terms she links to the structuralist anthropology of Claude Levi-Strauss. She depersonalizes her new relationship with a much older man through a series of concepts like *Structural Hatred*: "A single woman in her forties who wears high-collared shirt to conceal the thread sinews of her neck will structurally despise the twenty-three year-old girlfriend of a powerful male who not only employs said middle-aged female but is paying her way on this trip." This is followed by a string of additional concepts, "*Structural Resentment*," "*Structural Affection*," "*Structural Incompatibility*," and "*Structural Desire*," that in effect turn her relationship into a series of clichés she feels nevertheless willing to play out (48–9). This seems at once the author's reflection on the nature of representative fiction, and an evocation of the postmodern meta-analysis that many young people increasingly use to narrate their lives.

Unlike others who despair of the impact of new media technologies on language and lives, Egan suggests that with new languages of interconnectedness, new networks can be created. Her clearest demonstration of this is that one of the most moving chapters in the book is done in

PowerPoint format. Taking a mode of communication used primarily in mundane formulaic business encounters to tell a highly personal part of a family story encapsulates in many ways the hope of the novel, the hope in revealing connections thought lost, bringing to the surface emotional ties time and space had stretched but not broken. The chapter is told by a young girl trying to explain to an uncomprehending father that her autistic brother's fascination with and cataloguing of the pauses in various pop songs is a call for the dad to pause, acknowledge, and appreciate the different logic of his son's mind. In terms of style, the chapter uses the cool corporate tone of a presentation software to represent the father's world, and the implicit pauses between slides to underscore the insight of the son that pauses are necessary to meaning-making in music or any other medium of communication.

The penultimate PowerPoint chapter and the concluding one are both set in the near future, a bit of s/f that allows Egan to extrapolate about where digital communication might be leading us and our families. The final chapter hints that even a very reduced tech/text-speak can still be a mode for a real human connection. As one character asks, "if thr r children, thr mst b a fUtr, rt?" The novel suggests that the answer can be, Yes. (And Egan, despite declaring herself a bit of a technophobe, has suggested as much also by publishing another story entirely as Twitter tweets.[11])

At the same time, the final chapter touches on some serious ethical issues emerging from the digitized corporate takeover of privacy, and the cynical use of the notion of postmodern complicity to justify self-serving behavior. The chapter revolves around a dialogue between Alex, an unemployed would-be music industry professional, and Lulu, a young music promoter specializing in online buzz. She argues that Alex's reluctance to take part in a kind of pyramid scheme of promotion known as "parroting," getting his friends to spread seemingly spontaneous, word-of-mouth rave reviews of a musician, just reflects his outmoded ideals of authenticity, or "atavistic purism," as she labels it: "So," he said, "you think there's nothing inherently wrong with believing in something or saying you do for money?" "Inherently wrong," she said. "Gosh, that's a great example of calcified morality" (259). Alex loses the battle, gives in, and sends Lulu a list of his "contacts" (the people formerly known as friends). But ironically he wins the war, since it turns out the musician in question is an authentically talented, old-school analog guy who has long deserved greater recognition. Again, Egan reminds us, real emotional connections, and real kinships, can still be made despite the commercialized and digitized noise that constantly threatens them.

As Cathleen Schine suggests, Egan accomplishes this resistance to postmodern conditions through a reshaping of postmodernist style in *A Visit from the Goon Squad*, "a moving humanistic saga, an enormous nineteenth-century-style epic brilliantly disguised as ironic postmodern pastiche . . . [in which Egan] has employed every playful device of the postmodern novel with such warmth and sensitivity that the genre is transcended completely."[12] While it should be clear by now that "warmth and sensitivity" are present in more than just this one postmodern novel, Schine is right that Egan has matched condition to style harmoniously in this epic of dispersal and recollection. She shows us that with craft and care it is possible to make something meaningful—an album, a novel, a family, a life—even out of the jumbled, jangled, troubled, and troubling conditions of lives thrown into hyperdrive and dispersed across continents. Egan doesn't pretend to address some of the deeper, more troubling aspects of new technologies like frightening levels of surveillance and the dangerous proliferation of polarizing disinformation via new media (see Chapter 10), but she does suggest that new kinds of family can still be created and can still act as sanctuaries amid the mad swirl of techno-cultural transformations and space/time dislocations.

Indigenous Gothic, Sasquatch, and Community as Family: Eden Robinson's *Monkey Beach* (2000)

Haisla/Heiltsuk First Nations author Eden Robinson's *Monkey Beach* (2000) beautifully blends a coming-of-age story, a gothic ghost story, mystery tropes, and Indigenous lore in a three-generation family saga set in British Columbia, Canada.[13] The novel cuts rapidly between various eras of its protagonist's life, sometimes signaled, other times dropped in abruptly. Also interspersed are vignettes (like a disquisition on the mechanism of the human heart or an elegant description of a landscape) seemingly unattached to the storyline. The overall impact is to blur the lines between present and past, memory and dream, fact and story. But perhaps the novel's most postmodern feature, related to this compositional style, is its careful, tense interplay between white Western and Native Haisla ontologies or worldviews, including the use of sometimes untranslated words in the latter language. The narrating central character, twenty-year-old Lisamarie Michele Hill, appears to have abilities that the dominant culture calls supernatural, but that were once a taken-for-granted part of the Haisla world.

A relation between two worlds is established from the opening of the novel in a scene typically combining humor and tense concern. Lisamarie reports to her father that she had received a message that morning from some crows outside her window:

> "They were talking to me. They said *la'es*. It's probably . . ."
>
> "Clearly a sign, Lisa," my mother has come up behind and grips my shoulders, "that you need Prozac." (3)

The scene introduces not only Lisa and her parents, but also crows, who, along with their cousins, ravens, play a key role on the symbolic plane of the novel. All of these characters, human and otherwise, take part in the event at the heart of the novel, the search for Lisa's seventeen-year-old brother, Jimmy, who is presumed lost at sea in the Haida Gwaii sea (Douglas Channel in English) off the coast of British Columbia.

In using the term "symbolic plane," I am invoking only one kind of reading of the text. The novel can be read as a postmodern effort to challenge dominant epistemologies rooted in white European master narratives. Differing ways that readers interpret the novel highlight various possible relations to the Indigenous lore portrayed. As critic Michèle Lacombe argues, these issues also suggest tensions present between various strands of Indigenous literary/cultural theory as they relate to non-Native ones.[14] This tension in turn is symptomatic of a larger political struggle over the future of aboriginal cultures in and beyond North America. There has long been a debate between cultural nationalists, who stress specific locally based traditions, and those who see the need to articulate pan-Indian or pan-Indigenous elements that cross tribal/band borders. The politics of this debate has to do with the best strategies for maintaining and/or reconstructing Indigenous cultures in the face of ongoing efforts to absorb them into dominant cultures. Most Indigenous fiction writers acknowledge and address at least two distinct audiences with differing needs and interests: Indigenous readers and non-Indigenous ones. For the former, priority is often on stories that heal, while for the latter the hope may be to help generate external support for ongoing struggles for sovereignty and just treatment. And Indigenous authors are always subject to misreading as "primitive" or "superstitious" rather than as representing communities with fully developed different epistemologies.[15]

The key force in the attempt to destroy Native cultures featured in the *Monkey Beach* is the residential school policy. This government-sponsored, church-based system lasted in Canada for over 160 years (from the nineteenth century to the closing of the last school in 1996), using "aggressive assimilation" on over 150,000 Native youth. A deeply abusive system, the policy took Indigenous youth in Canada out of their home communities into boarding schools that aimed to teach "civilized" ways and "beat the Indian out of them." This horrendous system was belatedly apologized for by the Canadian government only in 2008, and a subsequent government commission that was set up to study its impact acknowledged it as "cultural genocide," though remedial action has remained very limited.[16] (A similar system of forcible boarding schools in the United States has generated no such formal governmental response.) Apologies and reconciliation efforts notwithstanding, the horrible impact of the residential school system (and its US correlative) continues to echo to this day in Indigenous communities and among urban Natives across North America.

If the residential school represents the disintegrating force in the community, it is family, kinship, which offers hope. In the novel, kinship that starts in the Hill family radiates out into an extended network that eventually includes virtually the whole Haisla/Heiltsuk community and its relationship to the land, sea, and creatures. This is not some easy, stereotypical Indigenous relationship to tribe and nature, but rather one that has to be cultivated amid the centrifugal forces of history and contemporary dominant culture. As is common in families faced with assimilation into another dominant culture, there are generational splits in the family between grandparents, parents, and their children. The novel depicts a wide range of attitudes toward Native traditions among the extended Hill family, from Ma-ma-oo (the grandmother) who is deeply immersed in Haisla beliefs, to Christian members of the family who utterly reject them, with most characters somewhere in between, mixing belief systems or, like Lisa, in a fraught search for greater understanding of ancient knowledge. When as a child Jimmy states his intention to go to Monkey Beach to take a photograph of what his grandmother calls the *B-gwu*, his father tells him that sasquatches are "make-believe, like fairies." Jimmy protests that "Ma-ma-oo says they're real." To which his father replies, "Your grandmother thinks people on TV are real" (10). Along with the Prozac joke, this is one of the first clues that Haisla beliefs have to some extent skipped a generation, with Lisa (and we later learn, Jimmy) attempting to recapture parts of their traditional culture that their father has left behind. For Lisa, the process seems to begin in the form of disturbing, seemingly prophetic dreams she starts to have as a young child before she has learned much about Haisla lore.

Lisa's Uncle Mick, a victim of the residential school system, also complexly mediates between generations. She is named after him, and there are hints he may even be her real father. Her attempts to regain some of the language and beliefs of her heritage are in part linked to her uncle's legacy as a member of AIM, the radical American Indian Movement that arose in the 1960s and 1970s to challenge a host of assimilationist and other attacks on Native peoples across North America.[17] At its best, AIM mixed dramatic political theater (like their occupation of the Wounded Knee massacre site), with quieter efforts to learn Native cultural traditions. Mick's militancy, or warrior spirit as he would call it, was partly sparked by his experiences in the residential system. In an argument over Christianity with relatives, Mick exclaims: "You're buying into a religion that thought that the best way to make us white was to torture children . . ." (110) Mick is the crazy, funny uncle Lisa loves, but over the course of the novel we learn more about the pain that to some degree drives his rebellious nature. But whatever its roots, his resisting spirit is honored. In contrast to Mick, his sister, Lisa's aunt Trudy, can deal with her memories of the brutal residential school only through the self-destructive act of drowning them in alcohol.

The novel also addresses the contrast between white and Indigenous cultures through its depiction of differing perceptions of the land. Early in the novel, we are given a brief lecture on Western map coordinates that marked, but also historically mislabeled, the various places the Native characters inhabit and visit.

> Find a map of British Columbia. Point to the middle of the coast . . . [W]hen the Hudson's Bay traders [arrived] with their guides . . . the name [Kitamaat] got stuck on the official records and the village has been called Kitamaat ever since, even though it really should be called Haisla. There are four or five different spellings of Kitamaat in the historical writings, but the Haisla decided on Kitamaat. To add to the confusion, when Alcan Aluminum moved into the area in the 1950s, it built a "city of the future" for its workers and named it Kitimat too, but spelled it differently. . . . Near the head of the Douglas, you'll find Kitamaat Village, with its seven hundred Haisla people tucked in between the mountains and the ocean. At the end of the village is our house. (4–5)

This passage names and mocks the arrival of whites, as well as the ongoing colonization by corporate capitalism, and is emblematic of the cultural misunderstandings that continue to this day. But it also suggests a way to recover what has been covered over by another culture's naming, and the continued existence of a "city of the present past" set against the corporate world's "city of the future."

As *Monkey Beach* progresses, the territory is gradually remapped as spaces of memory and local knowledge for the family and in Haisla lore. Beautiful descriptions of the natural environment, mountains "royal blue against the grey sky, tendrils of mist lifting through the trees like ghosts," Native stories about the Stone Man, *Weegit* (Raven), *D'sonoqua* (Ogre Woman), and the white monster guarding Douglas Channel/Haida Gwaii, run up against or entwine with a contemporary world layered upon an ancient cultural landscape: "the ripples [of the lake] spread, the mountain's reflection jiggling like a blurry TV reception" (117; 119). These two worlds coexist uneasily, but things like the fact that Lisa learns about her family and cultural history from her grandmother while they watch soap operas on TV suggests that she can find a way to bring those worlds into meaningful relationship (195–6). Likewise, Uncle Mick's love of Elvis Presley in no way undercuts his relation to Haisla culture and his Red Power vision for the future.

Lisa's journey over the course of the novel is complexly rendered amid contending forces of past and present, or rather the presence of the past as burden and hope. Her "gift" of second sight is encouraged by her grandmother, discouraged by her parents, and pathologized by her school counselor. She pretends to acquiesce to the counselor's view of her seeing of ghosts as a fantasy aimed at escaping personal problems. But we see her gradually come to better understand and harness her powers as their relation to Haisla culture, the abuses she suffers and the substances she abuses, and their role in her family story become clearer. In one lovely ironic moment that directly challenges the expected, stereotypic response, a friend asks if she "really sees ghosts," she answers, "Yeah, sometimes. When I'm sober" (313). Haisla reality also shapes the novel through parallels between a number of personal events in the novel and tribal lore. Lisa's grandmother complains that the next generation "cleaned up" the earthier dimensions of Haisla stories, and she encourages her granddaughter to embrace the versions that are both lustier and make more sense. And the sense is that tradition is not a static thing of the past but a living thing that can be, must be, refashioned for the living. In one dream sequence late in the novel, Lisa imagines her mother telling her to come home and "make me some grandkids," while her uncle tells her instead to go "give'em hell. Red Power!" (373) But can't she, mustn't she, do both? Isn't the reproduction of her community embedded in power struggles?

The novel's conclusion (no spoiler alert needed) is open-ended in several ways, including how to read the nature of Lisa's visions. How the novel resolves the mystery of the disappearance of her younger brother Jimmy itself remains a mystery. A dedicated, disciplined, and gifted swimmer with a chance of making the Canadian Olympic team, he is nonetheless unable to escape a haunted history of abuse passed on to his generation into the life of his girlfriend Adelaide (nicknamed Karaoke). We learn that his disappearance stems from an attempt to exact justice, but seemingly at great cost. That the meaning of his act and his subsequent fate remain something of a mystery at the end of the novel seems emblematic of the as-yet unknown future awaiting his kin and their wider community. That future will be decided by how the Native world and the surrounding dominant culture negotiate their coexisting story lines.

While *Monkey Beach* is unflinching in its depiction of the horrors unleashed on the Haisla by the ongoing invasion of their lands, throughout the novel the beauty of the landscape, the humor, the strength of family, and resistance efforts in the form of both radical activism (Mick's AIM years) and various efforts at Haisla cultural renewal, language recovery, and family/community reconstruction, belie attempts to reduce Natives to mere victims of settler colonialism. That Lisa lives to tell her story implies there is a new, better story to be written. In the twenty-first century, that spirit animates the vital Idle No More movement and efforts like resistance to the oil pipelines that cross and endanger lives on the sacred Indigenous land.[18]

6

(meta)Histories

The Past as Present

All fiction is historical fiction in the sense that a novel necessarily bears the marks of the era in which it is composed. History impacts us from the outside in, but we experience it from the inside out. We feel its effects even when we don't recognize them as history's mark upon us. Novelist William Faulkner told us that the past is never dead, and not even past. Fellow novelist James Baldwin pointed out the people are trapped in history and history is trapped in them. One critic, Timothy Parish, tells us that history is an ongoing event that bleeds into the present, and another, Ruth Berlau, reminds us that forgetting the past is no escape from it. Our connection to the inescapable past has both a quite personal side and a more structured side. The latter includes what the great critic Raymond Williams called "structures of feeling," transpersonal patterns of affect particular to a given time and place. Novelists are often far better at representing these emotional patterns than are traditional historians.

The works surveyed in this chapter highlight such patterns, and also highlight more directly than most novels the fact that historical writing and fiction writing are never fully separable. They underscore that "history" is both context and text. One important element of the postmodern emphasis on the central role of language in not merely shaping but to a large extent *inventing* reality has been the proliferation of works challenging "historiography," history writing, the professional writing of historians. Put simply, cultural theorists (and novelists) have examined the ways in which the narrating of putatively real historical events is subject to similar kinds of linguistic rules, strategies, tropes, and other determining features that critics use to analyze fiction. Theorist Hayden White, for example, in his magisterial book, *Metahistory*, shows how the great historians of the nineteenth century produced stories that conform to the same broad categories into which literary critics divided the novel: tragedy, romance, comedy, and satire. White showed how major historians crafted the morass of historical detail into stories whose "emplotment" parallels the plotting of novels. The significant body of work challenging realist historical writing in turn emboldened novelists to engage with historical events and figures in a range of new ways.

At the same time, from the literary theory side, critic Linda Hutcheon argued that a skeptical approach to history is central to what makes novels postmodern, suggesting that what she dubs "historiographic metafiction" may well be the most characteristic form of the postmodern novel. She might just as easily have called them "metahistorical fictions," since, like White's *Metahistory*, these novels try to lay bare the underlying literary techniques that turn the labyrinth of historical events into coherent, meaningful stories. They are metahistorical in reflecting on the writing of history, and metafictional in reflecting on the writing of fiction. As Hutcheon makes clear this does not mean, as some less careful critics assert, that history does not exist except as text. Like the much misunderstood comment by Jacques Derrida that "there is nothing outside the text," such a claim just means that we apprehend reality through its verbal, textual representation. This is true of reality in the present and even more fully true of previous historical eras since they are available to us almost exclusively in textual form—documents, public records, diaries, and so forth. It is not a denial of the fact that outside the text material reality and historical processes do certain things that no text can contain. The fact that history can only be known imperfectly through texts does not mean that texts alone make history. Texts of all kinds profoundly shape historical interpretation, but events always also exist outside of their textualization in ways that have force beyond what can be said about them. They determine certain parameters for what can and cannot be said about history's factuality. Reality, the full historical record, exceeds all interpretation.

Facts matter. But no fact has ever spoken for itself. Facts require a ventriloquist to give them voice. And the facts of history are given meaning, put into (con)text, most often by the ventriloquists known as historians. But historians are typically less conscious than fiction writers about how narrative strategies are essential to meaning-making of any kind. Postmodern novelists have used a variety of techniques to challenge naïve versions of historical truth, but their goal has seldom (if ever) been to replace truth with fiction. Rather the goal has been to get readers to become more aware of the narrative tricks by which certain historical truths have been told, and to draw attention to alternative truth claims by previously marginalized people, events, and ideas.

There are a number of different ways in which postmodern authors have challenged the overly simplistic line between history and fiction. Magical realist history, for example, uses the seemingly impossible to challenge the limits of historical imaginings. In this vein, Alex Kuo, for example, in his series of novels *Panda Diaries* (2006), *The Man Who Dammed the Yangtze: A Mathematical Novel* (2011), *shanghai.shanghai.shanghai* (2015), and *Mao's Kisses: A Novel of June 4, 1989* (2019), utilizes magical elements (like a postal worker who happens to be a panda bear) to trace postmodern China's evolution since the Tiananmen Square era. These works explore the complexities of the fictions created by Chinese authorities as they shape and are sometimes resisted in the everyday lives of Chinese citizens as no realist storytelling could.

Some other postmodern novels imitate the narrative rules of historical writing, then overtly violate those same rules through things like *obvious anachronisms* or *wholly implausible lines of causality*. A related type of postmodern historical narrative pushes this technique to the extreme of creating alternative histories, or *counterfactual histories*, in which well-known events (like the outcome of the Second World War) are rewritten in ways that clearly did not happen.

Other postmodern historical novels blend many styles and narrative forms while nevertheless hewing close to the archival record. They add levels of nuance that a single style of historical narrative often misses. Karen Tei Yamashita, for example, in her novel, *I Hotel* (2010), uses a range of conflicting and conflicted discourses embedded in ten novellas (each a different angle of vision on events in the title hotel as historical site), utilizing plays, poems, comic strips, transposed choreography and music, FBI files, movement documents, and much more, to capture the interplay of personal history and larger social change in the Asian American movement and related creative protest forces in San Francisco during the 1960s and 1970s. What makes this a difficult book but a truly radical history is the information it withholds, the ways in which it forces readers into the unknown present of historical actors rather than treating history as an accomplished thing of the past unfolding with a clear logic of causality. As Yamashita lyrically renders this: "Knowing the story's end does not necessarily imply completion or knowledge, for if many endings are possible, so also are many beginnings. History may proceed sequentially or, as they say, *must* proceed sequentially, but stories may turn and turn again—the knowing end kissing the innocent beginning, the innocent end kissing the knowing beginning" (301).

Other postmodernists create plots so filled with historical detail that no coherence can be made from them (a version of *maximalism*), or tell history through mixed genres or forms like the comic book that are thought to be highly inappropriate for the serious writing of history. Sometimes these novels incorporate *real historical figures alongside of or entangled with fictional characters*, often to complicate more general histories by pointing to the difficulty of representing the life history of even one historical personage, let alone representing an entire era. Novels like E. L. Doctorow's *The Book of Daniel* (1971) and *Ragtime* (1975) expertly employ this mix of real historical figures and fictional characters in politically intriguing ways.

An additional, quite direct form of postmodern historical challenge, the *nonfiction novel*, is treated in the chapter that follows. This seemingly oxymoronic concept entails using all of the tricks of the novelist trade but adhering as closely as possible to known facts about a given event in the recent or distant past. And, while they are beyond the scope of this book, I would also note that in response to postmodern theory and under the influence of these postmodern novelists, some professional historians have themselves taken up some new techniques of fiction writing, producing what some have called a *postmodern historiography* that bends toward the novel from the other side of this too neat of a generic division.[1] These works also underscore another key point made by Linda Hutcheon, that the critique of history writing is entwined with a critique of novel writing such that in "the postmodern novel the conventions of both fiction and historiography are simultaneously used and abused, installed and subverted, asserted and denied."[2]

While these various approaches differ in significant ways, they all have in common the intent to encourage readers to reexamine taken-for-granted ideas about the truthfulness of putatively objective historical accounts. As with other forms of postmodern skepticism, this is not the denial of truth (historical truth in this case), but rather a caution against *absolutist* belief in matters of fact that are always subject to a degree of interpretive perspectivism based in *situated knowledges* (see Chapter 2) that include previously marginalized voices and thus come closer to the impossibility of complete objectivity by acknowledging inevitable social biases.[3]

Chained to History: Toni Morrison's *Beloved* (1987)

Postmodern historical fiction includes many works in the magical realist tradition started by Latin American authors like Julio Cortázar and Gabriel Garcia Marquez. These novels address a range of historical eras and events, but in a US context, the era of slavery has proven of particular interest to magical realists. There are a number of such texts in the category labeled "neo-slave narratives." This genre includes such diverse works as Ishmael Reed's parodic *Flight to Canada* (1976), Octavia Butler's time-traveling s/f classic, *Kindred* (1979), Colson Whitehead's brutally surreal *The Underground Railroad* (2016), and Paul Beatty's *The Sellout* (2016) which imagines a twenty-first-century revival of slavery by a black man.[4] Each of these novels offers insight into the ways in which the historical institution of slavery continues to profoundly shape contemporary politics and contemporary lives, as the Black Lives Matter Movement makes clear. Each uses postmodern techniques to reanimate a set of issues by showing the ongoing life of the past in the present.

However, there is one neo-slave narrative that towers above all these, Toni Morrison's *Beloved* (1987), the novel that is largely responsible for securing its author the Nobel Prize in literature. *Beloved* is based on the true story of a slave, Margaret Garner, who murdered her own baby daughter rather than see her returned to the horror show that was slavery. The depth of love and despair that such an act implies led Morrison into her profound exploration of slavery as a form of subjecthood lasting long after its official abolition, lasting in fact into the present and foreseeable future. The novel is dedicated to "the sixty million," one estimate of how many Africans and African Americans died in the slave trade.

Beloved is a self-consciously deconstructive dive into the internal workings of minds under physical bondage. It is exquisitely sensitive to the postmodern perspective on language as a historically situated force that has done violence to certain human possibilities. Set a decade after the end of the Civil War and legal emancipation, with flashbacks to the slave era, it chronicles the many ways in which slavery haunts those upon whom it was perpetrated. The terror-filled past is partly embodied in a character, the Beloved of the title, who may be the ghost (or "revenant," in the novel) of a child sacrificed by her mother to save her from enslavement, or may be a young black woman escaped from years of brutal imprisonment by a white man, or somehow both. But the haunting is far more than that, and this horror story needs no paranormal activity. The "normal" practices of human enslavement provide the horror. And the focus is on the extraordinarily difficult task of exorcizing this evil. At the center of the novel is the concept of "re-memory." The term is meant to suggest a recovery process in both senses of that word. All of the characters, for obvious reasons, seek to repress their memories of slavery, including not only unfreedom but sexual violation. But that process proves impossible. The attempt at repression distorts, and in some cases destroys, personhood. The re-memory project is both personal and collective, communal, and can occur only through mutual recognition and creative re-imagining of the self.

The novel leaves the character Beloved's status ambiguous. Is her appearance a case of a kind of mass hysteria, a hallucination, or is it a case of mistaken identity, a different person on whom the sacrificed child is projected? Ultimately it does not matter, because Beloved in either scenario is an embodiment of the traumatic memories of slavery and captivity. The process Morrison invokes is not unlike the recovery from trauma that an individual under psychoanalysis undergoes, and each of the characters must undergo a version of this process to reclaim subjecthood. That project turns out to include recovering the flesh that has been stolen. This is not about denying reality but rather of re-membering the body, restoring lost body parts. The character Baby Suggs tells a group of assembled ex-slaves that "the only grace they could have was the grace they could imagine." In this sermonic passage, her words seek to work the magic of reclamation even as the horror they must overcome is evoked:

> In this here place, we flesh; flesh that weeps, laughs; flesh that dances on bare feet in grass. Love it. Love it hard. Yonder they do not love your flesh. They despise it. They don't love your eyes; they'd just as soon pick em out. No more do they love the skin on your back. Yonder they flay it. And O my people they do not love your hands. Those they only use, tie, bind, chop off and leave empty. Love your hands! Love them. Raise them up and kiss them. Touch

others with them, pat them together, stroke them on your face 'cause they don't love that either. You got to love it, you! And no, they ain't in love with your mouth. Yonder, out there, they will see it broken and break it again. What you say out of it they will not heed. What you scream from it they do not hear. What you put into it to nourish your body they will snatch away and give you leavins instead. No, they don't love your mouth. You got to love it. This is flesh I'm talking about here. Flesh that needs to be loved. Feet that need to rest and to dance; backs that need support; shoulders that need arms, strong arms I'm telling you. And O my people, out yonder, hear me, they do not love your neck unnoosed and straight. So love your neck; put a hand on it, grace it, stroke it and hold it up. and all your inside parts that they'd just as soon slop for hogs, you got to love them. The dark, dark liver—love it, love it and the beat and beating heart, love that too. More than eyes or feet. More than lungs that have yet to draw free air. More than your life-holding womb and your life-giving private parts, hear me now, love your heart. For this is the prize. (103–4)

Loss of ownership over one's body is profoundly tied to loss of the self, and each character must find or fail to find a way to throw off the lacerating language of the master discourse. And when that reclamation does not occur, it is passed on to the next generation, as has been done again and again as the ongoing impact of slavery shapes the body politic of the nation. The legacy of slavery shapes not just Black people but also poor and working-class whites compensated for a lesser status by being told they are superior to "Negroes."

Beyond the message directed at the legacy faced by each and every African American, Morrison's larger subject is the nation's historical recovery from the mass trauma inflicted through slavery. It is too easy, she shows, to blame the evils on Southerners. The North was complicit in the slave trade, and nineteenth-century science and social science each played a significant role in rationalizing the system. And the peculiar institution forever transformed both the slaves and those who took part in the enslavement or stood by as it occurred.

Whitepeople believed that whatever the manners, under every dark skin was a jungle. Swift unnavigable waters, swinging screaming baboons, sleeping snakes, red gums ready for their sweet white blood. In a way, he thought, they were right. The more coloredpeople spent their strength trying to convince them how gentle they were, how clever and loving, how human, the more they used themselves up to persuade whites of something Negroes believed could not be questioned, the deeper and more tangled the jungle grew inside. But it wasn't the jungle blacks brought with them to this place from the other (livable) place. It was the jungle whitefolks planted in them. And it grew. It spread. In, through and after life, it spread, until it invaded the whites who had made it. Touched them every one. Changed and altered them. Made them bloody, silly, worse than even they wanted to be, so scared were they of the jungle they had made. The screaming baboon lived under their own white skin; the red gums were their own. (198)

The novel ultimately asks whether the nation will ever achieve something approaching a just peace if the citizens of the United States do not fully engage slavery's continuing impact. Like the central character of the novel, only distorted life is possible in a nation where the trauma of slavery, its attendant brutalization, and the ongoing racism that arose from it are ignored. Whether it be the resurrection of the supposed glory of the Confederacy, or just the frequent call to "get over the past," the current state of the United States and other slavery-shadowed nations perpetuates this state of denial. Only by confronting the history that writers like Morrison brilliantly illuminate, will the future be one even vaguely approaching the claim of liberty and justice for all.

Of Butterflies and Dictators: Julia Alverez's *In the Time of the Butterflies* (1994)

The aftermath of colonization and slavery has been equally devastating in the Caribbean region, where racism, political instability, corruption, and authoritarian rule have continually disrupted efforts to instill democratic governance. A second strand of postmodern fictive history, one that novelizes important historical personages and events, has taken root in the region. The Caribbean has produced more than its share of this form of postmodern fiction, including many texts focused on the dissecting of dictatorial regimes that followed the official end of European colonialism on the island nations. Julio Cortázar, one of the forerunners of magical realism, was an early master of this type of novel. Jamaica Kincaid's uncharacterizable anti-travelogue, *A Small Place* (1988), gives a tourist trashing twist on postcolonial conditions on her island of origin, Antigua. Marlon James's novel, *A Brief History of Seven Killings* (2014), deconstructs corrupt Jamaican politics via a character always referred to only as "the singer" but clearly modeled on Bob Marley, the great Jamaican reggae musician and human rights activist. And Junot Diaz's *The Brief Wondrous Life of Oscar Wao* (see Chapter 5) brings the story to the United States, tracing the impact of the Dominican Republic's Trujillo dictatorship on a family driven to exile in New Jersey.

Among the most important and influential of these is Julia Alverez's novel, *In the Time of the Butterflies* (1994).[5] The novel tells the story of four female siblings in the Dominican Republic based upon the real-life Mirabal sisters, famous for their roles in resisting the dictatorial regime of Rafael Trujillo. Trujillo and his surrogates ruled the Dominican Republic for several decades, using the most brutal methods to suppress all criticism, let alone serious resistance. The Mirabal sisters became key symbols of opposition to the dictatorship, as well as feminist heroines throughout the Caribbean and Latin America.

The novel begins, in classic metafiction fashion, by calling into question the author via a first chapter telling of the encounter between a *"gringa dominica"* writer (a fictional stand-in for Alvarez who in fact did interview the surviving sister while composing the novel), and the surviving Mirabal sister, Dede. This metafictional dimension of the novel is more subtle than in many other postmodern texts, carefully crafted to not overshadow the known record of the women who actually made this history. Alvarez wishes to give new voice to women the dictator's regime sought to silence forever, but she does not want to silence the real women in the process. Additional interview segments, which often turn into Dede's interior monologues, are interspersed throughout the novel, reminding readers that the novel's story is in part a story told to the "real" author. At the same time, the Dede character more than once remarks on the unreliability of memory, making clear that her story like history is always filtered through years of subsequent events. This includes the fact that the sole surviving sister has in fact become the keeper of the Butterfly sisters' legacy, narrating and re-narrating their lives, telling some truths but not others, falling at times into mythic repetitions.

Dede remarks that the real sisters have become lost in the myth, and she tries, often through remembered everyday events not related to heroism, to recapture their humanity. The character "Dede" also expresses skepticism about the unnamed outsider author's motives and capacities to understand, especially given that the exiled Dominican writer barely speaks Spanish. She assumes that this one, like so many journalists and historians before, has just come to steal her sisters' story for her own purposes. Retelling her sisters' lives is a task Dede accepts but feels burdened by at times, and she is grateful that this *gringa* is asking new questions, seeking it seems to get beyond the legends. As readers of the novel we are thereby invited to take up this skepticism, to some degree, to see the truth of the story told as filtered through many layers of fiction/fact. Dede becomes a character in the novel as well as in the surrounding interview segments, and returns at the end of the novel in an "Epilogue" that reflects once more on the limits of the story told in part through her recollections as "the interviewee."

As the story of the martyred Mirabal sisters has become well known in certain parts of the Latin American world, their legendary status has turned them into abstractions, heroic beings above everyday life. In contrast, Alvarez's novel provides a far more complicated story than one of superhuman heroism. Each of the four sisters is depicted as a unique and uniquely conflicted individual for whom the decision to resist Trujillo came only through complicated inner turmoil and differing kinds of doubts that had to be overcome. The four stories also serve to undermine a simple historical viewpoint in that each character sees the reality of the historical events that are unfolding in a slightly different way, filtered through particular, personal but not simply individualized, angles of vision. The novel vividly captures the paranoia of living under a dictatorship, the sense that a neighbor, a friend, even a loved one may be an informer. It shows how a host of forces— religion, class privilege, gendered responsibilities, fear of harm to oneself or family—uphold the regime. And it shows how those forces can be turned against the regime in the form of religious morality, a sense of noblesse oblige, and family (especially sisterly) solidarity.

In life as in the novel, Dede Mirabal was the keeper of her sisters' legendary legacy for decades. And we may assume that in life as in the novel she is highly skeptical of those who know only the legend. She has become, as her character terms it, "the grand dame of the beautiful, terrible past. But it is an impossible task, impossible! After all, she is the only one left to manage the terrible, beautiful present" (65). Echoing perhaps W. B. Yeats' description of the "terrible beauty" of violent political upheaval, Dede too is torn between the legendary and the real sisters. Part of her historical legacy is raising the daughters left behind by the dead sisters. One of those daughters at one point in the novel cries out, with a spirit that ironically reminds Dede of the daughter's strong-willed mother, Minerva: "I'm my own person. I'm tired of being the daughter of a legend" (65).

Where political heroism, as portrayed in the media, can often distance ordinary people from figures made too perfect to emulate, Alvarez's novel, told in the intimate voices of each sister in turn, humanizes them, brings them closer to the way flawed, fragile human beings make difficult choices in political and personal lives. As Alvarez herself remarks in a postscript to a reissue of the novel in 2010, "such deification [is] dangerous, the same god-making impulse that had created [Trujillo]" (324). None of the sisters is deified or portrayed as experiencing a simplistic awakening to injustice. The power of the novel is in watching the gradual, spiraling process by which each of them is drawn, to one degree of another, into a political struggle they know is unlikely to succeed.

Patria, the eldest daughter, is also the most religious; she even once considered taking vows as a nun. Her struggle between this-worldly politics and other-worldly dedication to God transforms slowly toward a kind of liberation theology that joins her Catholicism to political resistance. Eventually she forms a Christian revolutionary group that merges with a more secular one co-founded by younger sister Minerva. Minerva, the third sister in age, is from the beginning of the story the most radical. She goes to law school to seek legal remedies for the Trujillo regime's violation of human rights, but is denied her degree by order of Trujillo himself. This further confirms her sense that only revolution can solve the nation's plight. The patriarchal power of Trujillo is made abundantly clear as his vendetta against the Mirabal family intensifies when Minerva resists the dictator's attempt to add her to the long list of his sexual conquests. The youngest sister, Maria Teresa, is initially very dubious about the resistance. She enjoys the material and social advantages of her economically privileged position, but eventually due to the arguments made by Minerva and Maria Teresa's husband Leandro, she joins the cause. The fourth sister, Dede, never fully overcomes her reluctance, worrying deeply about not only her sisters but her own children, and influenced by a husband who doesn't want her to be involved, she stays mostly on the sidelines. Yet she becomes a key figure in the process of creating the historical meaning of the sisters' resistance.

The butterflies in the title of the novel refer to "las mariposas" (the butterflies)—the code name the sisters were given in the underground resistance movement. Like that famous butterfly whose flapping wings, according to a popular representation of chaos theory, set a tornado in motion, these Dominican butterflies, against enormous odds, helped set in motion a hurricane that toppled a thirty-year dictatorship, an event that continues to inspire resistance to tyranny wherever their story is read. Alvarez's novel continues the sisters' work and Dede's work in keeping alive a current of resistance that is available to anyone who struggles against repressive forces.

Thanks to *In the Time of the Butterflies* (and a subsequent film of the novel starring Salma Hayek), their story became more widely known in North

America and the wider English-speaking world. A few years after the novel was published, the United Nations named November 25, the day that three of the Mirabal sisters were assassinated, as the "International Day for the Elimination of Violence Against Women" in their honor, a day that marks the first of sixteen days focused each year on resistance to gender-based violence around the globe.

In addition to its subtle portrayal of life under an authoritarian regime, *In the Time of the Butterflies* offers a larger insight—that history viewed as something abstract, out there, around us, teaches us too little. The novel suggests the need to remember that history is inside each of us, that it is the sum of choices each of us make in our daily lives. In her 2010 postscript, Alvarez offers a quote from Nobel Prize–winning American author Toni Morrison that sums up one key theme of a novel about young women who gave up their comfortable middle-class lives for a just cause. Morrison writes: "The function of freedom is to free someone else" (331).

Unstuck in Time: Kurt Vonnegut's *Slaughterhouse Five* (1969)

No historical subject seems to have attracted as much interest among postmodern novelists writing *counterfactual history* as the Second World War. A different outcome to that war has been the subject of numerous novels, including several by prominent postmodern writers including Philip K. Dick, *The Man in the High Castle* (1962), Philip Roth, *The Plot Against America* (2004), and Michael Chabon, *The Yiddish Policeman's Union* (2007). What several of these novels have in common is the use of counterfactual history to underscore the fact that while the United States may have been fighting a viciously anti-Semitic and racist Nazi regime, anti-Semitism and racism were very much a part of life in America, such that it is not that difficult to imagine a quite different historical trajectory. These what-if histories do various kinds of work, but perhaps most centrally they undermine too simple assumptions about the inevitability of historical development, reminding readers that many paths of historical development are always possible. Another type of counter-history takes the form of the time-travel narrative that seeks to rewrite history, or as Annalee Newlitz phrases it in her wonderful time-travel novel, *The Future of Another Timeline* (2019), "re-edit the past." This type of writing both challenges certain historical truths that have been edited out of the record, and, in the case of the Second World War counter-histories, cautions against the complacent belief that the outcome was inevitable. In focusing on the possibility that fascism had won out in the United States and in the United Kingdom, they seem particularly relevant in our time when authoritarianism is once again on the rise.

One of the earliest and most interesting works that radically combines history and counter-history, fact-based history and history that leaves facts in the dust, is Kurt Vonnegut's novel, *Slaughterhouse Five, or the Children's Crusade* (1969).[6] Vonnegut's humorous, sardonic, and direct style has kept him among the most consistently popular and widely read postmodernists. He also represents the fact that the counterfactual history genre owes much to s/f, with its central focus on alternative possibilities. *Slaughterhouse Five* grew out of the fact that Vonnegut was a prisoner of war in Dresden during the Second World War. He survived one of the most devastating bombing campaigns of the war, surpassed in carnage only by the atomic bombs dropped on Japan. The firebombing of Dresden by the United States and Britain destroyed one of the most beautiful old cities in Europe, and took the lives of close to 25,000 people, mostly civilian. Debate about whether the events constituted a justifiable military operation to shorten the war, a series of war crimes, or something in between, continues to this day (the debate is enacted in the novel as well). But Vonnegut, who experienced the events firsthand, saw it as a barbaric act without any possible justification.

In classic metafictional style, the novel begins with a mock preface in which the narrator/author lays claim to the realism of a story that is about to become as unrealistic as one can imagine. The very real Dresden bombing is the event around which the novel's various elements swirl, but the swirling eventually swirls well outside of facts and far into outer space. The protagonist, given the obviously symbolic name Billy Pilgrim, witnesses the firebombing and is deeply impacted by it. Partly as a result of the experience, Billy becomes "unstuck in time" (17), and the novel becomes a time-travel story that may or may not be the result of Pilgrim going mad or suffering from PTSD.

The novel jumps back and forth across time and space, from Billy's quiet life as a husband, father, and optometrist in mid-America suburbia to the Second World War to outer space. Pilgrim is transported to an alien planet whose inhabitants wish to study the peculiar creatures from Earth. These Tralfamadorians place Billy in a kind of zoo where his behavior can be closely observed, including asking him to "mate" with a porn actress named Montana Wildhack whom they also abduct for the purposes of this experiment.

The alien behavioral study trope affords just one of the many ways the novel offers commentary on the all too numerous follies and shortcomings of human beings in general, and American human beings in particular. For example, the narrator notes that

> Americans, like human beings everywhere, believe many things that are obviously untrue . . . . Their most destructive untruth is that it is very easy for any American to make money. They will not acknowledge how in fact hard money is to come by, and, therefore, those who have no money blame and blame and blame themselves. This inward blame has been a treasure for the rich and powerful, who have had to do less for their poor, publicly and privately, than any other ruling class since, say, Napoleonic times. (129)

But Vonnegut clearly sees the greatest of human follies to be our propensity for war, a propensity largely driven, the novel makes clear, by myths of heroic glory. The author is trying to counteract the fact that as one character points out, books and movies have a lot to do with keeping this myth alive. In his metafictional first chapter, the character named "Vonnegut" is railed against by the wife of one of his war buddies when he mentions that he is writing a novel about the war. She tells him, "You'll pretend you were men instead of babies, and you'll be portrayed in the movies by Frank Sinatra and John Wayne or some of those other glamorous, war-loving, dirty old men. And war will look just wonderful, so we'll have a lot more of them" (11). The Vonnegut character promises he will not do so, and adds that he will subtitle the book *The Children's Crusade* in honor of her insight. And so he does.

Playing off the role of Hollywood movies in glorifying warfare, and through what is clearly a wish fulfillment counterfactual close to his heart, Vonnegut uses the idea of a film played in reverse to undo the Dresden massacre:

> The formation flew backwards over a German city that was in flames. The bombers opened their bomb bay doors, exerted a miraculous magnetism which shrunk the fires, gathered them into cylindrical steel containers, and lifted the containers into the bellies of the planes. The containers were stored neatly in racks. The Germans below had miraculous devices of their own, which were long steel tubes. They used them to suck more fragments from the crewmen and planes. But there were still a few wounded Americans though and some of the bombers were in bad repair. Over France though, German fighters came up again, made everything and everybody as good as new.
>
> When the bombers got back to their base, the steel cylinders were taken from the racks and shipped back to the United States of America, where factories were operating night and day, dismantling the cylinders, separating

the dangerous contents into minerals. Touchingly, it was mainly women who did this work. The minerals were then shipped to specialists in remote areas. It was their business to put them into the ground, to hide them cleverly, so they would never hurt anybody ever again. (93–5)

Vonnegut turns this wish fulfillment into the basis for one of the strongest novelistic critiques of war ever penned. Some of Billy's fellow grunt soldiers, especially the character Lazarro, represent a kind of sadistic masculinity growing out of fear and a sense of powerlessness. And it is no coincidence that the novel was first published at the height of the Vietnam War when once again firebombing, this time using a horrific chemical called napalm, was wiping out soldiers, innocent civilians, and whole villages alike across Southeast Asia.

Another aspect of the novel's critique of war is a sense of perspective provided by a look at the long arc of human history. What that arc should provide is rendered even more trenchantly in another of his s/f novels, *The Sirens of Titan*. There a Tralfamadorian historian of Earth offers what may be the most humbling one-sentence reflection ever on our species: "Following the death of Jesus Christ, there was a period of readjustment that lasted for approximately one million years."[7] After the war, Billy Pilgrim becomes an optometrist, a humorous way of saying that he is offering the world a chance at a clearer vision. Between the imagined reversal of the Dresden bombing, and the perspective provided by this fictional alien race, Vonnegut seems to be saying, among other things, that looked at in the longer view of history the kinds of crusades that lead to war are petty, insane, and avoidable.

Neo-Hoodoo History: Ishmael Reed's *Mumbo Jumbo* (1972)

Few postmodern novels are as audaciously sweeping in their historical revisionism as Ishmael Reed's *Mumbo Jumbo* (1972).[8] The novel seeks nothing less than a rethinking of the entire history of the Western world, from its hidden foundations in North Africa to the second millennium. The novel brings together virtually all the various strands of metafictional historicizing. It is full of intertextual references, parodies, and partial rewrites of previous writers; it mixes real historical figures with invented characters; it uses repeated anachronism to remind viewers that history writing is always really about the present; it reflects on the question of whose history gets written and whose gets suppressed; it mixes the supposedly possible with the mystical to question the boundaries of factuality; and overall it offers a sweeping rewriting of the entire story of the Western, Judeo-Christian-Islamic religious and philosophical traditions allegedly traceable to ancient Greece.

As detailed by critic Henry Louis Gates, throughout *Mumbo Jumbo* Reed *signifies* upon his literary ancestors. Signifying is based in the African American vernacular practice, possibly derived from African trickster mythology, of wordplay aimed to show up another person's flaws or limitations.[9] Its most famous exemplar is the put down game called the dozens, a verbal trading of more and more clever insults, a game now largely folded into a certain strand of rap music. In the novel, Reed pays satirical homage to a number of key figures in the black literary tradition, including Richard Wright, Zora Neale Hurston, and Ralph Ellison. He parodies their styles, revealing the repeated tropes of realism and modernism each employed. He likewise mimics the rhetorical styles of a host of key black political figures including Marcus Garvey, Booker T. Washington, Alain Locke, W. E. B. DuBois, Elijah Muhammed, Malcolm X, and Martin Luther King.

Rich comic play with black literary and political history is one key strand of the novel, but like Jacques Derrida, Reed is after something much bigger, nothing less than the unraveling of Western metaphysics and the history of so-called Western civilization. Literary history is only one of several layers of historicizing (or "historifying," as Reed prefers to call it), going on in the novel. Composed during the late 1960s, the novel rewrites that decade as a subtext by juxtaposing all the key political currents of that time with similar ones in the 1920s, through character, event, idiom, and purposeful anachronism that open both eras to broader deconstructions of racialized history writing.

Paralleling the two decades does several kinds of work, including, most broadly, questioning recurring racialist paradigms and cultural amnesias. At one level, the comparison between the eras is about the similar ways in which the Jazz Age and the Rock'n'Roll Age both appropriate, or to put it less delicately, rip off black culture. The very name, the Jazz Age, given to the decade underscores this for the 1920s. But the 1960s were no less appropriative in Reed's eyes. The black-based genres of the blues and rhythm and blues were of course at the heart of the white rock and rollers who emerged to a new level of prominence and a new level of commercial viability in the 1960s, with little benefit accruing to African American artists.

The novel importantly begins before the copyright page, which comes some eight pages after the story has started. Here Reed is signifying on the ways in which copyright was abused in the 1920s with jazz and the 1960s with blues/rock to steal from African American originators. A similar gesture plays with the term in the novel's title, *Mumbo Jumbo*. The novel offers the following etymology for the phrase mumbo jumbo: Mandingo, "magician who makes the troubled spirits of ancestors go away: MaMa (grandmother) gyo (trouble) mbo (to leave)." The definition, in clear irony, is taken from *The American Heritage Dictionary* because readers will know that in US usage the term has come to mean nonsense. The fact that a Mandingo word has entered American English as a pejorative as opposed to a honorific, itself encapsulates the history Reed retells. Reed seeks to blow away much historical nonsense by chasing away a number of troubling ancestors.

At the start of the novel an epidemic called Jes Grew has broken out, starting in New Orleans and spreading rapidly across America. The epidemic causes people to lose inhibitions and start cavorting about in an agitated state. This agitated state, also known as dancing, is highly contagious, of likely "Negroid" origin, and unique among plagues in that it seems to "enliven the host" rather than enervating them.

> With the astonishing rapidity of Booker T. Washington's Grapevine Telegraph Jes Grew spreads through America following a strange course. Pine Bluff and Magnolia Arkansas are hit; Natchez, Meridian and Greenwood Mississippi report cases. Sporadic outbreaks occur in Nashville and Knoxville Tennessee as well as St. Louis where the bumping and grinding cause the Gov to call up the Guard. A mighty influence, Jes Grew infects all that it touches. (13)

Reed is here parodying the series of moral panics set off periodically in the United States by African American music; the novel mentions one outbreak in the 1890s (the era of ragtime), centers on the epidemic in the 1920s that "jes grew" out of early jazz and the blues, but also looks forward to the 1950s and 1960s when the moral panic set off by rock 'n' roll was also originally condemned as "Negro music," acceptable only in toned down cover versions sung by whites (cf. Elvis Presley's first hit, "Hound Dog" stolen from Big Mama Thornton). More recently, hip hop was declared to embody the end of civilization as we know it, especially once it started to be widely consumed by white youth.

The wild, genre bursting style of *Mumbo Jumbo* is a funky admixture of high art prose, a science fiction story, a fantasy tale, a detective story, a film script, a comic book, a manifesto, and a footnoted historical treatise (signifyin' on the footnotes to T. S. Eliot's poem "The Waste Land," first published during the Jazz Age). The deeply eclectic novel also throws in bits of song, erratic typography, photographs, necromancy, hagiography, Egyptology, voodoo theories of history, line drawings, halftone and woodcut illustrations derived from newspapers and magazines, a program from Harlem's Cotton Club, news photographs, snapshots and high art photographs, undigested newspaper clippings, gnomic symbols, and a host of other defamiliarizing or anti-illustrative devices.

These can, of course, be seen as typical elements of postmodernist literary form but they also use a diversity of media forms, genres, and subgenres to represent how cultural forms "jes grew" beyond any attempt to contain them. For Reed they are also clearly imitating jazz, particularly the wildly open form of 1950s bebop and 1960s free jazz associated with Ornette Coleman, Pharoah Sanders, Sun Ra, and others. Like free jazz that pushes maximum dissonance and polyphony, often produced without steady pitch, rhythm, or development, and so overabundant in thematic meaning as to approach chaos, *Mumbo Jumbo* is a gumbo full to the brim with ingredients. Jazz has long had radically deconstructive elements, but free jazz is arguably full on deconstruction avant la lettre.

The novel is built around the notion of several thousand-year struggle between the followers of Aton, and the practitioners of a force embodied in the Jes Grew epidemic. The bad guys in Reed's world are referred to as Atonists, that is followers of the Egyptian god Aton, the figure who for Reed signifies the birth of monotheism, long before the rise of the Jewish, Christian, and Islamic versions. From the point of view of the novel's central character, the hougan, or conjure man, PaPa LaBas (a play on the Haitian voodoo god, Legba), Atonism is the mistake of believing there is only one, rather than many gods. For PaPa LaBas, his ever growing, improvised neo-hoodoo pantheon of gods and spirits is a far more satisfying set of entry points into the sacred. The spirit of Jes Grew, of openness, improvisation, the Dionysian is set against Apollonian Atonism at all levels of society.

Among those countering the Atonists, are the Mutafika, a term allegedly from ancient Palestine that sounds suspiciously like the ultimate signifying term of derision in African American culture, the one imputing, shall we say, intergenerational intercourse of a more than discursive nature. The task of the Mutafika is to reclaim artefacts from ancient Egypt and Africa that have been stolen and are being held in what the novel calls Centers of Art

Detention—better known as museums. This is, in effect, the goal of the novel: to reclaim the history of the West as one deeply entwined with traditions arising from ancient Egypt and Africa, to free African and African American sources of creative vision from their captivity.

Resisting the modernist call for "fully rounded characters," Reed creates caricatures or cartoon figures. In this light, it is no accident that Reed dedicated *Mumbo Jumbo* to George Herriman, African American creator of the cartoon Krazy Kat. Krazy Kat had a modest following in the 1920s when the novel is set, but Herriman's greatest influence came with the rise in the 1960s of underground comic artists like R. Crumb, Art Spiegelman, and Richard "Grass" Greene, all of whom cite Herriman as an inspiration. Throughout, Reed mixes real historical figures with wholly invented characters, some of whom are meant to evoke other historical figures, others of which are wholesale inventions.

The intentionally ragged plotline jitterbugs around the attempt of PaPa LaBas to find the sacred text of the voodoo tradition. But when LaBas finally finds the chest putatively containing the text, it is empty. And of course this is a joke on the reader in two ways. First, he or she should have realized by now that an improvisational, living spiritual form can have no definitive text, and, second, the reader has such a text right in their hands, a mumbo jumbo literary gumbo that at once honors and chases away the troublesome ghosts of the ancestors. With the advantage of the perfect knowledge of a future that has already happened, PaPa LaBas says, "We were dumped here on our own without the Book to tell us who the loas are, what we call spirits were. We made up our own. I'll bet later on in the 50s, 60s, and 70s we will have some artists and creators who will teach Africa and South America some new twists" (130).

For Reed the celebration of radical pluralism is not a celebration of some kind of pure indeterminacy, if such could exist. His text is much too politically savvy and politically pointed for that. Radical pluralism, as opposed to the dominant liberal version, always remains rooted in an analysis of positionality, an analysis of uneven, situated power relations. Only the deconstructing of monocultural hegemony, the novel suggests, can make room for meaningful multiculturalism. But Reed's neo-hoodoo aesthetic, as he dubs it, does not need to wait for the revolution before the celebration can begin. Like Emma Goldman's apocryphal remark that she would only accept a revolution she could dance to, Reed wants no part in a revolution if you can't be dancing and playing jazz and writing jazzy novels full of play with dominant forms of historical writing that try to disguise a history of domination. As one critic notes, "In *Mumbo Jumbo* the zombie categories of modern history become literal in their persistence and recursion: Reed's novel at once figures the repressive work of zombification itself—the instrumental reason of slavery, colonialism, monotheism, and capitalism—as well as its spiritual countermeasures in jazz, experimental black writing, and Haitian Voudon."[10]

But for all Reed's celebration of multiplicity, there is one area where he is clearly mono-visioned, the realm of gender relations. *Mumbo Jumbo* is a relentlessly male-centered text. There are no significant female characters, historical or fictional, who make much impact on the story. The wisest correction to the blatant omission of female power in *Mumbo Jumbo* comes a few years later in the form of a novel by Toni Cade Bambara, *The Salt Eaters* (see Chapter 3), which puts women in their rightful place at the heart of black culture, black folk spirituality, black political struggle, and black literary production. Reed's story is radically incomplete without the ways in which Bambara and other black feminist authors like Toni Morrison, Gail Jones, Gloria Naylor, and Audre Lorde "signify" upon his limitations, but together they make a marvelous case for a spiritually informed radical politics at once close fisted, open-hearted and open-minded—a politics at once informed by an aesthetic disruption of dominant ideologies and grounded in concrete political realities of the current era.

Challenging Dead-eye Dog: Leslie Silko's *Almanac of the Dead* (1999)

In addition to postmodern critiques of *gran recits*, the big (hi)stories like Progress, there has also been a set of challenges to Western ideas about history from Indigenous communities around the world. Those challenges stem both from traditional knowledges and knowledge of what 500 years of colonization by the Global North have done to Native peoples. With equal ambition but a style quite different from *Mumbo Jumbo*, Leslie Marmon Silko's *Almanac of the Dead* (1999) presents a massive tapestry covering 500 years of history, several continents, more than 50 characters, and an extraordinary interweaving of themes, ideas, cultures, ideologies, and discourses. It demonstrates in rich detail the historical interconnections among commerce, culture, law, landscapes, politics, and aesthetics as they culminate in the crises of postmodernity.

The postmodernist nature of *Almanac* lies less in its style, which is deceptively realist in tone, but more in its challenge to the very idea of modern history and the novel as a record of conquest. The novel is also postmodern in being very much a story about stories and storytelling, one that highlights the ancient Native belief in the power of stories to make the world. It at once aligns those beliefs with the contemporary critical insight that all dimensions of social, cultural, and economic life rely upon narratives to do their ideological work, and challenges the superficial use of those ideas.[11] The historical scope and sweep of Silko's text is of crucial importance in establishing the foundation for her decolonizing intention. While deeply rooted in the present era, the text works not in terms of years or decades, but centuries. It presents a profoundly historical analysis, one in which history is not a backdrop but precisely what is contested.

The narrative simultaneously retells history from the point of view of those marginalized in dominant versions and challenges Western notions of linear history by evoking recurring cycles. *Almanac* makes the case that only by telling history properly, only by honoring the ancestors by telling past events from their perspective, can one think and act rationally in the contemporary world. Truthful storytelling handed down through oral tradition is an antidote to the deeply sick, sadistic contemporary world portrayed in the novel. From the title onward, *Almanac of the Dead* vividly counterposes the deadly repetitions of death-infused trauma in the form of colonialism, war, and personal and economic violence, with tribal prophecy, counter-memory, and ceremony as a way of structuring the past to make it useful while keeping faith with the wisdom of ancestors.

There is no more dominant theme in the novel than the need to return all Indigenous lands. Variations on this phrase appear over and over in the novel, beginning even before the text proper in the form of words inscribed on the map that serves as prologue: "Sixty million Native Americans died between 1500 and 1600. The defiance and resistance to things European continue unabated. The Indian wars have never ended in the Americas. Native Americans recognize no borders; they seek nothing less than the return of all tribal lands" (14–15). But while this theme is starkly clear from the beginning, each reiteration in the text adds new complexity. The notion of "returning" or "restoring" all Native lands includes at least three levels. First, returning "home" lands to particular tribes; second, restoring a sense of sacredness to the land and/or communal ownership, rooted in Indigenous traditions; and third, most expansively, restoring a sustainable Earth in the wake of devastating colonization via resource extraction, severance of people from place, and racialized capitalist industrialization. This third and most comprehensive definition exists as a synthesis of, and the ultimate trajectory for, the other two meanings. *Almanac* makes clear that only a thoroughgoing economic decolonization process can undo the devastating social and environmental impact of the European imprint on the Americas (and the rest of the planet), and reverse the impact of climate change. *Almanac* ties these threads together in a critique of toxicity, militarism, patriarchy, and economic exploitation.

From the beginning of the European colonial era to the present, dominant cultures have argued that the lands of Indigenous peoples are underdeveloped and empty (*terra nullius* as it was known in Australia) and that the people living on them are less than human, less than "civilized." The counterclaims of Indigenous peoples have been growing more insistent for decades and are at work in the twenty-first century through movements like Idle No More and the massive protest against the environmentally dangerous Dakota Access oil pipeline that was rerouted onto Native lands, led by Standing Rock Sioux, Ponca, Santee, Omaha, and Winnebago peoples.[12] The wasting of peoples and lands has, as Silko's map shows, gone on unabated but was always resisted, from the expropriation of Native lands by guns and disease in the sixteenth century to the toxic colonialism of the twenty-first century imposed on, for example, the Shoshone people, whose resistance to the dumping of nuclear waste on their non-waste lands Valerie Kuletz has richly documented.[13] As Kuletz and other environmental justice scholars have meticulously demonstrated, the supposed "natural" wastelands are actually lands laid waste by militarism and capitalism, places that seem inevitably to coincide with the boundaries of Indian reservations (and the ghettos and barrios and poor white neighborhoods outside the protected circle of wealthy whiteness). As Indigenous activist and former vice-presidential candidate Winona LaDuke trenchantly asks, "What happened when the best scientific minds and policy analysts in the world spent 20 years examining every possible way to deal with problem of nuclear waste? They decided the solution was to ship the radioactive stuff thousands of miles from all over the country and dump it on an Indian reservation" (LaDuke is referring to Yucca Mountain, Nevada, a sacred site of the Shoshone people, chosen as the main nuclear waste site of the military-industrial-scientific-governmental colonizers).[14]

This story of land and waste is embodied in the novel in the juxtaposition of a "giant sacred stone snake" (whose reappearance is among the signs of a coming postcolonial era) with the open-pit uranium mine on Laguna land.

In one of the novel's many self-consciously ironic moves, the sacred object, lost for many generations, is uncovered because of digging around the mine. At the beginning of the novel, the Laguna character Sterling is banished by his Tribal Council for unintentionally facilitating the desecration of the stone snake by a Hollywood film crew. The act is associated with a theft of two sacred stone figures that occurred eighty years earlier; this theft functions as a stand-in for several generations of anthropological expropriation of Native "artifacts" and the ongoing struggle to repatriate thousands of stolen pieces of Indigenous cultures. Sterling's story frames the novel. His banishment leads him back into the nontribal world where his role as a gardener suggests a diminished land stewardship.

Sterling's reappearance at the end of the novel offers a simple, unheroic witness to a revolution that seems to bring the story full circle, but with a difference. Silko is well aware of various ironic meanings of revolution as a full turn of a wheel that can bring not justice but just another form of oppression. *Almanac* reveals that the associations of the poor white, nonwhite, and the Native with waste must not simply be reversed symbolically and materially by changing oppressors for oppressed; they must instead be resisted through new, yet very old, narratives in which land and peoples are intimately connected. To do this, the white noise of the dominant culture must be tuned out, and different voices tuned in. To hear these voices, however, Indigenous people and others must struggle to block out the domination resounding in their heads, and must fight terrible forces unleashed in the colonial era Natives in the text call the reign of "Death-eye Dog." *Almanac* puts forth a spiritual-social-psychological theory of human evil that is at once thoroughly Indigenous and resonant with Freud's notion of the "death instinct." While the text is concerned with the Death-eye Dog/death instinct of the era of European colonization, neither evil nor resistance to it is reductively racialized. Indeed, how could it be, since "race" itself is a concept invented by Europeans largely as a rationale for colonization?[15] While the novel depicts aspects of the white-dominated world as deeply disturbed and depraved, Anglo allies form part of the resistance forces. Key among these is the white woman Seese—she "sees" the ancient vision and "ceases" to be part of colonialism—who enters the ancient "data" from the almanac onto computer disks.

By the same logic, Native cultures are not spared implication in this mode of evil. As the Native character Yeome notes, "Montezuma and Cortés had been meant for each other" (570). Nevertheless, while the Destroyers arise cyclically in all cultures, this bloody mode of existence has been brought to icy perfection and death-delivering efficiency by capitalist modernity. Death-eye Dog has gone global in the modern capacity to utterly destroy the environment and humanity with it. The prophetic hope in *Almanac of the Dead* is that the outcasts of the world will soon bring to an end the current, 500-year reign of Death-eye Dog: the era of colonialism.

There is nothing remotely sentimental in *Almanac*'s vision of Indigenous people leading a multiethnic alliance to resist and reverse this ecological, economic, and social devastation. These are not Indians as ultimate ecologists, or New Age Natives closer to "Nature" by virtue of their uncorrupted "spirits." Healthy communities can constrain, if not wholly contain, evil. But healthy communities are few and far between in the postmodern world, even in its Native portions. The colonized in the novel as well as the colonizers (and those who are both) are subject to the distortions bred of oppression. For every visionary revolutionary like the Native characters El Feo and Angelita, there are ordinary, culturally confused characters such as Sterling (with his fascination with gangsters like John Dillinger) and utterly corrupted "Indians" as well. The drug trade, in which many of the novel's Native characters are involved, is both literal cross-border trafficking and a metaphor for the deeply addictive economic form that is capitalism. The Yaqui character Calabazas, for example, has ancient practical knowledge of the earth and its healing herbs, but is also deeply entangled with drug dealing and arms trading. He is far from innocent. His story alludes to another key element of global environmental justice cultural criticism, a critique of corporate colonization in the form of the "bio-pirating" of everything from Native "pharmacology" (herbal medicines) to the warehousing of Native DNA.[16] Like the imperfectly preserved, arcane almanac that gives the novel its title, in all these characters much has been lost and nothing in their cultures was ever pure. Resistance to colonization is never pretty or easy.

In this novel/almanac, which Silko claims was in part dictated to her by "the ancestors," networks of resistance to neocolonial capitalism are symbolized by the intersecting forces of the Army of the Homeless, a rag-tag group of lucidly crazy Vietnam vets of various races fighting gentrification of their Tucson neighborhood, and the Army of Justice and Redistribution, an Indigenous-led band of insurrectionists emerging from the Chiapas region of Mexico (several years before the "real-life" Zapatista Native resistance force came into existence, partly in response to *Almanac*).[17] These forces of resistance must struggle with their own imposed demons even as they challenge the deeply disturbing, dehumanizing forces arising from racist capitalism's increasing objectification, commoditization, and degradation of people and environments. The logic of economic objectification (and the text's strategy of countering it) is apparent even before the novel officially begins, in the map that precedes the first chapter. Mapping was one of the key objectifying strategies that enabled colonialist expropriation, and thus might seem a strange place for the text to begin. But this map is quite subversive. While it shows that imaginary line called a border, it labels only Mexico. The map is hardly to scale, and it is covered with names of characters and pithy encapsulations of prophecies that foretell "the disappearance of all things European" from the Americas and a revolutionary "return of all tribal lands."

The embeddedness of European and US cultures in the logic of Death-eye Dog is apparent in everything from sexual to aesthetic to political practices—all are reduced to the economic nexus. The death logic of objectification and commoditization infects even the realm reserved in the West for beauty, as seen in the aesthetic praise and monetary value heaped upon the "Eric Series," a group of photographs made by an "artist" of his former lover's remains as splattered about by a suicidal gun blast. This is clearly a slap at the aestheticization of violence in contemporary mass culture from torture porn films to first-person shooter video games.

Almanac uses the actually existing lucrative transnational market in human organs harvested from the poor (including babies) to save the lives of the rich, as an all-too-real marker of the ultimate commodification and exploitation of the human body.[18] What the West calls "Nature" is equally commodified, reduced to an economic resource and denied the wild creative agency with which the other-than-human world is credited in most Indigenous cultures (as seen, for example, in Coyote stories). While the novel offers no easy way out of this situation, it is clear that the reduction of all things to their economic value in the marketplace must be replaced by a process in which human and environmental needs are at the center.

In the novel, sexual fetishism (first theorized by Freud) and the fetishism of commodities (first theorized by Marx) are set against the spiritual uses of the fetish in Indigenous traditions as the creative animation of what the West considers inanimate, a process in which natureculture is not divided (natureculture is Donna Haraway's term to signify that nature and culture must always be conceived as interwoven). Critics who bemoaned the fact that *Almanac* is not rooted in Native rituals, like Silko's earlier novel *Ceremony*, miss the fact that *Almanac* too is a ceremonial enactment. But its ceremonies are embedded in a much more complex social matrix. The almanac of the title is the lost, scattered ancient almanac the characters in the narrative seek to restore. And it is also the novel itself. Silko's *Almanac* enacts a kind of historical shamanistic exorcism that requires that the evil spirits be fully evoked and dramatized before we can collectively banish them

The novel may be rooted in the past and profoundly critical of the devastation wrought by modern industrial civilization, but it is not afraid of the new and is more than willing to turn the West's high technology against itself, as in Seese's transferring of the almanac onto disks and in the Asian character Aw Gee, who, like the "hacktivists" of the global justice movement, turns those computing machines, born of militarism and corporate exploitation, toward the revolution. The novel's evocation of the coming revolution offers no blueprints or predictions as to how events will unfold. According to Silko, the revolutionary forces will be a rainbow:

> Nothing could be black only or brown only or white only anymore. The ancient prophecies had foretold a time when the destruction by man had left the earth desolate, and the human race was itself endangered. This was the last chance the people had against the Destroyers, and they would never prevail if they did not work together as a common force. (747)

The text ends without showing us any of these events or heroic actions. Instead we return to the quiet character Sterling, back on his beloved Laguna Pueblo, where he discovers "why the giant snake had returned now; he knew what the snake's message was to the people. The snake was looking south, in the direction from which the twin brothers and the people would come" (763). Silko suggests the forces will arise from what used to be called the Third World and now the Global South, but also from the Fourth World of Indigenous peoples all across the planet, and from those in the First and Second Worlds, who recognize radical changes must occur, not only to provide long overdue justice for oppressed people but also for human and ecological survival.

7

Re-Visions

Novels Rewriting Novels

If historical writing inevitably includes an element of fictiveness, as discussed in the previous chapter, it is equally the case that fiction always contains elements of history. That is one key reason that a number of postmodern novelists have rewritten earlier novels or parts of those novels, incorporating story lines that are in effect revisionist histories based on a rethinking of the historical context of the original novels. These novels go beyond mere *intertextual* references to previous literary works, and instead offer sustained reconceptualizations of their predecessors. They emphasize that all novels are time-bound, history-bound, even if they also contain certain "timeless truths." Each generation of readers interpret even the oldest, most classic texts in new ways stemming from new social realities. Postmodern realists have used this insight as the basis for writing works that speak directly to earlier novels.

Revisionary texts also embody this insight through new novels that reflect upon older works by including angles of vision left out of or marginalized in previous works. This can take many forms: works that pretend to be prequels or sequels; classic works that imitate the style of those earlier works; works written from the perspective of a figure in the classic work who is marginalized, often by their class, gender, or race; or works set indirectly in the same context but clearly in dialogue with a previous novel. The latter, for example, would include *Things Fall Apart* (1972), by African novelist Chinua Achebe. Achebe takes on the history of European imperialism, but via an oblique response to one of the most celebrated novels of the modernist era, Joseph Conrad's *Heart of Darkness* (1899). Conrad's book is, not incorrectly, read as a critique of the racist enterprise of colonization of Africa. But Achebe's novel makes clear that Conrad, by leaving African characters out of his work except as extras to be manipulated by Europeans, reinforced notions of helplessness and backwardness, and failed to embody their subjective humanity. Achebe's novel locates itself intimately in the daily life of an African village in the time and place of Conrad's novella in order to show the rich, complex lives Conrad could not imagine.

These types of novels might be called revisionary in the dual sense that they act as historical revisionism and they are visionary glimpses into the future of the past. History includes the history of literature, and postmodern fiction, even more than most other bodies of fiction, often reflects intensely on the past life of literary forms. The genre includes a number of light, playful works with titles like *Pride and Prejudice and Zombies*, *Android Karenina*, and *Sense and Sensibility and Sea Monsters*, as well as works whose playfulness goes a bit more seriously into revising texts based upon new historical perspectives. This often entails varying degrees of *intertextuality*, references to, and sometimes overt thefts from, other novels, extending from Borges's word-for-word recreation of the original *Don Quixote* to Kathy Acker's pla(y)giaristic mash-up *Don Quixote* (see Chapter 3) to Salman Rushdie's metafictional *Quichotte* (2019) reflecting on our post-truth historical moment. These novels require us to re-imagine novels from the past in light of subsequent historical events that change their meaning.

Other revisionary fictions take the form of rewriting parts of an earlier novel from the point of view of a character who was marginal to the original story. This can be a subtle, slowing dawning revelation as in *Wide Sargasso Sea* or obvious from a title like *Ahab's Wife*, or slightly less obvious in a work like *Foe* (1986), in which J. M. Coetzee rewrites Daniel Defoe's eighteenth-century novel, *Robison Crusoe* by turning Defoe into the character Foe in recognition of the original novel's misogynistic and racist elements.

I will concentrate on literary rewrites, but other art forms have also undergone revisionary exploration. Angela Davis-Gardner's *Butterfly's Child* (2011), for example, is a kind of literary sequel to the Puccini opera "Madame Butterfly," one that mixes fictional characters with real historical figures and includes a metafictional moment when the central character attends a showing of Puccini's opera in Tokyo. Like the revisionary play "M Butterfly," the novel brings to the foreground issues of race and gender hidden in the background of the original opera. Similarly, one of my examples in this chapter, Jessica Hagedorn's *Dream Jungle*, revises both literary (*Heart of Darkness*) and cinematic (*Apocalypse Now!*) history.

Most of these revisionary works have in common a critique of certain privileged storytelling perspectives, and an attempt thereby to broaden historical vision. You can see things from the edge of the frame in an older novel not visible from the central narrative. And sometimes, as Toni Morrison argues, a revisionary reversal can occur: "I stood at the border, stood at the edge and claimed it as central. Claimed it as central, and let the rest of the world move over to where I was."[1] In the 1960s, just as postmodern fiction was coming into its own, a movement among historians, referred to as "history from the bottom up," sought to get further away from the "great man" theory of history and from history as told by the victors—those whose version of reality won out, at least in political terms. The works of fiction I highlight in this section likewise seek to illuminate angles of vision from outside the frame of what have become canonical stories of the past. For example, *Lavinia*, by Ursula K. LeGuin (2008), whose narrator marries Aeneas after he leaves Dido, tells the true history of the founding of Rome, disputing one of the earliest historians, Virgil. While this is serious work, it can also be done with more than a hint of absurd fun as when Julian Barnes critiques biblical history by having a woodworm on Noah's Ark narrate parts of his novel *The World in 10 and 1/2 Chapters* (1989).

Barnes's novel not only challenges the Bible but also makes fun of textbooks that claim to tell the entire history of the world in a handful of chapters. In this, he is in the company of other revisionaries who challenge whole subgenres of the novel and other writing forms too. This includes genres like the noir detective story in Robert Coover's satirical, *Noir* (1995), or Angela Carter's rewriting of the fairy tale form in *The Bloody Chamber* (1971), or, in a lighter but still quite serious vein, James Lever's send-up of the gossipy celebrity autobiography in *Me Cheeta* (2008), narrated by the chimpanzee who starred in a series of *Tarzan* films.

Virtually every era and style in literary history has been the subject of one or more revisionary novels. No earlier story is too sacred to be rewritten, and the revisionary impulse can even be applied, as it is by A. S. Byatt, to other postmodern novels. Several of the novels treated in other chapters of this book might also have been included here, including, for example, Daisy Johnson's retelling of the myth of Oedipus in *Everything Under* (2018), discussed in Chapter 4. Many have rewritten the story of "Hamlet" but none in a more outrageously postmodern way than Ian McEwan, whose novel *Nutshell* (2016) turns Shakespeare's most famous play into a satirical thriller narrated by a snarky fetus inside Gertrude's womb. In utero, this proto-Hamlet eloquently decries the climate crisis, the rise of fake news, the excesses of certain de-politicized identity politics, and the rise of right-wing nationalisms.

Decolonizing the Literary Past: Jean Rhys's *Wide Sargasso Sea* (1966)

Perhaps no literary genre or era has received as much attention from radical revisers as the nineteenth century. Not only the many zombies added to Jane Austen's oeuvre, but a host of other Romantic and Victorian era novels have proven to be especially attractive cannon fodder for postmodernists.

Gothic fiction of the romantic era has been a particularly rich terrain for revisionary writers. There is, for example, a large body of work spinning revisions on Mary Shelley's novel *Frankenstein* (1818). In 2018, on the 200th anniversary of the novel's publication, for example, Twitter was alive with a "Frankenreads" thread. In addition to Shelley Jackson's hypertext *Patchwork Girl* (see Chapter 4), the Frankenstein story has been reimagined recently by Jeanette Winterson's novel, *Frankissstein* (2019) (see Chapter 10).

Undoubtedly the text that set in motion the reimagining of the Gothic novel is Jean Rhys's short novel, *Wide Sargasso Sea* (1966).[2] It focused not on *Frankenstein*, but upon a different, equally famous novel from that era, one that in the interest of avoiding spoilers I shall leave unnamed. Rhys's novel is set in the then British colony of Jamaica soon after the British government officially ended slavery in 1834. At the center of the novel is Antoinette Cosway, a woman who carries in her very body the dichotomy between master and slave, England and its empire. She is Creole, which in this historical context means not a person of mixed race but rather a white person long in residence in the Caribbean. As a white person of French descent who has lived in close proximity to blacks, her identity is tainted in the eyes of white British newcomers. Her family's long association with black slaves is enough to undercut her whiteness, though some characters in the novel suggest there may be miscegenation in her lineage.

As a Creole, Antoinette finds herself despised by both sides of a black/white racial divide. The novel was ahead of its time in representing race as a cultural and class construct, not a biological given. As a child a black playmate succinctly tells the truth of her condition: "Plenty white people in Jamaica. Real white people, they got gold money. They didn't look at us, nobody see them come near us. Old time white people nothing but white nigger now, and black nigger better than white nigger" (24–5). The abolition of slavery brought a crash in Antoinette's family fortunes, and as she sinks deeper into abject poverty her only path out comes in the form of a young English gentleman too new to the land to fully understand its caste system.

That gentlemen eventually absorbs the prejudices of his class, and Antoinette comes to realize too late that he views her more as a beautiful possession than a sentient being. He plays upon her fragile sense of self until she see herself through his eyes and begins to doubt not just her identity but her sanity. In an act of patriarchal power, he renames her Bertha, a gesture that enrages her: "Bertha is not my name. You are trying to make me into something else, calling me by another name. I know, that's obeah too" (148). Obeah refers to syncretic religion of the Caribbean that is known colloquially (and problematically) as voodoo. Antoinette is throwing back at her English husband the claim that black magic is being used by her beloved black nanny, Christophine, the moral center of the novel. And she is right. At another point her husband calls her Marionette Antoinette—he is turning her into a doll (155). The sense of self she clings to amid tragic circumstances in the first third of the novel that she narrates—the burning down of their home, the death of her brother, the madness of her mother—appear increasingly weakened in the second part told mostly by her husband.

The novel stands alone as a beautifully lyrical, exquisitely crafted tragic tale. But it is also cleverly structured in that only in the last dozen pages of the novel is the reader likely to realize that it is also a prequel, the backstory to one of the most revered novels in nineteenth-century British literature. In this part of the novel, the abusive husband, having driven Antoinette near madness, returns to England where he locks her in the attic of his stately home. *Wide Sargasso Sea* climaxes when Antoinette/Bertha escapes from the attic and sets the mansion afire. What was unexplained madness in the nineteenth century original is rewritten as an act of vengeance against patriarchy and colonial domination, mimicking the burning down of her former plantation home by its slaves. Like the id beneath the tame ego, another story erupts beneath the domestic tale of the earlier British novel. The personal in the original version turns out to be political as *Wide Sargasso Sea* explores the subtextual colonial darkness inside the dark literary genre known as Gothic romance. It is a move that can be read as spreading its message of repressed racial and gender history across the whole expanse of British literature in the era of its empire, and it helped unleash a host of postcolonial novels.[3]

Globalizing the Past: Bharati Mukherjee's *The Holder of the World* (1993)

Postcolonial literatures of various kinds are a major part of the wider postmodern fictional world, and some of these novels are written in revisionary form. Bharati Mukherjee, for example, a self-described "American writer of Bengali-India descent," approaches postcolonial issues in a couple of different ways in her retelling of a story from one of the most famous texts of American literature. Mukherjee once wrote that once she settled in as a fiction writer in her adopted land, her literary credo became: make "the familiar exotic (Americans won't recognize their country when I get finished with it) and make the exotic—the India of elephants and arranged marriages—familiar."[4] She accomplished the latter in novels like *Jasmine* (1989) that show the deeply "American" values held by many Indian immigrants to the United States. And her efforts to do the former, to "make the familiar exotic," included revisioning one of the founding novels of American literature, Nathaniel Hawthorne's *The Scarlet Letter* (1850).

Mukherjee's literary revisionary text, *The Holder of the World* (1993), is a kind of time-travel novel set in three locations in time/space: twentieth-century Boston, seventeenth-century Mughal India, and colonial era Salem, Massachusetts, the historical time frame of Hawthorne's novel.[5] The meta-narrative frame involves a twentieth-century woman tracking down the mysterious appearance of a gem from the Mughal empire that has turned up in a small New England museum. In this it mimics the nineteenth-century *Scarlet Letter*'s time travel back to the seventeenth century. Mukherjee adds a further element as well such that her novel is structured via the parallels between three women, each of whom engages in a cross-cultural love affair: a contemporary woman, and two from the colonial era, one a Puritan woman who marries a Nipmuc native, the other, her daughter, who becomes the "Salem Bibi," lover of a Mughal royal.

The contemporary narrator, Beigh Masters, is a woman with a New England ancestry dating back to the colonial era. She is an "assets hunter," a kind of detective whose job it is to find valuable objects for wealthy collectors. But as the novel develops, it is clear that Beigh is actually interested in a more traditional kind of detective work, tracking down a person. She is helped in her dual project of tracking down a famous gem and the seventeenth woman who owned it by her lover, Venn Iyer, an MIT computer programmer of Asian Indian background. His work, "out there, beyond virtual reality, re-creating the universe," sets the frame for the novel. He is in effect trying to use "big data" to create an interactive virtual reality time-travel machine (3). He admits that even by inputting massive amounts of information about a single day of an historical era, he will only create a simplified replica. That prompts Beigh to offer the following: "Every time-traveler will create a different reality—just as we all do now. No two travelers will be able to retrieve the same reality, or even a fraction of the available realities. History's a big savings bank [that allows] infinite reality withdrawals" (6). This is, in effect, what Mukherjee is doing with Hawthorne, making a different reality withdrawal from the same (imagined) database in seventeenth-century America. Beigh also points out that Venn's time traveler will have to answer a thousand-point questionnaire to create a "personality genome" in preparation for their visit to the past. This is, in good postmodern fashion, both a critique of naively objective historiography and an implicit acknowledgement that what any reader takes from the "database" of Mukherjee's novel will depend greatly on who they are and what they bring to the reading process.

Due to "genre-ism" (Kurt Vonnegut's term for the literary equivalent of racism or sexism as applied to popular genres by literary elitists[6]), *The Holder of the World* is not characterized as science fiction. But that surely is one of the genres into which it fits. The premise that by loading enough data bits about a given time period into a computer program, plausible time travel is possible is nothing if not s/f, and like most s/f, it is more about the present than the future. The novel begins with a speculation on the impact of information overload in the digital era. The narrator remarks that her life in postmodern America "has gotten just a little more complicated than my ability to describe it. That used to be the definition of madness, now it's just discontinuous overload" (7).

Mukherjee invents a character, Hannah Easton, who might plausibly have been a part of the colonial New England world invented by Hawthorne, but with a twist that she is quite literally a woman of the world, one whose insights point to the limits of an American point of view on the wider world. Puritan New England was a drab, provincial place compared to the richness and dazzling beauty of seventeenth-century Mughal India. Beigh, on a visit to a New England maritime museum, notes "in adjoining cases cups of translucent jade fitted with handles of silver and gold; bowls studded with garnets and sapphires, pearls and emeralds; jewel-encrusted thumb rings; jewel-studded headbands for harem women; armlets and anklets, necklaces and bangles for self-indulgent Mughal men; scimitars rust dappled with ancient blood" (8). The novel plays with the mutual misunderstandings and prejudices of these two cultures worlds apart, and undercuts the American hubris that justifies its current empire. The narrator imagines a Cub Scout or Brownie leader looking at this case full of Mughal extravagance and telling the children, "We beat those Asians because our pots are heavy and black and our pothooks contain no jewels" (12). The "gaudiness of Allah" lost out to the plain "porridge of Jehovah" (9).

The intricate play of history and fiction takes on its final twist when the novel "reveals" that the story of Hannah and her daughter, Pearl, was the inspiration for Hawthorne's novel. Mukherjee plays with the adultery-signifying scarlet "A" of Hawthorne's novel, imagining in its stead an "I" for Indian-lover or India-lover that could equally adorn Hannah or her mother. She extends her intertextual literary play by fantasizing that Hannah, "encoder of a secret history" (60), should have been called "V" like the mysterious, nameless title character of Thomas Pynchon's breakthrough postmodern novel, V (1963). Mukherjee references the fact that Pynchon's family is one that traces its lineage back to Puritan New England and makes one of the novelist's ancestors one of Hannah's unsuccessful suitors. Mukherjee is suggesting that complicated literary continuities and discontinuities across wide swaths of history link Hawthorne and Pynchon as quintessentially American yet also worldly, and underscores that leaving Asia out of American history, or American literature, distorts the past, and impoverishes the present. As it turns out, the real time-travel machine at play in The Holder of the World is one that is centuries old, the literary imagination in novel form steeped in historical research.

The parallels between old and new eras of globalization are clearly intended as a swipe at the arrogant belief that the West has always been the seat of advanced civilization: "while the Taj Mahal was slowly rising in a cleared forest on the banks of the Yamuna, . . . [a young Puritan] was erecting a split-log cabin adjacent to a hog pen" (11). But no culture escapes unscathed, and none is a very hospitable place even for an extraordinarily bold and gifted woman like Hannah. The novel's take on Europeans in India is typically both harsh and sympathetic to their plight.

> What we're seeing is progressive derangement. God-fearing, land-starved, profit-seeking Welsh and English and Scottish and Irish second sons, jilted by primogeniture, sexually repressed, passion denying, furtively engaging the favours of native women, girls, and boys, all unfolding in the midst of septic heat, rain, disease, squalor, and savage beasts, while being waited on, cooked for, fanned, massaged by servants a thousand times more loyal, submissive, and poorly paid than any in the world, in the middle of the biggest real estate boom, jewel auction and drug emporium of the past five hundred years. No wonder they went a little crazy. (106–7)

In this and numerous other ways, both literary history and historiography are rewritten in the novel. Mukherjee subtly critiques the recent focus on the alleged newness of *globalization*, both by showing that the world has been globalized for centuries, and by suggesting that the current version of globalization is fatally limited because it looks at the world almost solely through the eyes of the West, rather than from multiple positions around the globe. Hannah's husband, Gabriel Legge, goes from being an employee of the seventeenth-century British East India company to becoming a pirate, a transition that seems logical and underscores that mercantile capitalism was just piracy by another name. And to complete the parallel, the narrator compares Legge's type to contemporary "buccaneers," "the arbitraguers, leveragers, junk bonders" of Wall Street today (102). Neoliberal capitalist globalization arrogantly fails to recognize that the current empire, like all those of the past, will also fade into history.

Sacred Revisions: Salman Rushdie's *The Satanic Verses* (1988)

Certainly the most controversial entry into the revisionary realm is Salman Rushdie's *The Satanic Verses* (1988).[7] Among many other themes, it offers a comic magical realist take on the sacred texts of Islamic religious history. It has the dubious distinction of being the only revisionary novel that required its author to go into hiding under threat of death. In a backhanded compliment to the power of fiction, *Satanic Verses* elicited not only protests but book burnings, riots, and finally a *fatwa* by Iran's Ayatollah Ruhollah Khomeini, who called for the death of Rushdie and his publishers. While the author escaped this fate, his Japanese translator was stabbed to death, and assassination attempts were made on the lives of his Italian and Norwegian translators.

The irony of this tragic reception is that this largely comic novel was as critical of the West as of the Islamic East. The novel strongly critiques the long history of British imperial rule in India and the Middle East, and offers a rich portrait of the trials faced by immigrants to the UK. *The Satanic Verses* addresses a host of issues around bicultural identity, the confusion and alienation faced by all migrants, and the sense of disillusionment many feel toward both their culture of origin *and* their adopted homeland. (Since Rushdie himself is an immigrant to the UK, the novel has elements of surreal allegorical autobiography.) As Rushdie himself phrases it, "If *The Satanic Verses* is anything, it is a migrant's-eye view of the world. It is written from the very experience of uprooting, disjuncture and metamorphosis (slow or rapid, painful or pleasurable) that is the migrant condition, and from which, I believe, can be derived a metaphor for all humanity."[8]

Rushdie accomplishes his allegory of immigrant experience primarily through a frame story involving two actors of Indian Muslim background, Gibreel Farishta, a Bollywood star ironically famous for playing Hindu gods, and a far from famous assimilated Indian, Saladin Chamcha, reduced to doing voice-over acting in Britain. The two experience apparent death when a hijacked plane they are traveling on explodes in mid-air. But magical realism takes over as the two are somehow miraculously saved. At that point, the novel transitions into a series of dream sequences associated with one or another of the two actors. In being shaken from their life paths by a violence akin to entering a new, alien society, the two protagonists have fantasies that radically entangle worldviews normally set in isolated opposition. In good postmodern fashion, the text mixes literary and pop culture allusions with sacred texts. Through these sequences the novel playfully deconstructs several varieties of political and religious extremism, and at the same time attacks the spiritless materialism of much Western consumer culture.

Citing the long history of the novel as a hybrid genre, Rushdie has made clear his intent in *Satanic Verses*:

> Between religion and literature, as between politics and literature, there is a linguistically based dispute. But it is not a dispute of simple opposites. Because

whereas religion seeks to privilege one language above all others, the novel has always been about the way in which different languages, values and narratives quarrel, and about the shifting relations between them, which are relations of power. The novel does not seek to establish a privileged language, but it insists upon the freedom to portray and analyze the struggle between the different contestants for such privileges.[9]

This is very close to Russian literary critic M. M. Bakhtin's definition of the novel as a carnivalesque form in which discourses normally set apart are put into dialogue—a task likely to be central to our survival as societies, if not as a species, in the near future.

By this definition, true novels are inherently opposed to fundamentalisms of all kinds—religious, political, philosophical, or otherwise. In this case, the dialogue Rushdie opened, that led to his targeting by Islamic fundamentalists, was his revisioning of ancient legends told about the prophet Muhammad having been tricked by the devil into including certain questionable, satanic verses in the holy Q'uran (Koran). Raising the possibility that sacred scriptures might be imperfect, might include not only the voice of God or Allah but also the contrary voice of his devilish nemesis is to throw a very considerable heap of doubt into the textual foundation of the religion. Clearly, such doubt, if taken to heart, would require far more humility on the part of scriptural interpreters than anyone claiming fundamental knowledge of truth. That was something those who called for Rushdie's assassination could not abide.

Re-envisioning the Postmodern University: A. S. Byatt's *Possession* (1990)

From Vladimir Nabokov, *Pale Fire* (1962), to John Barth, *Giles Goat-Boy* (1966), to J. M. Coetzee, *Disgrace* (1999), to Zadie Smith, *On Beauty* (2005), to Julie Schumacher, *Dear Committee Members* (2014), the university campus has been a site for postmodern literary play. Given that the university is the main source from which most ideas about postmodernisms and postmodernities have emanated, the pleasures, pretenses, paradoxes, and politics of postmodern university life (as specific site but also as microcosm) can help place the theories woven into this book. Postmodern university novels range from those disparaging cultural theory as the bane of contemporary education to those that seek to give vibrancy and embodiment to those very theories, but each grapples with academe as a key site where postmodern conditions are both experienced and theorized. Universities are not only places from which much discussion and production of postmodern fiction arises, but also institutions whose nature has been profoundly changed by such postmodern phenomena as increasing corporatization, changing global demographics, and the impact of new communications technologies.

Until the end of the Second World War, universities in the United States, the United Kingdom, and much of the rest of the Western world were very much elite spaces inhabited primarily by the upper-class whites. But after the war, a process of expanding higher education took hold such that the percentage of the population receiving college degrees skyrocketed. In the United States, for example, the numbers went from less than 4 percent in 1940 to more than 30 percent by 2018. Massive new public institutions arose, while the major private universities were gradually opened up to scholarship students from a variety of social classes and ethnic backgrounds. Prior to this era Jewish students and students of color were largely excluded or marginalized in higher education institutions. This expansion continued into the mid-1970s when contractions in the global economy gave birth to a new kind of free-market fundamentalism that in turn led to "austerity programs" that soon started a long process of defunding public education. By the 1980s, the implications of having too many educated folks from less privileged backgrounds had begun to make conservatives nervous. By the beginning of the twenty-first century, public universities that had once been funded almost wholly by federal and state governments found themselves largely bereft of public funding, forced to rely increasingly on private and corporate money that often came with strings attached.[10]

This ongoing process led to an increasing bureaucratization that conceptualizes universities as corporations and students as consumers, an increasing vocationalization that downplays the value of critical thinking as taught in the social sciences and the humanities, ever-more draconian austerity measures often aimed at cutting funding for the most politically progressive programs in the curriculum, and all manner of related right-wing political attacks on the very idea of publicly funded higher education.

A. S. Byatt's epic Booker Prize–winning novel, *Possession* (1990), stands out among novels of academe for its complex treatments of postmodernism and postmodern education.[11] The book does many different things, but I will stress three ways in which it is revisionary. First, it reworks the genre of the campus novel. Second, it is about the postmodern era's revisionary relation to another historical era, the mid-nineteenth century. And third, it is an oblique comment on another postmodern novel, John Fowles's *The French Lieutenant's Woman* (1969), a book often considered to be a founding text of the British branch of postmodern fiction.

Like Fowles's novel, *Possession* centers on paralleling the lives of two couples, one from the late twentieth century, the other from the nineteenth-century Victorian era. In Byatt's case, the contemporary couple are academics working in an Oxbridge-like university. Her postmodern couple are professors of English literature, Maud Bailey and Roland Mitchell, each researching another couple, nineteenth-century poets Christabel LaMotte and Ralph Henry Ash, respectively. Byatt also throws into the fray some real-life English scholars like F. R. Leavis. The novel utilizes a dazzling array of kinds of invented texts—diaries, letters, poems, historical, and literary critical writings—in an effort to show the inevitably fictional element in the complex task of truth seeking. In addition to being a novel of academic life, the text also flirts with a number of other literary genres, including literary biography, the romance, the detective novel, the historical novel, the novel of adultery, and Gothic horror, including a little grave robbing (in the name of academic research, of course). All these and other metafictional elements place the book squarely within the postmodernist camp. But the novel also explicitly offers a critique of certain strands of postmodern theory, and certain assumptions about postmodern fiction and postmodern life.

The detective aspect of the novel concerns the modern-day researchers' (at first reluctant) collaboration to uncover and prove a hitherto unknown relationship between the two nineteenth-century poets each had been separately researching. In a satirical take on the competitive "publish or perish" world of postmodern academe, Maud and Roland are pushed into an obsessive effort to outrace any potential professorial rivals in order to be the first to document and write about such an important affair. The worst of academic excesses are blamed largely on Americans, a small army of cultural imperialists who use obscure jargon and vast sums of research money in an effort to rob the treasures of English literature. In Byatt's rendition, the Yanks have even infected some British scholars. The worst of these figures, given the not very subtle name Fergus Wolff, is a full-bore postmodern theorist, who sniffs out the gist of his colleagues' find and tries predatorily to snatch it up to feed his own voracious need for academic accolades. Wolff is at once a sexual predator and a predator upon literary history. Another rival, given the equally villainous name, Blackadder, has an equally predatory, but quite different, desire to capture the past exactly as it happened, contrary to Wolff's postmodern sense of history as text. (The name, in calling up for some readers the buffoonish character on the British sitcom "Blackadder," a show that, like *Possession*, pretends to re-create earlier historical eras, turns this professor's literal-mindedness into a joke.) A third competitor, Professor Cropper, whose name is a British slang for failure, seeks to possess the past as fetish, collecting various objects once belonging to the nineteenth-century poets, an approach one critic characterizes as "suffused with elements of sexual domination: voyeurism, pornography, and finally necrophilia."[12] These characters embody the transformation of universities in the era of neoliberal market fundamentalism into corporations where competition has replaced scholarly collegiality, and where innovative theory is quickly turned into a marketable commodity. In this economic context, the object of the professors' search, a piece of the past, is treated also as a commodity.

Each of the academic characters in the novel is engaged in some degree of historical reconstruction, and Byatt is equally critical of those who simply impose their present critical theories on the past and those who believe they can somehow perfectly retrieve the past without being shaped by the present. This initially includes her two main protagonists who are steeped in contemporary literary theory, but as the novel progresses, Maud and Roland are changed by their encounter with their nineteenth-century counterparts. They enter into a mutually informing dialogue with the past, one not based in absolutely true reconstruction, but in a richly embodied fictional re-creation. Byatt's exquisite imitation of the poetic styles of Ash and LaMotte are possible because she has engaged deeply with the models for these characters, especially poets like Robert Browning and Alfred Tennyson for Ash, and Christina Rosetti and Emily Dickinson, for LaMotte. Byatt also pays attention in the text to the major intellectual and political currents that shaped nineteenth-century culture. As Lynn Wells argues, Byatt's technique resembles that of

> the historian [who] relinquishes monologic control over historical representation, and accepts that her or his own voice is in fact produced through the dialogue with the past, through the response to what is different from the self in its present context. This discovery generates both "self-critical reflection," as postmodern historical theorist Dominick LaCapra points out, and awareness of the past's discrete and audible voice.[13]

The novel suggests that it is not necessary (or possible) to tell the past "exactly as it was," the goal of positivist history. But it *is* possible to have a deeply enriching encounter with another time period. This approach is aimed as a critique of a tendency in some circles of postmodern life to embrace *presentism*, the false belief, driven by consumer culture, that the newest is always better. The failure to become immersed in other times and other modes of thought reduces all the past to a sameness with the present that impoverishes experience. Byatt's theme returns again and again to the multiple meanings of her title. In this case, she is suggesting that any attempt to *possess* the past is doomed. It cannot be owned. Just as possessiveness can destroy one's relationship to a lover, so too a desire to own the past like a commodity will fail. Instead, what we need is an open-ended dialogue with the past, a dialogue in which we make our (post)modern assumptions vulnerable to those of another era.

Italian literary theorist and novelist Umberto Eco, writing on love in the postmodern era a decade before Byatt, describes a problem that is in many ways a central focus of *Possession*:

> The postmodern reply to the modern consists of recognizing that the past, since it cannot really be destroyed . . . must be revisited, but with irony, not innocently. I think of the postmodern attitude as that of a man who loves a very cultivated woman and knows that he cannot say to her "I love you madly," because he knows that she knows (and that she knows he knows) that these words have already been written by [cheesy romance author] Barbara Cartland. Still there is a solution. He can say "As Barbara Cartland would put it, I love you madly." At this point, having avoided false innocence, having said clearly it is no longer possible to talk innocently, he will nevertheless say what he wanted to say to the woman: that he loves her in an age of lost innocence.[14]

This is a classic description of postmodern *double-coding*, and the technique as employed by Byatt allows the novel to develop the relationship between Roland and Maud in loving detail, without sacrificing linguistic self-awareness, as when Roland "slept curled against her back, a dark comma against her pale elegant phrase" (424). There are many kinds of irony, some of which lead to cynical distancing, condescension, and self-satisfied narcissism, but others of which open up multiple horizons of thought and feeling.

Possession is subtitled "A Romance," and whether this alludes to the contemporary bodice-ripper genre or the more serious literary form, it is one quite removed from simple realism. Thus when Roland senses near the end of the novel that he "was in a Romance, a vulgar and High Romance . . . one of the systems that controlled him, as the expectations of Romance control almost everyone in the Western world, for better or worse" (425), he is torn by this realization: "Roland thought, partly with precise postmodern pleasure, and partly with a real element of superstitious dread, that he and Maud were being driven by a plot or fate that seemed, at least possibly to be not their plot but that of others" (421–2). This is at once a sly allusion to the postmodern device of a character in a novel realizing they are a character in a novel, and, within the plot of *Possession*, a reference to the characters' entanglements with the lives of their research subjects. Roland continues, thinking that he is probably experiencing

> an element of superstitious dread in any self-referring, self-reflexive, inturned postmodernist mirror-game or plot-coil that recognizes that it is out of hand, that connections proliferate apparently at random, . . . not controlled by conscious intention, which would of course being a good postmodernist intention, *require* the aleatory or multivalent or "free," but structuring, but controlling, but driving to some—to what?—end. Coherence and closure are deep human desires that are presently unfashionable. But they are always both frighteningly and enchantingly desirable. (421–2)[15]

In this passage, Byatt plays the postmodern trick of having her text and eating it too. She can make fun of a certain kind of oft-repeated postmodern trope, and deploy it to add another level of pleasure to her novel. More important, she is also making the (realist?) point that even as we lead postmodern lives, even as some of us are drenched in postmodern theory, we may still deeply desire closure and coherence. (The contemporary popularity, not to say cult status, of the great nineteenth-century novelist Jane Austen may be exemplary of this desire.) Ironically, it is the postmodernist villain, Fergus Wolff, whose recommendation initiates what becomes the love connection between Roland and Maud. And this is quite apt, since a novel rich with love—love of literature, of the past, of another person—is in part the postmodern product of Byatt's critique of the excesses of some strands of postmodern theory. In a final twist, she proves it is quite possible to lovingly pastiche nineteenth-century poetry (she writes 1,500 lines of it in the novel!), the fiction of other postmodern novelists, and still tell a decidedly postmodern tale that exposes the true fakery that is always the essence of fiction.

Dark Hearts: Jessica Hagedorn's *Dream Jungle* (2003)

Among the many things that Jessica Hagedorn accomplishes in her novel *Dream Jungle* (2003) is a doubling of the revisionary practice—she revises a text that itself revises a key modernist text, Joseph Conrad's *Heart of Darkness* (1899).[16] *Dream Jungle* satirizes Francis Ford Coppola's *Apocalypse Now* (1979), a film that incorporates themes and passages from Conrad's novella.[17] (In Chapter 8, I discuss Brian Fawcett's *Cambodia: A Book for People Who Find Television Too Slow*, which also reflects brilliantly on both Conrad's and Coppola's texts.)

Hagedorn's novel is set in the Philippines during the time when Coppola was there to film his Vietnam epic. She sets up a plot implicitly paralleling Coppola's "invasion" of the Philippines to make his movie about Vietnam, and the war on Vietnam itself as a continuation of US colonial wars dating back to the founding of the republic.

In *Apocalypse Now*, the intelligence dossier on the anti-hero Colonel Kurz includes the datum that he received an MA at Harvard for a thesis on the Philippine Insurrection, the war waged by the United States on the island nation between 1899 and 1902. That Conrad's fiction came out the same year as the US-Philippines War began provides another ironic and iconic connection between the narratives. These connections animate Filipina-American author Hagedorn as she satirizes both *Apocalypse Now* (barely disguised as "Napalm Sunset" in her novel) and *Hearts of Darkness: A Filmmaker's Apocalypse* (1991), a documentary film about the making of the fiction film that includes material shot by Coppola's spouse, Eleanor Coppola. This is intertextuality with a vengeance, though Hagedorn's vengeance is tempered by knowledge that no one escapes complicity in the postmodern, postcolonial era.

The "Napalm Sunset" story line is entangled with a different fictionalized true life event that may itself have been a fiction, the "discovery" of a lost tribe in the remote jungle of Mindanao. The novel raises the question of whether the find is real or a lie concocted by the corrupt Philippines government (run at the time by dictator Ferdinand Marcos). Could it be just a pretext to spy on and attack rebel guerillas in the region where the tribe was allegedly found? The search is led by Zamora Lopez de Legazpi, Ivy League–educated son of one of the five richest men in the Philippines who lives in the suburbs of Manila in a mansion he calls the Hollywood Hills. Zamora thinks of himself as a good man because he doesn't beat his servants and waited till she was seventeen before deflowering one of their daughters, while dreaming of strangling his "Teutonic goddess" trophy wife, Ilse. He also represents anthropologists, and much humor is made of the failed attempts of the "civilized" to understand "primitives" who seem much more reasonable and ethical than their "discoverer." The novel is exquisitely attuned to the racialized and gendered dimensions of the colonial caste system of a country where the layers of Spanish, then American, domination set hierarchies in place that remain little changed in the postcolonial era but that are at times subverted, and even reversed, if only as partial victories.

The filmmaker story and the lost tribe tale entwine like fast-growing jungle vines. The link between the two plot lines, and the star of the novel, is Rizalina, the brilliant daughter of Zamora's cook. Rizalina is forced by poverty and abuse into prostitution, but uses her beauty and wits to transcend her sleazy milieu. She becomes the lover of the aptly named Vince Moody, a supporting actor in "Napalm Sunset." Meanwhile, director Tony Pierce struggles to make his film amid breakdowns and warfare between members of his cast and crew, as well as environmental catastrophes and the threat of an actual military incursion onto his set. The novel hopscotches between a host of characters, switches between third- and first-person narration, and moves rapidly between locations and time frames to capture something of the fragmented, multilayered fictions being staged by the various protagonists. It also captures the contrast between the languid jungle culture and the frenetic pop culture–driven scene in the capital city of Manila. These include the machinations of journalist Paz Marlowe (Marlowe is the narrator of Conrad's *Heart of Darkness*), the metafictional voice of the author, who works to expose both the lost tribe hoax and the grandiose hubristic efforts of the film company.

Each character is living in a different dream jungle, a tangled web of illusion, truth, fear, hope, and possibility. The novel forces the reader to ask a series of questions about the relations between fiction and reality, and who benefits from certain ways of confusing the two. Is Zamora a discoverer of new worlds, the perpetrator of a hoax or the victim of one? Is his Native guide a conman or an honest cultural translator? Is Jinx, as Rizalina renames herself, in love or just using Moody as her way to a better life? Is Moody using her or is he duped by the hooker with a heart of gold myth? Is Paz an investigative journalist or continuing her work for a tabloid magazine? Is the director a visionary like the Conrad he periodically quotes, or a Hollywood egomaniac enacting not a critique of the war on Vietnam, but just a smaller scale imperialist venture of his own? Is he exploiting the locals he hires as servants and extras or is he providing them a welcome break from being exploited more fully by the Philippine government? We as readers need to dig in to answer these questions, unless of course we are just looking for an exotic journey and easy answers that do not challenge our own dream jungles.

Reds, Whites, and Reservation Blues: Sherman Alexie's *Lone Ranger and Tonto Fistfight in Heaven* (1993)

"Postindian" Anishinaabe writer and critic Gerald Vizenor claims that postmodernism was invented hundreds of years ago by tribal "authors" in figures like the trickster,[18] a wildly wily creator who storytells the world into existence. Vizenor's claim is embodied not only in his own postmodern novels like *The Heirs of Columbus* (1992) which portrays Christopher Columbus as a Mayan trying to return home, but also in a number of other contemporary Indigenous writers. Canadian-American Native writer Thomas King, for example, has likewise written richly humorous postmodern Coyote novels like *Green Grass, Running Water* (1993), in which four Native elders named Lone Ranger, Ishmael, Robinson Crusoe, and Hawkeye—all allusions to literary and pop culture non-Native figures implicated in "Indian" stereotyping—escape from a mental institution. All four turn out to actually be female Native supernatural beings. Likewise, Haisla/Heiltsuk First Nations author Eden Robinson's novel *Monkey Beach* (2000) (see Chapter 5) creatively intermixes Indigenous spirituality, Gothic tropes, and magical realism.

Each of these writers and other fictionists of Indigenous descent have created a specifically Native form of literary revisionism, one that often revises a centuries-old oral tradition in the cause of a resistive and restorative form of postmodernist fiction. The Indigenous author who has brought a postmodern sensibility to the widest audience is Spokane-Coeur D'Alene writer Sherman Alexie. In a manner reminiscent of the works of the great modernist writer William Faulkner, Alexie has created a set of characters who recur across a number of his books. His work resists conditions imposed on present-day Natives through a pointed sense of humor directed with word arrow precision at the long sordid story of settler colonialism. Alexie's work has many moods and modes, but overall the work suggests that humor is the most perfect weapon for disarming oppressors. His readings often resemble stand-up comedy as much as literary presentation, and the humor liberates as few other approaches to a tragic history can.

The book I will focus on, *The Lone Ranger and Tonto Fistfight in Heaven* (1993), is sometimes treated as a story collection, but I think it can be better read as a novel in fragments, one that refracts the fragmenting of the lives of many contemporary Indigenous people. As the title suggests, Alexie is also rewriting the genre of the Western, and doing so in a style that might be called "trickster realism." In spirit, it draws upon the kind of wild mix of the probable and the improbable found in Plains/Prairie Native "coyote tales." One of his friends dubbed Alexie "Shaman Perplexie," because like the trickster Coyote, these works diverge from a certain level of the real in order to tell deeper truths. But these are far from traditional tales. Traditions can become traps if they are not adapted to new conditions, and are easily co-opted by whites for profit. (Alexie loses few opportunities to launch direct assaults in his essays, interviews, and performance-readings on "new age" white folks looking for their "inner Indian," while selling "authentic" sacred crystals, sweat lodge experiences, vision questions, and dream catchers at outrageous prices.) That is one reason that Alexie's postmodern style draws a good deal on contemporary pop culture, such that the hilariously incompetent cartoon spirit of Wile E. Coyote can be as much an inspiration as ancient Coyote tales.

The Lone Ranger and Tonto Fistfight in Heaven (1993) confirms Faulkner's observation that "the past is never dead, it is not even past." On almost every page, the book reminds readers of the ongoing impact of forces set in motion by the lost Italian sailing under a Spanish flag who happened upon lands he misidentified as India and thus misnamed its Native inhabitants. The place where most of Alexie's work is set is the Spokane Indian reservation in Washington State. Wildly comic stories set amid an often tragic reservation landscape draw upon and deconstruct every stereotype of "Indians," while showing how history intrudes into every life lived on the reservation. From the title onward, it is clear that Hollywooden Indians (like the Tonto of the title) and other misrepresentations shape not only the external but also the internal world of Indigenous residents of the not very United States.

To say, for example, that a story in which the nineteenth-century Sioux warrior, Crazy Horse, appears in a late twentieth-century Spokane, Washington coffee shop is anachronistic is to misunderstand both history and the present. Alexie makes clear that language is the best weapon available to those who have been otherwise disarmed by history.

> Driving home, I heard the explosion and thought it was a new story born. But, . . . it's the same old story, whispered past the same false teeth. How can we imagine a new language when the language of the enemy keeps our dismembered tongues tied to his belt? How can we imagine a new alphabet when the old jumps off billboards down into our stomachs? . . . I want to rasp into sober cryptology and say something dynamic but tonight is my laundry night. How do we imagine a new life when a pocketful of quarters weighs our possibilities down? (152)

Much of the trickster realism is in the style of Alexie's work, but one recurring character, Thomas Builds-the-Fire, actually embodies the trickster. As Alexie phrased it in an interview, "[Thomas] comes from a long history of . . . indigenous trickster figures. . . . When he's telling his stories, [we are so] used to seeing a stoic Indian storyteller standing up on a mountain that I'm not sure they're even listening to him. He's lying, telling jokes, making fun of people, manipulating them." Like all literary fiction writers, Thomas lies to tell the truth. And truth-telling is never appreciated by oppressors.

"The Trial of Thomas Builds-the-Fire" begins with Thomas under arrest for no apparent reason. But soon a Bureau of Indian Affairs official tells his fellow officials what the problem is: "Builds-the-Fire has a history of this kind of behavior. . . . A storytelling fetish accompanied by an extreme need to tell the truth. Dangerous." Thomas turns out to be dangerous indeed because "he had once held the reservation postmaster hostage for eight hours with the idea of a gun and had also threatened to make significant changes to the tribal vision" (93). It is the latter role as revisionary that sends terror into the hearts of government officials and the judge presiding over his trial, because his vision calls for a truer form of justice. In his defense, Thomas tells, in the voice of a pony, the true story of Colonel George Wright, who in 1858 massacred 800 horses in order to further deter the Spokane Indians from resisting encroachment on their lands, and then, in the voice of Qualchan, one of the tribe's leaders, he tells of his hanging along with his wife and four others by Wright.

When asked the point of his story by the judge, Thomas replies, "Well, the city of Spokane is now building a golf course named after me, Qualchan, located in that valley where I was murdered." While the tribe members present cheer, the judge grows so "red-faced with anger . . . he almost looked Indian" (99). Even the postal employee who had once been held hostage by Thomas's "idea of a gun" made "a leap of faith across the room" to support him. Thomas is of course found guilty (of "the crime of being an Indian in the twentieth century," as another story has it), and is given two life sentences. But of course, life sentences are what literature is all about. As the story ends, Thomas is traveling to prison with fellow inmates who together represent the communities that make up most of the prison population in the country with the highest rate of incarceration in the world.

> "I know who you are," the Chicano said to Thomas. "You're that Indian guy did all the talking." "Yeah," one of the African men said. "You're that storyteller. Tell us some stories, chief, give us the scoop." Thomas looked at these five men who shared his skin color, at the white man who shared this

bus which was going to deliver them into a new kind of reservation, barrio, ghetto, logging-town tin shack. He then looked out the window, through the steel grates on the windows, at the freedom just outside the glass. He saw wheat fields, bodies of water, and bodies of dark-skinned workers pulling fruit from trees and sweat from thin air. Thomas closed his eyes and told this story. (103)

Like Thomas, like crazy world-maker Coyote, Alexie believes in the transformative power of storytelling:

Do you believe laughter can save us? All I know is I count coyotes to help me sleep. . . . Imagination is the politics of dreams; imagination turns every word into a bottle rocket. . . . Imagine every day is Independence Day and save us from traveling the river changed; save us from hitchhiking the long road home. Imagine an escape. Imagine that your own shadow on the wall is a perfect door. Imagine a song stronger than penicillin. Imagine a spring with water that mends broken bones. Imagine a drum which wraps itself around your heart. Imagine a story that puts wood in the fireplace. (152–3)

8

True Lies

Nonfiction Novels and Autofictions

The critique of the solid line between literature and history in postmodern theory has fostered the proliferation of genres that purposely blur that line. These genres go by names like "nonfiction novel" and "autofiction." The use of novelistic techniques in nonfiction is as old as the novel itself. Works like *The Anatomy of Melancholy* (1621) or Rousseau's *Confessions* (1782) are often said to be more literary than narrowly factual. John Hersey's *Hiroshima* (1957), a magnificent and troubling literary-journalistic treatment of the lasting impact of the US atomic bombing of that city, lies somewhere between these older works and the new twists given to fictional nonfiction forms at the birth of the postmodern era in the 1960s.

The term "nonfiction novel" was a purposely provocative one widely used in the 1960s and 1970s for works by Norman Mailer, Tom Wolfe, Hunter Thompson, Truman Capote, and Joan Didion, among others. More recently, the term has been largely supplanted by the more neutral term "creative nonfiction."[1] That term seems not only bland but a bit insulting, since all good nonfiction is creative. It also lacks the disruptive, thought-provoking power the seeming oxymoron "nonfiction novel" retains. Were it not for its more common meaning, Truman Capote's term "faction" (fiction/fact merged) might be an even better term for this body of work.

Postmodernist true fictions would also include Jamaica Kincaid's searingly beautiful postcolonial anti-travelogue *A Small Place* (1988). Another more recent work that seeks to restore some of that lost disruptive power of the nonfiction novel is *Human Smoke* (2008), Nicholas Baker's stunning documenting of the complicity of Western leaders in the rise of Nazism prior to the Second World War. The true fiction category also includes works in the partly fabricated memoir genre sometimes known as *autofiction*. Though it sounds like it might describe novels about cars, "autofiction" is actually a term invented in 1977 by French writer/theorist Serge Doubrovsky to name a kind of autobiography or memoir with an overtly fictional element. It names a variety of texts that build upon personal truth, but apparently do not confine themselves exclusively to factuality. *Apparently* is the key word here, since there has never been an autobiography that did not include fictional elements. Autofiction just seeks to bring the tension between personal truth and fiction to the textual foreground. One pioneering work in this form in English is Audre Lorde's *Zami: A New Spelling of My Name* (1984). Lorde called her book a "biomythography," an arguably even more fitting term for the genre that became increasingly popular among writers after the turn of the twenty-first century. It can be seen as part of a complicated desire to return to the real (but not to realism) in an era when truth seems more and more difficult to come by.

This trend is referenced brilliantly in David Shields's manifesto, *Reality Hunger* (2010), a work consisting primarily of quotes from other authors, with occasional glosses by Shields.[2] That book is remarkable in being at once a thoroughgoing deconstruction of "realism" as a concept in writing, yet nevertheless a call for the greater use of real things in fictions. From my perspective, this is a call for more postmodern realism, perhaps with an even more explicit recognition that raw facts become entangled with an inevitable element of fictionalization. Note that such entanglement does not invalidate the need to search for the most truthful approximation of reality, one that recognizes that the real can only be called forth when situated knowledge is taken into account, when the relative social power of those making truth claims are factored into interpretation of the narrative.

Empire's Tracks: Maxine Hong Kingston's *China Men* (1980)

Maxine Hong Kingston's National Book Award–winning *China Men* (1980) is a true fiction rife with stories within stories within stories in which a blend of historical facts, personal memories, tall tales, bits of classic Chinese literary works, proverbs, folk songs and folktales, are reimagined into a novel telling of the truth about the history of the men in her family that encapsulates a larger history of men of Chinese descent in America. Conceived as a companion volume to her widely acclaimed *Woman Warrior* (see Chapter 5), it focuses especially on the period from the mid-nineteenth to the mid-twentieth centuries, the generations of the author's father and grandfather, with a brief treatment as well of her brother's service during the Vietnam War. The story line eschews chronological development, and instead jumps back and forth in time to show the embeddedness of history in later times. *China Men* builds up its portrait through overlapping, sometimes contradictory, beautifully rendered narratives that demonstrate that rewoven folktales, legends, and personal memories are as much a part of history as the statistics and documents she also presents and discusses.

Perhaps for the benefit of those who did not first read *Woman Warrior*, before she tells these tales of male woes and triumphs Kingston makes two contextualizing gestures. Her first is a short, reimagined folktale that tells of a man who undergoes transformation into a woman, including the excruciating practice of foot-binding inflicted on generations of Chinese women. And the second story has children (presumably Maxine and her siblings) misidentify a man walking by their house as their father, evoking at once an emotionally distant patriarch, and underscoring the lonely anonymity of Chinese men in an alien country.

The book signals its fictiveness with its first sentence that begins "Once upon a time . . ." But if Kingston is telling fairy tales, it is because reality is in part a fairy tale woven from hundreds of disparate threads of narrative. Even before that first sentence, the book's title begins the process of countering the hi/story told by the dominant culture. In place of the racist term "chinaman" that lumped all males of Chinese descent in America into a single, often vilified and stereotyped bloc, "china men" is plural and points to the many different men whose stories are about to be told. Members of Kingston's family had been going to America and returning for many generations, even before the California Gold Rush of 1849 brought a large wave of Chinese men (and a much smaller number of Chinese women) to the North American West Coast. The Gold Mountain Sojourners, as those returning from America were known, often puffed themselves up with tall tales of streets paved with gold and streams gleaming with nuggets one could simply reach down to grab. Kingston's grandfather challenged one such storyteller, only to be chastised for bringing bad luck by suggesting it was not true (41–2). The sojourners brought back to poor villages just enough gifts to make their stories plausible, while leaving out the many hardships of mining, including the frequent robbery, claim jumping, and even murder, that compatriots suffered at the hands of the "white demons." The desire to believe was stronger than the desire for evidence. But songs popular with wives left behind also told of those who never returned, lost at sea or in the wilds of Gold Mountain, or in the arms of an imagined new wife overseas.

By the late 1800s, "sojourners" in cities like San Francisco and Vancouver found that Chinese merchants and entrepreneurs of all kinds had begun to build vibrant, if segregated, communities. Gold Mountain's first Chinatowns offered to new arrivals some of the familiar elements of the home country, including possibly an encounter with someone from their own village. Kingston's grandfather was one of the thousands of Chinese workers who formed a second wave after the Gold Rush, the generation crucial to the building of the railroad that turned America into a transcontinental empire. Without these "illegal immigrants" the uniting of the states would likely have taken decades longer. That massive undertaking tracks a wider historical process of cultural warfare in which exploited Chinese laborers were indentured to an imperial project of "racial capitalism" that also displaced Cheyenne, Lakota, and Pawnee Natives.[3] (This was true initially as well for the Irish laborers on the eastern portion of the project who were for a time also treated as an inferior "race."[4]) Working against the long-standing stereotype of Asian males as small and weak, Kingston's stories of the railroad-building crew stress the incredible bravery, strength, and physical endurance that work entailed. But her tales of heroism also detail the often ugly effects of discrimination and deprivation, including those created by the fact that Chinese women were largely excluded from the immigration process, except as a small number of prostitutes. This limitation colored the experiences of Asian women (and men) in the United States for generations to come.

Largely in response to the achievements of Chinese rail workers, in 1882, the Chinese Exclusion Act made illegal all immigration by Chinese laborers ("coolies" as they were derisively labeled); Chinese women had already been banned in 1875. Exclusion was surely a bitter "reward" for the heroic efforts of Chinese men on the rail line. But it was a key part of the effort of politicians like California Governor Leland Stanford to use racism to divide the white working class from potential nonwhite allies.[5] The act was not fully revoked until 1965. But in another historical twist, when most public records in the city were destroyed in the great San Francisco earthquake and fire of 1906, the largest concentration of Chinese in America could no longer be identified as "aliens"; each could claim to be among the few who had obtained legal citizenship. As Kingston notes in an interview, after that disaster "an authentic citizen . . . had no more papers than an alien. Every China man was reborn out of the fire as a citizen."[6]

The Chinese Exclusion Act meant that the men like Kingston's father could only enter the United States illegally. But as the novel details, many forms of violence, including the Japanese invasion of China prior to the Second World War, and the terrible famine of the Maoist era meant the push to leave was stronger than the fear of doing so illegally. One of the ways that *China Men* makes clear that history, including personal history, always contains fictive elements is through such narrative devices as telling five different versions of her father's passage to America. These differing stories each contain some truth for some people, and since it was common for members of her father's generation to invent fake stories for the authorities, she is slyly honoring tradition. Moreover, the method captures the truth that after a time memory mingles with fiction for all of us.

One version of the crossing vividly evoked in *China Men* involves a trip via Cuba and stowing away in a wooden crate. "The ship docked in Cuba, where the surf foamed like the petticoats of dancing ladies." Her imagined father earned money for the next part of the trip by working in a Havana cigar factory. Then he becomes a stowaway

> inside a crate with no conspicuous air holes. Light leaked through the slats that he himself had nailed together and the bright streaks jumped and winked as . . . friends hammered the lid shut. Then he felt himself . . . carried to a darker place. Nothing happened for hours so he lost his bearings. . . . Various futures raced through his mind: walking the plank, drowning, growing old in jail, being thrown overboard in chains, flogged to tell where others were hiding . . .
>
> Suddenly—a disturbance—a giant's heart came to life, the ship shook and throbbed. (48–9)

As it turns out, after his death, when he could no longer be subject to deportation, Kingston revealed that this version was closest to the facts. Her father made three attempts at this perilous crossing to America in 1924. He traveled from China to Cuba via the Panama Canal, then, just as in *China Men*, he stowed away in a suffocating dusty crate on the leg from Havana to New York, where he was caught and deported twice before finally succeeding on a third try.

After a fifteen-year separation, her father won a visa for his wife in a gambling game, and brought her to the United States, eventually settling in Stockton, California. Her father had been a poet and teacher in China, and her mother a midwife, but in America they eked out a living first by opening a gambling house, then a laundry. This history for Kingston helps explain, though not fully justify, a bitterness passed on to her generation, including her father's misogyny. The rich, lyrical storytelling of history in *China Men* plays an important role in the process of imagining a truer past for Americans of Chinese descent. As critic/historian Jinqi Ling summarizes, the negotiated historical stance Kingston adopts in *China Men* refuses simple stories, matching the class, racial, and gender injustice her ancestors endured to the joys and creative reimaginings entailed in building a new homeland, contrasting "complex, multilayered and variously entangled Asian American identities to convenient categorization."[7]

The very category "Asian American" covers over the diverse history of Japanese, Vietnamese, Korean, Cambodian, Thai, East Indian, and a dozen other immigrant groups from Asia who have over subsequent generations struggled with both unique and repetitive forms of discrimination, misrepresentation, and, in the case of Japanese Americans, incarceration in internment camps, as brilliantly evoked by Julie Otsuka in *When the Emperor Was Divine* (2003).[8] Each group and new wave of immigration has found their postmodern literary voices, from early magnificent works like Teresa Cha's evocations of Korean and Korean-American history in *Dictee* (1982) to twenty-first-century novels like Karen Yamashita's *I Hotel* (2010), with its intricate tale of the Asian American political alliances in 1960/1970s San Francisco, and Viet Thanh Nguyen's *The Sympathizer* (2015) with its retelling of the Vietnam War and its aftermath from multiple Vietnamese, American, and Vietnamese-American points of view, as well as many more postmodern realist novels.

History as a Novel, the Novel as History: Norman Mailer's *Armies of the Night* (1968)

The title of this section is the subtitle of a book by Norman Mailer chronicling the "siege of the Pentagon" in 1967 by thousands protesting the war on

Vietnam. In *Armies of the Night*, Mailer uses two counterpointed narratives, one seemingly more "objective" and historical, the other seemingly more "subjective" and novelistic.[9] I say "seemingly" because in the course of the book, these poles of objectivity and subjectivity are called into question as we come to understand that a higher objectivity can sometimes emerge by going more deeply into the subjective.

The events portrayed in the book, and the book itself, were part of a large shift in sensibility in the United States (and around the globe) driven by the rise of a host of new social movements in the 1960s. The Civil Rights and Black Power movements, parallel civil rights and ethnic power movements led by Latino/a/xs, Asian Americans and Native Americans, the women's and gay liberation movements, and crossing all these the student and anti-Vietnam War movements shook many in the country free from quiescent obedience to cultural and political authority. The hippie counterculture was another sign of alienation from mainstream, materialistic, and repressive values. These movements, with their profound critiques of the so-called American Dream, also became in certain respects entwined with a widespread cultural shift toward a postmodernist sensibility.[10] The importance of *Armies of the Night* lies in the various ways in which it describes, analyzes, and through its form embodies a shift toward new forms of *postmodern politics*.

At the level of style, the shift to postmodernist devices can be easily traced in Mailer's career, in that he began by employing a style close to classical realism in such novels as his Second World War epic, *The Naked and the Dead* (1948). Like the trajectory of so many writers who began to write in a realist vein after the war, Mailer came, over time, to embrace styles and forms more aligned with postmodernism in their questioning of our ability to fully capture reality in texts. *Armies of the Night* was a particularly important step along that transformative journey, in that it confronted several of the central areas of cultural contention in the era when postmodernism emerged in literary and cultural life.

Armies is structured through a double interpretive framework in which Mailer, as participant-interpreter in/of the events of the march (in which he played a minor part), is portrayed in the third person by a narrator-interpreter who further mediates the reality represented. The two "books" of the text treat the relationship between these two "Mailers" somewhat differently, and are formally distinct in other ways as well. They alternate between first and third person to emphasize our existence as both self-knowing individuals and the subject of larger historical forces. The longer of the two parts, Book 1, "History as a Novel: The Steps of the Pentagon," resembles a novel, and is written in the third person about a "character" named "Norman Mailer." This section also relies fairly heavily on such novelistic devices as imagined dialogue, literary allusion, elaborate conceit, and so on. Book 2, "The Novel as History: The Battle of the Pentagon," resembles contemporary mainstream historiography or journalism by attempting to step back and view the events related in Book 1 from a panoramic, "objective" viewpoint rather than that of individual, embodied consciousness.

This means that *Armies* is structured in such a way that the problem of reading the text and the problem of reading the events illuminate each other. These interpretive questions are interwoven with an attempt to point out some of the theoretical, rhetorical, and strategic questions facing the progressive social movements of the era—the protests against the Vietnam War, the civil rights, women's liberation, and other movements by groups seeking an equal space in society.[11] Its twofold structure, along with other literary devices, throws into question the authority of the author/text, and thereby grants a certain degree of autonomy to the demonstration itself as a drama that enacts and embodies key political questions. That drama included one of the most massive marches in US history till that time, a surrounding of the Pentagon building and a mystical attempt to levitate it, and a small but intense pitched battle in which a fraction of the protesters tussled with troops defending the Department of Defense fortress.

In particular, the book embodies and analyzes the problem of authority faced by the social movements of the 1960s. It looks at how the new social movements dealt with the strategic issues of violence versus nonviolence, leadership versus anti-hierarchical structures. These debates are summarized in the novel history as the "action faction" (those advocating spontaneous revolt) and the "praxis axis" (those supporting more carefully strategized nonviolent actions). The character "Mailer" fails to think of a way to resolve these conflicts, as did the New Left itself, which imploded in the late 1960s precisely around these issues. But perhaps the nonfiction novel itself does suggest a way out, in that the text itself is both structured and open-ended, both a factual account and novelistic questioning of that account. As such it embodies a new mode of postmodern political action that came to fruition in self-consciously postmodernist activist groups like ACT-UP in its fight against homophobia during the AIDS epidemic.[12]

Mailer's characterization of what he calls the "aesthetic" of the Pentagon march and siege captures a portion of the New Left in transition into the confrontation-based politics of its late phase (roughly 1968–70). In that phase, a small, but influential, component of the "action faction" began to turn "action for action's sake" into the "aesthetic" of the movement, arguing that "revolutionary action," not techniques used by the tradition of nonviolent protest, would speak for itself. This view has repeatedly been taken up by sectors of postmodern movements. For example, the Black Bloc of the global justice movement and the Anti-fa (for anti-fascist) movement embrace street fighting and property damage as revolutionary action, thinking it epitomizes a more radical stance. But this style of street fighting alienates potential recruits to the movement, confuses physical with moral courage, violence with meaningful confrontation, symbolic with literal assault, and downplays the fact that action seldom speaks unambiguously. As *Armies* makes clear, such action must be read, and interpreted. And it is seldom read as intended but rather just seen as unjustified rioting, senseless vandalism, and meaningless assaults.

Street fighting plays into the hands of authorities who can falsely equate this violence with the far greater violence of war and social repression, linking it to terrorism, a tactic that is in fact almost exclusively practiced by right-wing groups of white supremacists. If violence is a useful tactic in a democratic context, why do government agencies try so hard to provoke it, as they did in the illegal CIA/FBI COINTELPRO campaigns[13] of the 1960s and the 1970s, and similar efforts to provoke violence by the police and intelligence agencies in recent years? Violence-provoking infiltrators have worked inside social change organizations for decades, not only encouraging senseless acts that allow the repression of movements but also sowing dissent and paranoia within them as questions arise about who in the group might be an informer.

Armies makes clear that a positive interpretation of actions like the Pentagon siege is not an inevitable consequence of proximity to or even immersion in the event itself, but comes only through a careful interplay of rhetorical strategy and context (that is what Mailer means by the "aesthetic" of the protest). In the case of the Pentagon march, this kind of contextualizing was part of what "praxis axis" organizers, who planned the protest, offered. "Revolutionary action" or "confrontationism" in the late 1960s and since, may for a brief time be successful in increasing the notoriety of the movement. But those successes are not generally accompanied by, and often undermine, serious attempts to cultivate the roots, to build a critical democratic community through collective political (re)education.

Armies suggests that the text/event at the Pentagon takes the path of both intensifying and replacing the (sur)reality of everyday life. The event is not only drama itself but also includes some self-consciously surrealist theater by the Yippies, something of the American version of the French avant-garde revolutionists, the *Situationists*,[14] who believed in turning everyday life into art. Such surrealist play, including the mostly tongue-in-cheek attempt to levitate the Pentagon and exorcise its demons, was one mode of action among many in the march, one with an important, but limited, audience. Humor and play, theatricality and educational slogans, are strong threads in new social movements, and one which sidesteps the problems with "revolutionary action" and recognizes that they can disarm adversaries and attract new supporters.

While sympathetic to the playful side of the protests, Mailer's treatment suggests that neither realism nor surrealism are sufficient when pursued singly, but work best when set alongside or against one another. As the first generation raised fully under the hegemony of the then new medium of television, Mailer argues that the children of the 1960s were being socialized as surrealists, a view even more relevant in our digital era.

They had had their minds jabbed and poked and twitched and finally galvanized into surrealistic modes of response by commercials cutting into dramatic narratives, and . . . flipping from network to network—they were forced willy-nilly to build their idea of the spacetime continuum (and therefore their nervous system) on the jumps and cracks and leaps and breaks which every phenomenon from the media seemed to contain within it. The authority had operated on their brains with commercials, and washed their brains with packaged education, packaged politics. (103)

Mailer partly applauds the surrealist moment, the new nonlinear mode, but also sees its limits, sees its complicity in the maintenance of the system that needs to be overturned. In a surreal world, a world in which reality is carved up into commodity chunks placed between, but indistinguishable from, commercials, a sense of narrative, of history, becomes a powerful and necessary element in a subversive movement. Mailer worries that already signs of a "packaging" of surrealist politics are on the horizon. In a postmodern world where mass-mediated (sur)reality seems at once to be random and utterly programmed, spontaneity may be an essential subversive quality or it may be part of the program. Political spontaneity without imaginative strategy quickly devolves into highly conventional, passively consumable, co-optable forms. These questions continue to vex radically democratic social movements to this day.

At its best, Mailer's nonfiction novel follows the spirit of the movement in the 1960s in calling its readers to make history themselves through political action. As such, the text offers a history very much pointed toward the present, a novel history calling readers to think through possible paths to a more democratic society. The heirs of those movements today call for a decentralized society where political power is more in the hands of those it impacts, a society more accountable to communities built on mutual respect for diverse values and ways of living, and fueled by renewable forms of energy.[15] This kind of postmodern politics seeks a balance between individual and collective identity, tries to avoid the traps of ideological rigidity, and rejects using unjust means to achieve just ends.

Historical Sideshow: Brian Fawcett's *Cambodia: A Book for People Who Find Television Too Slow* (1986)

Mailer caught a key aspect of the Vietnam War (or the American War, as the Vietnamese call it) story as it shaped the United States in the 1960s, while Canadian Brian Fawcett's true fiction, *Cambodia: A Book for People Who Find Television Too Slow* (1986), takes readers deeply into one of the most tragic trajectories of that war.[16] Fawcett's book is as innovative and bizarre as its title suggests. Each page is divided in two, with a series of thirteen chapters combining essay and story on the top two-thirds, and on the bottom third a single historical commentary that runs the entire length of the book. I have added a "U" for upper or a "L" for lower to each parenthetical citation below to indicate the quotation comes from the upper stories or the lower essay (this split page was similarly utilized a couple of decades later by the Nobel Prize–winning writer J. M. Coetzee in his 2007 novel *Diary of a Bad Year*). Fawcett's baker's dozen story-essays (for lack of a better term) are deeply strange, sometimes short story-like, sometimes essayistic, usually with elements of each. The topics, ranging from baseball player Reggie Jackson to lost Tibetan monks to chicken nuggets to the meaning of the Trojan horse, make the word "eclectic" seem too tame a descriptor. But in one way or another, all of the top-of-the-page essays deal with the impact of postmodern mass media and consumerism on our individual and collective lives. The sometimes seemingly trivial topics covered in the story-essays also embody the notion that cultural trivia and mass media distraction turn the profoundly important kind of issues addressed in the bottom-of-the-page analytic long essay, such as the roots of our capacity to commit horrible massacres and genocide upon our fellow humans, into a mere footnote.

The book's structure embodies the principle of postmodernist realism that fiction must be (con)textualized by reflection on real sites of historical action and real modes of reader interpretation. But to a degree unusual even for postmodernist realisms, Fawcett makes this goal quite explicit in a preface to the book and in discursive disruptions to several of the stories. This includes numerous asides to the reader about how they read the world and how they should read his—his what? Can it be called a novel? Maybe. In fact maybe it is more of a novel than most of the other ones discussed in the book since the word after all means "new," and this book is certainly newer in form than most of what passes as a novel these days. And remember that according to literary theorist M. M. Bakhtin, what distinguishes the novel is precisely the fact that it can include all forms of discourse within itself (see Chapter 2).

Fawcett's most extended discussion of the nature of the novel occurs in the tenth essay in which he, or at least a narrator who presumably speaks for him, enters into a conversation with the British novelist Malcolm Lowry (despite the fact that he is deceased) about the role of the novel under postmodern conditions. The Fawcett character argues that the personal-psychological modernist novel, the kind Lowry wrote, played a liberating role when personal life was subject to intense social repression, but now makes little sense, given the way in which contemporary capitalist consumerism fosters free expression of emotion as the be-all and end-all of existence. Fawcett seems to share the view Foucault takes toward free sexual expression, that this alleged end to emotional repression is just as programmed as was expression in more repressive eras.[17]

The character (ghost?) of Lowry argues that "the novel was a great gift to humanity. A democratic invention of enormous intellectual force. It provided a sense of individual complexity to a civilization caught up in class structure—one that wanted to classify people according to who their ancestors were and how much wealth they possessed." The narrator grants this as once true but then replies:

> For the last thirty years there have been bombers flying over each of our heads twenty-four hours a day, each plane loaded to capacity with nuclear weapons, and a certain percentage never more than a few minutes [from detonation]. And I'm expected to confine my artistic investigations to how people feel about their bodies or their disappointments over not getting a better job . . . [The novel] today takes the writer out of his or her moral

imagination . . . and it takes the reader out of social and intellectual structures that lead to change. (163–5U)

This can stand as a mini-manifesto for the alternative kind of novel that is *Cambodia*. In support of postmodernist realism, Fawcett argues that popular writers like Danielle Steele and Robert Ludlum are "surrealists in the literal sense of the word" (28–9U) because they literally avoid the reality of our time.

To make his analysis, the novel breaks most of the laws of fiction, all the laws of objective journalism, and a host of rules about discursive prose. The whole two-level structure immediately challenges the reader's complacency by raising the question of how to read it. Should you read the "footnote" essay first, by itself? Last? Along with the stories, in case it affects your reading of the story-essay material, as footnotes often do? The story-essays likewise include metafictional observations such as the remark in another chapter that it is doomed because it "lacks" an exciting story or other "conventional aspects of narrative" (27U). Or, as Fawcett notes in one chapter, he is offering "no plot, no dialogue and the action [is] frequently off-stage" (45). He is drawing attention to these alleged "lacks," deliberately resisting the thought-crushing onrush of sped-up narrative that has become a defining feature of postmodernity. The novel's subtitle, in contrasting a "book" and "TV," hints at its interest in challenging the multimedia reality fostered by postmodernity.

In one way of reading, the book begins by paralleling two stories thousands of miles apart, one in the United States, the other in Cambodia. The link to US foreign policy is immediately apparent, but the full meaning of that link will become clear only slowly as the book proceeds. The first story-essay on the top recounts the killing by US National Guard troops of four American nonviolent student anti-war demonstrators at Kent State University in 1970. The students were there to protest after the revelation that the US armed forces had been secretly bombing Cambodia, allegedly as a necessary part of the Vietnam War effort. That bombing proved to be a key factor in the rise of the Khmer Rouge regime in Cambodia, a regime that during the 1970s murdered millions of its fellow citizens. That the story of this genocide dominates the lower section of the novel embodies the fact that in the United States those events are treated as a mere footnote to the war on Vietnam, or, as one of its foremost chroniclers puts it, treated as a mere "sideshow."[18] How, the book asks, could the brutal murder of millions be a mere footnote to America's story about itself?

While this question is vital, Fawcett's ultimate target is larger than America's cultivated historical amnesia, or the general populace's widespread indifference to suffering in other countries unless it directly hurts them. He is out to diagnose a form of *global amnesia*. First he has to unspool the story of what happened in Cambodia after the US incursion brought the Khmer Rouge to power. The horrific details of the logic behind the assassinations and mass murder by the Khmer reveal that they were designed to remove all traces of memory of any time before the rise of their regime. They sought in effect to erase their nation's history. And to a brutally effective degree they did so by especially targeting historians, intellectuals, artists, students, Buddhist monks, doctors, journalists, anyone fluent in a foreign language, or who had traveled abroad—in sum, anyone capable of articulating a contrary view to the regime's desire to return to a mythical pre-technological past (71L).

In juxtaposing this true horror story to the impact of electronic media Fawcett is noting that mass media can turn even war and genocidal massacre into just another spectacle alongside a celebrity wedding or a great football goal. As their first major action, the Khmer regime emptied the cities, and sent people to the countryside where they sought to empty the minds of their citizens of anything outside of Khmer ideology. They "began to obliterate the identities of Cambodians in the name of efficiency, simplicity and purity," and Fawcett argues, "I would like you, my readers, to consider that, in a less direct and violent way, the Global Village is doing the same thing to us" (63L).

What at first seems a bizarrely over-the-top analogy is illustrated by both the content and the form of the novel. As a key component of his argument, Fawcett uses this term "Global Village," a term coined by media theorist Marshall McLuhan to describe the impact of television, but which is an even more accurate description of what the internet has made possible. He no doubt likes the term "village" in this context as it echoes with the villages of the decimated Cambodia. But there is something else that is key to that usage. Fawcett is from a small town in British Columbia and he loves villages, loves their quirky local flavor, the differentness of one from another. To him, a global village is an oxymoron, is the opposite of a village. It is the spreading of sameness across the globe. Several of his essays deal with the damaging results of things like the rise of franchise chains which assault our sense of place by making all places seem the same. He remarks in "Universal Chicken" that the franchised planet puts in place an "anti-memory device [that] keeps pounding images into your head that tell you what to buy or what's fashionable. And while it is doing that it wears away your sense of who you are, where you are and where you're going by convincing you that you're just like everyone else and that all places are the same" [58U]. Anyone who has traveled will have had this experience of sitting in a McDonalds or a Starbucks and forgetting exactly which city you are in. What Fawcett might have added is that to compensate for this sameness, the market provides you with a myriad of slightly different brands to allow you to express, or rather to purchase, the "unique you." This is what the great cultural theorist Theodor Adorno called the "freedom to choose what is always the same." Whether you choose Nike or Reebok, Sony or Samsung, McDonald's or Wendy's, indie rock or pop, Netflix or Hulu matters not a whit in the big picture of the consumer paradise we live in.

McLuhan's argument, as repurposed by Fawcett, is about how the nature, not just the content, of electronic media is crucial to demolishing key aspects of human personality and consciousness in ways far subtler, but analogous, to those of the Khmer Rouge murderous campaign of "reeducation." Fawcett is taking up in a serious way the concept that McLuhan put forth through the phrase "the medium is the message." This is the notion that it is less the content of media than its mode of operation, its structural nature that largely determines its impact, quite apart from the intent of media users.

> Complaining about the shallowness of the Global Village, mourning the paradise of the old world, or [refusing to use] the new technological advantages will not make much of a difference . . . to the fate of the planet. . . . What does matter is the degree to which we understand what the Global Village means, how it has created a new Imperium for the post-modern world, and what that Imperium will take away from us if we do not defend ourselves and our planet against it. Why, because . . . Cambodia is the subtext of the Global Village, and that the Global Village has its purest apotheosis yet in Cambodia. (54L)

The attempt by the Khmer Rouge to assassinate anyone capable of remembering or documenting the cultural past of Cambodia are linked for Fawcett to what the "information revolution" is doing to the minds in so-called advanced, developed countries.

Cambodia argues for and represents a "democratic" art that openly connects to real-world representations, and raises serious questions about what mass-mediated reality is doing to our capacity to imagine, remember, and grasp political truth. One of Fawcett's story-essays has Marshall McLuhan debate with the Christian apostle Paul on the road to Damascus.

Paul is portrayed as a bureaucratic administrative genius whose great "revelation" is to imagine a "cybernetwork directly linked to the cosmos and divinity" (49U). Fawcett suggests that when McLuhan named this cybernetwork the Global Village he should have foreseen, as the apostle did, that a corporate takeover of the internet would emerge. The Global Village we now inhabit daily has been largely reduced to a consumerist playground in which the worship of trivia triumphs, and capitalism, becomes, as cultural critic Walter Benjamin phrased it, "a purely cultic religion, perhaps the most extreme that ever existed."[19]

While the book was written when digital media was just emerging, it has become even more relevant in the era of social media, fake news, and the rest of the cyberscapes of the contemporary world. Fawcett anticipated these phenomena at a time when computers were not much more than room-sized business machines. He noted cogently that

> the quality of information produced by electronic systems is totally dependent upon the quality of information originally provided to them, and the quality and intention of the data processing. On the one hand, garbage in garbage out. On the other, the narrower the interpretive conduit and the larger the flow of information, the more absolutely the law of the lowest common denominator applies. (56–7L)

His work was an early warning that garbage data going into a Global Village communication system whose structure allows no critical filtering is a deadly thing, causing citizens to lose historical memory, empathetic imagination, and the human capacity for thoughtful judgment. The medium creates a sameness, an onrush of 0s and 1s that make all scenes, whether of teen love or warfare equivalent, and all arguments equal, regardless of how brilliant or insane they are. Given the increasing amount of terrorism, war, and authoritarianism since the publication of the book, as well as the devastation the climate crisis is bringing, the issues this media onslaught raises are more pressing than ever.

Graphic Trauma: Art Spiegelman's *Maus* (1986)

Like the horrors for Africans that was slavery, the decimation of Indigenous peoples, or the mass murder in Cambodia, the Jewish holocaust has been the subject of postmodernist historicizing. And no postmodern text on this subject has received more praise and more condemnation than Art Spiegelman's graphic novel *Maus* (1980–91; 1986).[20] The success of *Maus* did much to open up the whole terrain of the graphic novel as a more respected and widely read medium where creators like Noelle Stevenson, Allan Moore, Guy Delisle, Marjane Satrapi, Howard Cruse, Alison Bechdel, and many, many others have flourished. But the initial response in some quarters was brutally negative. The condemnation stems in large part from the form of the work, a graphic novel, or comic book as its detractors would call it, one in which Nazis are portrayed as cats and Jews as mice. The very idea of treating so serious a subject using a form then largely associated with adolescent fantasy was seen as heretical by the solemn. But as the subtitle of the work, "A Survivor's Tale: My Father Bleeds History," suggests, this novel form of truth-telling takes history seriously. In fact it enabled a vividly revelatory approach to a topic rendered opaque by numbing layers upon layers of cultural representation in books and film. It also shows, in particular, how historical trauma is enacted within a family, and how the family is at once an agent of history and subsumed by history.

Spiegelman based much of his graphic novel/memoir on taped interviews he made with his father, Vladek, a survivor of the Auschwitz concentration camp. That process of interviewing brought to the surface a family history that is very much larger than the family, but also allowed Art to transform his family trauma into art in a way that, while not healing the wounds of his life experience, transformed the pain into a source of illumination for himself and others.

The postmodern qualities of the text include not only its graphic nature, where text and image sometimes reinforce, sometime contradict one another, but also via the play among the many voices and sources of truth in the text. In metafictional fashion, Art is both a character and the author. He gives up some authorial control to his father's narrative, but he also points out errors of omission, contradictions, and other inconsistencies in Vladek's account, and draws upon other historical sources that work with and against his father's history. His father's account is one kind of history, and has its own truth. But it is not the only truth and its relation to Art's truth, as son, as character, as author, is never resolved into a singular Truth. It is also a book filled with humor, even in the darkest of circumstances, and a plea to downplay heroism as the only way to portray survivors of the Nazi terror.

One of the things a graphic representation can do, and *Maus* does particularly well, is to use another form of language, body language, to disrupt the flat surface of textual language, expressing feelings, thoughts, and ideas that the written text can't do. Perhaps Spiegelman is saying that in the case of the holocaust, especially since bodies were so violated, this additional language is necessary.

In one extraordinary moment, Art interrupts the style of *Maus* with a section from another of his works, "Life in Hell," created years earlier in response to his mother's suicide and done with a markedly different aesthetic. It is as if that trauma was so great as to require its own, different form. And as if Art could not once again write of that trauma but instead chose to include a previous graphic rendering of it. The novel suggests that traumatic wounds are not meant to fully heal over because they are marks of history, marks of the self in time. But with artful reflection, the text shows, we can place trauma into a form that expresses, rather than represses, aspects of the self, and thereby allows us perhaps to learn from (our) history, rather than being condemned to repeat it.

Crude Awakenings: Olivia Laing's *Crudo* (2018)

In a preface to his autofiction, *A Heartbreaking Work of Staggering Genius* (2000), novelist Dave Eggers notes that "Most of what follows is true," and then inverts and satirizes the usual legal disclaimer:

> Any resemblance to persons living or dead should be plainly apparent to them and those who know them, especially if the author has been kind enough to have provided their real names and, in some cases, their phone numbers. All events described herein actually happened, though on occasion the author has taken certain, very small, liberties with chronology, because that is his right as an American.[21]

These disclaimers and the phrase "most of what follows is true" might well serve as the disclaimer for all those works labeled autofiction, works that in the twenty-first century take up an increasing amount of the English-language literary landscape.

Books like Will Self's *Walking to Hollywood* (2010), Maggie Nelson's *The Argonauts* (2015), Michael Chabon's *Moonglow* (2016), several of Ben Lerner's novels, Rachel Cusk's trilogy *Outline, Transit,* and *Kudos,* Michelle Tea's *Black Wave* (2017), Catherine Fatima's *Sludge Utopia* (2018), Sheila

Heti's *Motherhood* (2018), Terese Marie Mailhot's *Heart Berries* (2019), among many others, are building a new wing on the anglophone edifice of this originally francophone construction. And they are joined by prominent twenty-first-century writers in other languages, such as the Swede Karl Ove Knausgaard and the German W. G. Sebald. The new anglophone wave can be understood, in large part, as an attempt to grapple with both the fluidity of the postmodern self and the wider issue of "truth" in an era when "truthiness" and outright lying seem ever-more prominent in public life.

The English-language piece of autofiction that I will focus on is Olivia Laing's *Crudo* (2018).[22] The work is particularly intriguing in the context of this book, in that it is autobiographical, and yet the autobiographical central character is not named Olivia Laing but Kathy Acker, the by then long-dead postmodern novelist/provocateur. *Crudo* seamlessly blends elements of Acker's life and persona with those of Laing in such a way that the two selves cannot be wholly separated. Given Acker's role as literary impersonator, purposefully pla(y)giarizing Cervantes, Dickens, Rimbaud, and many other authors (see Chapter 3), she is an apt choice for Laing to incorporate as her alter-ego in what turns out to be a wild ride through a short period of Laing's life.[23]

Crudo, Laing tell us, was written in "real time," by which she means that she wrote it during and only during the time covered in the novel—roughly seven weeks during the summer of 2017. She wrote every day and allowed herself only minor editing. The term "crudo" refers to fish eaten raw, and it is the power of this rawness, the novelty of the literarily uncooked as it reflects the rush of the postmodern world, that the author bets on with this technique. The novel's metafictional component acknowledges the strangeness of her compositional method:

> Kathy was writing everything down in her notebook, and had become abruptly anxious that she might exhaust the present and find herself out at the front, alone on the crest of time—absurd, but sometimes don't you think we can't all be moving through it together, the whole green simultaneity of life, like sharks abruptly revealed in a breaking wave? (8)

Early parts of the novel capture the overly precious insularity of the writer's privileged upper-middle-class life, with some of the notations too personal to be clear. But as the book evolves, that insularity gives way to ever-greater pressure from the wider world.

The rapid writing process underscores *Crudo*'s uncanny ability to capture the breakneck pace of life in the era of social media and the twenty-four-hour news cycle that constantly bombards anyone with a TV or internet connection. "Kathy" is introduced as author (co-author?) in the first sentence of the book, "Kathy, by which I mean I, was getting married" (1). As one reviewer notes, "Laing as Acker is not a literary device—it is literary detonation. Everything accelerates from there."[24] Laing explained in an interview that she found it impossible to write another kind of book

> because the world was changing too rapidly. Because of Trump, because of Brexit, because of the rise of fascism and the attack on concepts like truth and democracy, I just couldn't write the kind of nonfiction I'd done in the past. To write from a stable point of view meant losing the feeling of chaos and perpetual disruption that was the signature of summer 2017. I needed a perspective that wasn't me, a character that could observe the turbulence in an exaggerated, frenetic, paranoid way. Writing as Kathy, as this hybrid Frankenstein composite of me and Acker, was immediately liberating.[25]

The adoption of Acker's persona, a woman famous not only for impersonating others but also for living her life at a dizzying pace, makes perfect literary sense. It also allows Laing to bounce her own sense of self off the late author's often self-mythologized one in ways that illuminate an era in which inner and outer worlds seem increasingly chaotic. The hope seems to be that Kathy can liberate Laing a bit from her own identity (one of Acker's novels, after all, is entitled *In Memoriam to Identity*) in politically and personally useful ways. Sometimes Acker's words (not set off in quotation mark but acknowledged in endnotes) flow seamlessly in the text's development. At other times, they abruptly disorient that story line. This blurring of boundaries likewise embodies the increasingly intrusive ways in which external realities impinge upon the self in the media-saturated postmodern world. And the external realities of the summer of 2017, as relayed in the novel, are emblematically surreal, mystifying, unbelievable, and frightening.

The novel also represents a moment of major transition in its forty-year-old author's life. In her widely acclaimed works of nonfiction, Laing has portrayed herself as a "typically British," diffident, insecure, self-deprecating person who is nevertheless a restless seeker of new experiences with a reasonably checkered romantic past. But compared to the wild, unpredictable, sexually voracious, crude, and irresponsible Kathy Acker, Olivia Laing is angelic. Laing has made clear she doesn't want readers to attempt to sort out her biographic truth from Acker's, that the character "Kathy" is neither of them or both of them, but more importantly is centrally a vehicle for telling certain truths.

As the novel opens, Kathy is making arrangements to marry a much older man (in "real life" the never-named poet Ian Patterson became Laing's husband during the time covered in the novel). Marriage holds out the terrifying and tantalizing prospect of greater stability in "Kathy's" life. The narrative duality sets up Kathy as a kind of evil, but not unwise, twin. Can Olivia convince her Kathy-self that marriage will not be the end of her independent spirit and creativity, and convince her to be more bold in her approach to life even as she enters what might seem a less adventurous coupled life?

The book's approach also seems implicitly an acting out of, or a demonstration of, the ways that reading fiction can shape and reshape our lives. The central character's doubling of identity would be interesting on its own terms, but what takes the novel into postmodern realist territory is that this internal struggle is intertwined with and interrupted by constant incursions from the wider world of politics and social disruption. The election of Donald Trump, the Brexit referendum, neo-Nazis marching in Virginia, the rise of authoritarianism in other parts of the globe, the ever-increasing threat posed by the climate crisis, nuclear brinksmanship with North Korea, poor people incinerated in the Grenfell Tower disaster, these and other events threaten to overwhelm Kathy's individual problems. As a blurb for the novel on Laing's official website phrases it, "Is it really worth learning to love when the end of the world is nigh? And how do you make art, let alone a life, when one rogue tweet could end it all?"[26]

As best she can, Kathy uses humor—sometimes dark, sometimes light—to try to hold off this onslaught. As a good middle-class woman temporarily ensconced at a vacation resort with the very rich, Olivia/Kathy is deeply irritated by a patrician Brit sitting next to her in the hotel bar. "His name was Henry, she didn't even need to ask, she could just tell." She mutters "Dick" under her breath when he disses the Labor Party, and describes him as looking "like an untrustworthy fox in a Disney film" (12). She can also turn this snarkiness on herself, noting of her upcoming wedding ceremony, for example, that her friends had "doubt that Kathy would be willing to share the spotlight long enough to actually make her vows" (12).

Kathy at the age of forty is newly in love and about to be married for the first time. It was the happiest moment of her life to that point, and yet all those horrendous events that were happening at a distance felt like they were happening in her room.

> How had all this happened? Some sort of gross appetite for action, like the Red Wedding episode only actual and huge. It didn't feel actual, that was the

problem. It felt like it happened inside her computer. She didn't watch the news or listen to the radio, in fact she'd imprisoned the TV inside a cupboard she'd had specially built. If she walked away from her laptop what was there: a garden, birches, that Malcolm XXX man chatting in the queue. Walk back, Armageddon. A bird had landed in the tallest birch. She couldn't make it out with her glasses on, or with them off. 40, not a bad run in the history of human existence but she'd really rather it all kept going, water in the taps, whales in the oceans, fruit and duvets, the whole sumptuous parade, she was into it thanks, she'd like that show to run and run. (48)

Kathy has mashed together anxiety about her own wedding and the horrific one on *Game of Thrones* that entailed mass assassination. But what kind of world is it, the novel asks, when the first analogy that comes to mind for the threatened end of the world by nuclear holocaust is a fictional massacre by knives on a TV show? And what a strange one in which she sees herself as the showrunner of her own life, while momentous events don't feel real but rather feel like they were happening inside her computer.

Of the increasingly obvious climate crisis, she writes "What a waste, what a crime, to wreck a world so abundantly full of different kinds of flowers. Kathy hated it, living at the end of the world, but she couldn't help but find it interesting, watching people, herself included, compulsively foul their nest" (69–70; 18). Is it a writer's perspective on the world that makes her feel like someone who can't not look as they pass an automobile pile-up, or something worse, our collective passivity in the face of a world seemingly spinning out of control?

The novel is set at the pace of life in the privileged postmodern digital realm, moving at the speed of a Twitter feed, with its stream of consciousness mix of her life and Kathy's constantly in danger of flowing off into random meaninglessness. That randomness is dizzying, disorienting and frightening, and finally numbing. Kathy worries that "Numbness mattered, it was what the Nazis did, made people feel like things were moving too fast to stop and though unpleasant and eventually terrifying and appalling, were probably impossible to do anything about" (87). The whole world seems as unstable as cell service on a desert island. *Crudo*'s narration makes us feel how new media have greatly intensified the wider world's intrusion into our private lives.

Knowledge of the world's horrors seem unavoidable but that knowledge is coming in strange forms, with inner and outer worlds collapsing into one another. There is a growing sense of disaster, and yet also unreality, because the era keeps assaulting truth in ever-more deeply disturbing new ways.

Kathy/Laing wakes up one day to learn that the month proposed for her wedding should be enjoyed because "August she read on a site she'd only opened to read a book review: conspiracy theorists say it might be your last month on Earth" (41). Was this possible? Maybe because

> People weren't sane anymore, which didn't mean they were wrong. Some sort of cord between action and consequence had been severed. Things still happened, but not in any sensible order, it was hard to talk about truth because some bits were hidden, the result or maybe the cause, and anyway the space between them was full of misleading data, nonsense and lies. (62)

This struggle between the incursion of a world that seems to be going mad or hurtling toward chaos, and her attempt to lead a good, ethical, maybe even happy, life is what animates the best of *Crudo*. "Each day she sensed something creeping nearer. If it was happening to someone, it being unspeakable violence, how could she be happy: the real question of existence" (112). Does "Kathy" have an answer to this question? Maybe, maybe not. Maybe what the book offers is something of a method for thinking and acting that each of us has to pursue in our own way. Amid its many uncertainties, *Crudo* offers a compelling sense that there is no place to escape from history. The novel makes clear that the dizzying digitally delivered discourses that may be leading us toward disaster must be resisted collectively, that our choices as individuals, privileged or otherwise, will allow our lives to remain personally meaningful only as part of the collective action supported by compelling stories of a better world that is possible but far from guaranteed.

9

Displacements

Exiles, Diasporas, and Returns

The era of postmodernity has seen a massive displacement of people, both internally within nation states and as a time of unprecedented migration. In particular, the various large-scale processes that go under the collective term "globalization," or more properly corporate or neoliberal globalization, have had a profound impact on postmodern life and thereby on postmodern fiction. Dislocations caused by globalization and related political forces have rendered virtually every country on earth more ethnically diverse. Economic changes due to multinational corporate restructuring within nations have likewise caused massive insecurity and movement within countries, a phenomenon sometimes called in-migration. A sense of dislocation and even placelessness has also been driven by new technologies, including the rise of the internet and "cyberspaces" as virtual places to inhabit, as well as sources of knowledge that have disrupted long-standing traditions previously sustained by isolation. And, finally, the growing climate crisis is displacing thousands more each year.

Postmodern authors have represented a variety of approaches to the increasing amount of cross-cultural interaction brought about by the latest phases of globalization. They show the virtues of diversity and the creative interactions of cultures, as well as the reactionary nativist resistance to newcomers. In a typically postmodern way, they refuse the easy binary of melting pot versus bounded ethnic identities. They represent characters who live in the middle ground between a rigid insistence on retaining pure cultural or ethnic identities, and an equally rigid insistence on assimilating cultural differences to sameness. While depicting the dizzying array of cultural patterns and influences available to identity seekers in a postmodern context, they do not simply celebrate or condemn these displacements. They seek instead to present various strategies by which people navigate these complexities through practices tailored to the particularities of individual lives and communities.

Processes of globalization and its attendant dislocations have been represented in fiction in a variety of ways, sometimes directly, more often indirectly. Part of this is the greater global circulation of literatures such that the mutual influence of writers from around the world has intensified. Euro-American realisms, modernisms, and postmodernisms of all sorts have changed and been changed by literary currents flowing from local sites all around the globe. Beyond literary influence, the social conditions of postmodernity brought by globalization have been challenging all narrowly national traditions and the representation of national experience as unique to one place. While this has sometimes encouraged a certain kind of modesty in regard to claims that literature embodies "universal" experiences, it has also recognized the growing impact of cultural imperialism in which Western pop culture, and with it to some extent Western obsession with consumption of cultural and other products, has become more pervasive. (Japan has played a similar cultural imperialist role in relation to the rest of Asia as well, and made some serious inroads into North American culture.) This element of globalization has created a kind of global culture, but the more perceptive among the authors who try to represent this commercialized global culture note that such culture is consumed quite differently in differing national, regional, and social contexts.

In many respects, urban life has been the site of the most intense impact of postmodernity and the displacements it has engendered. Cities have been the site where all the varied forms of postmodern experience have hit most directly, sites where old imagined communities and identities have fallen and new ones have arisen at a staggering rate. This has, of course, been true for centuries but the postmodern era has brought it to a new level of intensity. Multicultural cities like London, Toronto, LA, Sydney, Singapore, New York, Lagos, and Tokyo have been reimagined by postmodern fictionists. Dislocations have occurred both from nation to nation, and within countries. Postmodern urbanization has driven millions of new people from the countryside to cities, mostly dramatically in China, and also in countries all over the globe. Meanwhile rural areas—due to television, the internet, and the arrival of displaced people—have been exposed increasingly to postmodern cultural overload and displacement as well.

Best known as a steam punk writer, China Miéville has been a great chronicler of urban life. His brilliantly rendered novel, *The City and the City* (2009), expresses the essence of postmodern cities as sites where the conflicts of ideology and identity get played out and can serve as a metaphorical embodiment of displacement. The premise of the novel is that two different cities exist in exactly the same geographic space, divided not physically like East and West Berlin were divided, but ideologically and psychologically by learning to "unsee" the other. For both good and ill, postmodern cities entail a good deal of unseeing of the other. They are broken into enclaves where in-migrants, immigrants, and longer-term residents spend much of their time isolated from one another or refusing to engage with each other. But as in *The City and the City*, where this process breaks down and the cities leak into one another, in all postmodern cities unplanned exchanges of experience create interactions that transform all parties.

Cities and the urban novels that represent them enact and reenact encounters across lines of social difference again and again. In Teju Cole's *Open City* (2011), the Nigerian immigrant physician who narrates the novel via wandering along the streets of New York makes visible a host of communities and individuals whom nativists would prefer remain unseen. Likewise for the LA of Karen Yamashita's *Tropic of Orange* (1997), the Toronto of Dionne Brand's *What We All Long For* (2005), the Lagos of Chris Albani's *GraceLand* (2004), the Johannesburg of Lauren Beuke's *Zoo City* (2010), the London of Zadie Smith's *White Teeth* (2000) or Bernardine Evaristo's *Girl, Woman, Other* (2019), or the Sidney of Michelle de Kretser's *Questions of Travel* (2013), among many, many other cities given postmodern literary embodiment.

Increasingly in the twenty-first century, precarious economic and environmental conditions have led to greater amounts of migration both between and within countries, most often in search of employment or a more livable climate, a process that has also fueled nativist politicians seeking to deflect blame for neoliberal austerity by enflaming anti-immigrant sentiment. It is important to realize, however, that for many people dislocations began long before the postmodern era. With that in mind, let's look at the ongoing impact of a dislocation that, while decidedly postmodern in form, began 500 years ago.

Foreigners in Their Own Land: Tommy Orange's *There There* (2018)

For Native people of the Americas, the displacements of globalization began in 1492 and have never ceased. In that sense, displacements on to and off of Native reservations and First Nations reserves in the postmodern era are new only in kind and degree. The devastation and displacements over the 500 years of the European colonial era have been resisted at every stage, and the postmodern era has seen both increased displacement and increased resistance. Literature has played a significant role in that resistance.

As devastating as the reserve/reservation system has been for Native North Americans, and similar restrictions for Aboriginal Australians and Indigenous South Americans, the alternative, relocation to urban areas, has often been a worse form of displacement. Urban Indians have long been a part of Native literature in works by Janet Campbell Hale, James Welch, Sherman Alexie, Leslie Marmon Silko, and Louise Erdrich, among others. But this body of work has often been less acknowledged or celebrated than reservation-based fictions. However, the first two decades of the twenty-first century have seen a growing body of fiction dealing with the lives of urban Indians including works like Erika Wurth's *Crazy Horse's Girlfriend* (2014), Chip Livingston's *Owls Don't Have to Mean Death* (2017), Theodore Van Alst, Jr's *Sacred Smokes* (2018), and many others representing the Indigenous presence in cities.

The most celebrated of these works is no doubt Tommy Orange's *There There* (2018), which offers a kaleidoscopic view of Native life in the city of Oakland, California.[1] Orange writes, "Getting us to cities was supposed to be the final, necessary step in our assimilation, absorption, erasure, the culmination of a five-hundred-year-old genocidal campaign. But the city made us new and we made it ours" (8).[2] The novel includes twelve main characters each of whom has a series of chapters to themselves. What at first appear to be random individual stories slowly begin to connect as the novel progresses, till eventually all the characters arrive in the same place, geographically if not emotionally. The characters are all Native, but represent different amounts of, and relation to, Indian ancestry, and vary in gender, age, economic status, and a variety of other points of social difference. The stories are told in first person, third person, and even in a rare second-person narration, and are told in flashbacks, flashforwards, and in varying order, all of which underscores the sense of unsettledness, constant displacement that pervades the lives of all the characters. There is much humor mixed with the often tragic story lines, as when, for example, a character muses that his sisters' Aqua Net hairspray impacted the ozone enough to bring about the apocalypse of climate change predicted in Revelations, or when a narrator wonders was it "entropy, or was it atrophy or was it apathy" that was bringing on the crisis (213).

All the characters must deal with the feeling that they are "foreigners in their own land" (52), as Orange phrases it, while also being questioned as to their authentic "Indianness." The novel is filled with families and individuals that are broken, rebuilt, and broken again. The novel plays with the metaphor of the spider's web, a web that can be either a trap or a source of nourishment depending on who gets to play the spider, and who the prey. The search for a stable, or at least a life-sustaining, identity is at the heart of each character's portrait. Survival requires some kind of core knowledge of one's place in the world, and such places are extremely difficult to find. "Indianness," for all its connection to a deeply tragic history imprinted onto each character's life, proves, nevertheless, to be for most of them at the root of finding that stable grounding. Reservation/reserve contexts may not always provide an easy continuity of identity or a passing on of tradition, but the sources for urban Indians are far fewer, culturally thinner, and more ambivalently offered. *There There* shows brilliantly that Native folks off the rez have to improvise their lives to a great degree, but that Indigenous identity, however imperfectly embodied or represented, or denigrated by the white majority culture, can often be the key lifeline.

There are metafictional elements in the text, but they are largely unobtrusive. Two of the characters seem as though they could be authorial voices, one a Native kid seeking a grant to make a movie based on relatively random interviews with Oakland Natives (interviews which may or may not be the chapters of the book), the other a would-be writer who seems blocked by self-consciousness. The latter, a character named Edwin Black, listens to

A Tribe Called Quest, a First Nations group based in Ottawa who make electronic music with samples from powwow drum groups, and then notes:

> It's the most modern, or most postmodern, form of Indigenous music I've heard. . . . The problem with Indigenous art in general is that it's stuck in the past. The . . . double-bind . . . is this: If it isn't pulling from tradition, how is it Indigenous? And if it is stuck in tradition, in the past, how can it be relevant to other Indigenous people living now? (77)

There There is a work of art that answers this question in multiple ways. The burdens of history and the power of tradition bang up against the internet-driven present on every page.

While no character's evolution can be called typical, and each of the main twelve characters takes a different route, the development of Native identity in the character Orvil Red Feather contains many of the common elements. After the death of his mother and disappearance of his grandmother, Orvil is raised by a great aunt who studiously avoids talking about his Indigenous roots. Perhaps because it was implicitly forbidden, as a teen Orvil develops a deep interest in everything Indian, eventually finding dance regalia in his aunt's closet, and learning powwow dancing from some YouTube videos. The novel is pervaded by digital culture, with several of the characters finding resources there to build their identities, connect with distant family, and learn some history. It is also the source of much danger, including a digital 3D printer that brings tragedy. More than that, cyberspace is where many Natives now reside: "Plenty of us are urban [Indians] now. If not because we live in cities, then because we live on the internet" (9).

Orvil's missing grandmother turns out to be Jacquie Red Feather, a woman whose displacement includes being driven from Oakland by the haunting grief of not being able to save her daughter from self-destruction. Suicide rates among Natives are astronomical, at least three times the rate for non-Natives. Jacquie, a recovering substance abuser who is now an abuse counselor, attends a conference of Native health workers where an older Native man delivers a devastating critique of efforts to deal with this issue.

> Kids are jumping out of the windows of burning buildings . . . [a]nd we think the problem is that they are jumping . . . . Convince them that burning alive is better than leaving when the shit gets too hot for them to take . . . . They're making the decision that it's better to be dead and gone than be alive in what we have here, this life, the one we made for them, the one they've inherited. How do we instill in our children the will to live? . . . [T]here has to be an urgency, a do-whatever-at-any-cost . . . spirit behind what we do. (104–5)

When someone uses the phrase "drunken white guy" it is about a single drunken white guy. But when someone uses the phrase "drunken Indian" it covers a whole community, a community under the weight of a stereotype. As the novel points out, the idea of a biological predisposition of "Indians" for alcoholism is a long-standing, now debunked, myth. But there is in fact a key correlation that does explain much alcoholism—poverty. Every poor community—white, black, yellow, brown, red (to use the standard misnomers)—has a much higher level of alcohol and substance abuse rate than wealthier communities of the same mislabeled pigmentation. And Natives are by far the poorest communities in North America. Jacquie's fight against her addictions is emblematic of many such struggles in the novel and outside of it that seek to get beyond portrayals of passive victimhood.

Another Native character, Blue, is adopted and raised by wealthy whites in the affluent Berkeley Hills district above Oakland. Because of the cultural context in which she is raised, she feels white inside,

> I knew I wasn't white. But not all the way. Because while my hair is dark and my skin is brown, when I look in the mirror I see myself from the inside out. And inside I feel as white as the long pill-shaped pillow my mom always made me keep in my bed. . . . So I grew up with money, a pool in the back, an overbearing mother and an absent father. I brought home outdated racist insults from school like it was the 1950s. All Mexican slurs, of course, since people where I grew up don't know Natives still exist. (197–9)

In a kind of recapitulation of the history of race as a concept, racism *creates* her racial identity. The casual racism endemic to her school and community shapes her sense of self, despite the privileges accorded by her economic status. From her eighteenth birthday, when she is told the name of her birth mother, Blue too begins a process of becoming Indian. As an adult, her privileged background is of little help in fending off the spousal abuse she encounters, a fact that allows the novel to raise the horrendous issue not only of domestic abuse but also of the several thousand "missing and murdered" Native women in Canada, the United States, and Mexico, a staggering phenomenon that remains largely ignored by mainstream political institutions.[3] After many years of struggle, Blue shakily finds her identity and ends up being the head of the Powwow committee.

Thomas Frank is a character who seemed to have been born sad and had sadness reinforced by a hundred life events, including the confusion of being half white, half Native. Thomas had a white evangelical Christian mom and a "100% Indian" dad, one parent each representing a "people who took and took and took," the other the "people taken" (216). By the time of their divorce, his mom is calling his father's spirituality "demonic." Eventually, Thomas finds something in a Native drum circle that transforms him: "Old songs that sang to the old sadness . . . . This is what it sounded like to make it through those hundreds of American years, to sing through them. This was the sound of pain forgetting itself in song" (212).

All of the richly varied portraits of contemporary urban Natives drive incessantly toward the moment of communal celebration that is the powwow. Powwows are a relatively recently invented "tradition" that mixes tribal histories, the "authentic" and "fake" and authentically fake, the stereotypically invented and the creatively contrary, commerce and community, all for the benefit of "full bloods," "half-bloods," and all lesser "blood quantum" folks from tribal lands and cities all over North America. The fractioning of identity known as "blood quantum" perfectly expresses the dilemma of Indigenous identity. Blood quantum was invented as part of a genocidal federal policy (aptly named Termination) that, alongside Relocation (the stealing of Native kids from their parents in the United States, Canada, and Australia, and the decimation of reservations and reserves) hoped to eliminate "Indians" altogether over several generations of intermarriage with "civilized" (i.e., white) people.[4] Yet, as it evolved in the United States, blood quantum became the sole measure of who might gain the status of an enrolled member of a tribe, and through which only certain Indigenous communities were eligible for the meager, but often life-sustaining, benefits provided by the US government. Those outside the quantum circle had to fight to achieve their identity. And as they fight against this long history of redefining and displacing Natives out of existence, most of the characters in the novel have made parts of the city home. But now they must face yet another new threat of displacement, increasing gentrification by white hipsters and wealthy professionals who are slicing away chunks of their hard-won bits of "Indian country" in Oakland, a process replicated in many cities with significant urban US Native populations like Denver, Chicago, and Minneapolis.

The powwow as a culminating event is foreshadowed throughout the novel, as each character develops some role in or makes plans to attend it:

We all came to the Big Oakland Powwow for different reasons. The messy, dangling threads of our lives got pulled into a braid—tied to the back of everything we'd been doing all along to get us here. We've been coming from miles. And we've been coming for years, generations, lifetimes, layered in prayer and handwoven regalia, beaded and sewn together, feathered, braided, blessed, and cursed. (135)

Despite all the foreshadowing, it can be said of the ending that no one gets what they expect.

In a sense, everything about *There There* is there in the title. The title is on one level a reference to a famous comment by modernist/proto-postmodernist author Gertrude Stein. She wrote of her former home, Oakland, that "there is no there there." The remark is often taken as a put down of provincial Oakland in contrast to Stein's cosmopolitan adopted home of Paris, or perhaps in relation to its more glamorous neighboring city, San Francisco. But as one narrator of *There There* notes, this reading is only possible out of context. In context, Stein is regretting that the city had changed so much since her youth (38–9). This latter interpretation ties into the attempt in the novel by the various characters to make even the poorest parts of the Oakland their home. Resistance to so many displacements has led to a search for the home ground, and a desire to fend off the city's gentrification, that is also a search for the kind of comfort carried in the calming words "there, there." But "there there" are weak words delivered to generations caught in an ongoing genocidal process. The possibilities for better futures for the kind of urban Natives portrayed in the novel are deeply fraught, but *There There* refuses despair and offers not only glimmers of hope but also models of how such a better future might be built.

Migrant Doors of Reception: Mohsin Hamid's *Exit West* (2017)

There are at least seventy million refugees in the world today, and thousands more are forced into exile every day. The causes—war, terrorism, political repression, poverty, climate change—may vary, but the experience of being driven forcibly from one's homeland to start life anew in a strange land is often remarkably similar whether the refugee be from eastern Europe, Middle East, Africa, Pacific Islands, Asia, or Latin America. The displacement of global populations has transformed a number of major cities into unprecedently culturally diverse places. Depending on a number of factors, but especially class and ethnicity, these spaces have proven to be more or less hospitable to newcomers. But over the last decade, the rise of ethno-nationalisms in many countries means that greater and greater hostility has come down upon folks in the places they chose as a sanctuary.[5]

No single work, or even set of works, can encompass these massive processes. Each route on the map of migration has particular perils and possibilities that postmodern realist writers have sought to capture. The vicious real and symbolic battles on the US-Mexico border, for example, have been chronicled in brilliant novels like Valeria Luiselli's *Lost Children Archive* (2019). Luiselli, who has worked as a translator and volunteer court reporter for Latin American migrants, brings this experience in her nonfiction work, *Tell Me How It Ends* (2017). Written in the form of answers the forty questions she asked migrant children as she interviewed them to help with their entry forms, it concludes that "It is perhaps not the American Dream they pursue, but rather the more modest aspiration to wake up from the nightmare into which they were born." *The Lost Children Archive* as a novel deepens themes treated in her nonfiction, using a variety of formal elements to capture the many facets of the personal and larger political dimensions of the crisis. This includes a metafictional component that raises key questions about the ethics of representing such vulnerable people. Similar works treat the increasing border wars in Europe.

Mohsin Hamid's *Exit West* (2017) is among the most intriguing novels written about the vast sweep and complexity of postmodern migration as it tries to capture certain truths virtually all immigrants face.[6] Using the magical realist device of doors that automatically transport a person hundreds or thousands of miles away from where they enter, *Exit West* makes clear that the existence of multiple realities is not science fiction but a fact people experience every day. For migrants, the theory of the multiverse is a fact of their lives. The doors represent both the migration process and the magic carpet that is the internet. Multiple realities are virtually formed by the new technologies that allow access to so many other spaces around the globe. One character, a young man in Tokyo, muses that his fondness for Irish whisky might stem from the feeling that "Ireland was the Shikoku of a parallel universe" (29). Parallel universes might well have been the title of the novel, because these universes are all here, now, and the doors suggest what it feels like to leap into a new one, both via the imagination and through physical relocation. Throughout the novel place names are often absent, a device that allows for a greater sense of the generalization of experience across locations, but that also forces the reader to experience the sense of dislocation of migration.

Exit West captures the interrelated desires for a homeland, a romantic relationship, family, and selfhood, with the necessities of survival in deeply hostile conditions. It seeks to break down the image of Middle Easterners as either captives of insane regimes or refugees, seen only as poor, desperate, and limited to basic survival. Instead it gives a rich set of portraits across classes and age groups, and humanizes all by showing their everyday lives full of food, sex, the internet, prayer, avoidance of prayer, political argument, and avoidance of argument, while their lives are radically transformed by the utter disruption that is forced exile.

We meet the two main protagonists, Nadia, a deeply sensual and independent young woman, and Saeed, her more conservative and religious boyfriend, living in a large city in an unnamed Middle Eastern country. Nadia is a rebellious young woman estranged from her family. Saeed, who works in an ad agency, is the son of a professor father and a former schoolteacher mother. That two people coming from fairly privileged backgrounds face the hardships detailed in the novel, can suggest the far worse issues facing those with fewer resources.

As the novel begins, the city's life is interrupted only by the occasional rat-a-tat of automatic weapons in the distance. But soon the city is thrown into an increasingly dangerous civil war. Nevertheless, the initial meeting of Nadia and Saeed has an almost rom-com ordinariness to it (emphasizing ordinariness in extraordinary conditions is one of the novel's themes) as they sit together in a college class whose topic is corporate identity and product branding. Nadia wears a veil to ward off predatory males, but Saeed misreads its cultural meaning and assumes she is a religious traditionalist. In light of this, he gets the first of many shocks regarding her nature when she rides off on a motorcycle after gently turning down his offer to go for coffee.

Back at his job in an advertising agency, Saeed is unable to get Nadia out of his mind. The story then abruptly shifts to an upper-middle-class house in Sydney, Australia. One room of the otherwise sunlit home has a "closet doorway that was dark, darker than night, a complete darkness—the heart of darkness" (8). Out of that darkness steps a dark-skinned man with wooly hair. He gently sidesteps the bed of a sleeping woman and exits out a window. We then return to Saeed shopping for dinner, and soon we hear of his second encounter with Nadia. Saeed, still curious about what seems to be her contradictory cultural role, asks why since she has said she doesn't pray, does she wear the long black robes of a devout woman. "So that men don't fuck with me," she replies, with a smile (17). The remark is another of the many aimed at shooting down the West's stereotypical notions about women raised in traditional Muslim countries.

After their initial meetings at school, the relationship between Saeed and Nadia develops much of its early energy online, an environment of great importance in a country so full of restrictions on movement. The doors of the internet opened in a million places, and in that one place of intimacy they were building together.

Nadia and Saeed's courtship is cut short as random violence gives way to an all-out civil war in their city. Like many others, they feel they must leave their homeland behind. They are driven to choose exile as represented by those seemingly magical doors. The doors lead to a variety of other places on the planet, but as is true for most refugees, those passing through cannot know their ultimate destination. This device allows readers to understand the precarious choices refugees with few financial resources are left with. They must dive into the unknown, with little-or-no knowledge of where they will land and what reception they will receive. Like refugees themselves, the text journeys in seemingly endless, relentless movement as hopes rise and fall, possibilities open and are slammed shut. "[W]hen we migrate, we murder from our lives those we leave behind" (98). Migration is all about the crossing of borders, but geographic borders are at most the symbol of a rather more important crossing, from wealth to poverty, sacred to secular, homeland to strange land, family to network. Borders of sex/gender, ethnic identity, religions, and many more are also crossed in complicated ways.

We are given the visceral details of the city's descent into a civil war fought intimately on the streets, in the schools, in the shops that days before had been a neighborhood. Feelings that would be called paranoid if they were not fully justified by circumstance begin to shape the life of the city. Battle lines are murky, enemies may have become friends, friends enemies. Food grows scarce, and in lines for goods Nadia experiences random acts of sexual violation. Normalcy dies quickly. Windows, as openings onto the wider world, become problematic as bullets fly: "One's relationship to windows now changed. A window was a border through which death was . . . most likely to come" (71). Soon rumors of magic doors begin to be heard (72), changing perception of another everyday aperture. The novel tells of Nadia's experience of facing her first such door: "drawing close she was struck by its darkness, its opacity, the way it did not reveal what was on the other side, and also did not reflect what was on this side, and so felt equally like a beginning and an end" (103).

When the two get the courage to enter, this first leads to a refugee camp on one of the Greek islands, representative of many such overcrowded way stations between homeland and a hoped for new home, and ironically a place filled with wealthy tourists in the summer but now covered

with hundreds of tents and lean-tos and people of many colors and hues—
many colors and hues mostly falling in within a band of brown that ranged
from dark chocolate to milky tea . . . [people] speaking in a cacophony that
was the languages of the world, what one might hear if one were a
communications satellite, or a spymaster tapping into a fiber-optic cable. . . .
In this group, everyone was foreign, so, in a sense, no one was. (106)

Over the weeks they are stranded there, their money running out, they enter
into the desperation felt by so many others around them. In the overcrowded
tent city they find that the "doors to richer destinations were heavily guarded,
but the doors in from poorer countries, were mostly left unsecured, perhaps
in the hope that people would go back to where they came from—although
almost no one ever did—or perhaps because there were simply too many
doors from too many poorer places to guard them all" (106).

From the island camp, the text suddenly shifts again, to an unnamed
young woman in Vienna who wears a number of badges signaling her
support for various marginalized groups, including immigrants. This woman
sets off to help form a "human cordon" to shield migrants at an anti-migrant
rally. She finds herself on a train surrounded by male countrymen "who
looked like her brothers and her cousins and her father and her uncles,
except that they were angry, they were furious" at her support for foreigners.
The woman feels "animal fear, terror, and thought anything could happen."
This domestic terror moment putatively aimed at terrorists from abroad was
provoked by "militants" from Nadia and Saeed's homeland who, by attacking
Viennese citizens, had "hoped to provoke a reaction against migrants from
their part of the world," a reaction they hoped would drive them at least back
home if not into the militant's ideological camp. Such, the novel shows us, is
the cycle of terrorisms fueling terrorisms (109–10).

A seemingly more promising door leads Nadia from desolation to a
beautiful house with a fine bathroom where the towels are "so plush and fine
that when she emerged she felt like a princess using them, or at least like the
daughter of a dictator who was willing to kill without mercy in order for his
children to pamper themselves with cotton such as this" (125). These kinds
of juxtapositions occur throughout the novel in ways that give a deeply
visceral sense of the contrast between seemingly safe worlds and the worlds
of pain created by authoritarians, wars, terrorism, ethnic cleansing, and
climate change.

In one vignette, London in the near future is described as two cities, one
bathed in light, the other electricity-starved and dark. In the latter the
common tongues are various Englishes that have evolved in the migrants'

various respective homelands. Partly because they have a better command of English, in "dark London" Saeed and Nadia begin to drift apart as he desires the comfort of his countrypersons, while she enjoys the freedom of being among those who do not share her history. The two come to embody the choice faced by all migrants—how far to move away from one's origins toward the new.

Housed as squatters, Saeed and Nadia feel the growing presence around them of nativists and a government bent on destroying their dark city. Finally, violence breaks out, the army destroying a church in which hundreds of people, mostly children, are killed. The migrants are terrified that this is the beginning of a massive massacre. But something else happens, the government forces and the nativist gangs draw back, the crisis is averted, perhaps because in destroying the church the self-destructive nature of targeting others was revealed (166).

In the wake of a near massacre, a plan is put in place to let the migrants work to build a "halo city" on the outskirts, laboring to earn their "forty meters and a pipe," a minimal living space and access to utilities (170). While echoing the "forty acres and a mule" given to slaves at the end of the American Civil War, the gesture is not portrayed cynically. Saeed and Nadia come to enjoy the hard labor of building this new ex-urb, and the novel shows their intense relief. Partly because they feel themselves continuing to grow further apart, they decide to once more pass through one of those "jet-black" doors. I will leave unspoiled the story of their final adventure, in Northern California.

Nadia and Saeed are the only characters given names, as if all the others who emerge in a variety of interspersed vignettes—Nigerians, Somalis, Guatemalans, Indonesians, a family from "the borderland between Myanmar and Thailand," and many more—are, like the refugees on our TV and computer screens, nameless. The novel's balance of beauty and brutality, imagination and limitation, the personal and the universal gives a face, a mind, a body, and five senses to the statistical facts of migrant life. While the conditions portrayed are often bleak and always painfully disruptive, even for those who "make it" to relatively safer spaces, the novel is one of hope. The quietly luminous beauty of the prose, the everyday bravery of those facing inhuman conditions, and the presence of characters who welcome newcomers make clear that it is still possible to pull back from an all-out war on migrants.

There is a steady, calm tone to the prose, even when describing deeply troubling events. It is as if the entire novel is trying to turn down the heat of the current deeply divisive political moment. In setting the text in the near future, it even seeks to prepare us for the strong likelihood that worse is yet to come due not only to the weakening of democracy but also due to the pressures of ecological collapse. In "places both near and far, the apocalypse appeared to have arrived and yet it was not apocalyptic . . . life went on, people found ways to be and people to be with, and plausible desirable futures began to emerge, unimaginable previously but not unimaginable now" (217). Imagining a plausible future for a world in the midst of massively disruptive transformation is a great gift to the present.

An Epidemic of Displacements: Rabih Alamenddine's *Koolaids: The Art of War* (1998)

In his novel *Koolaids: The Art of War* (1998), Rabih Alamenddine turns his experiences during the Lebanese civil war of the 1970s and the "war" on gay men in San Francisco during the rise of the HIV/AIDS epidemic in the 1980s and 1990s into a complex meditation on exile, death, and transcendence.[7] *Koolaids* is composed of numerous kinds of discourses, including diary entries, letters, news articles, dreams, mini-plays, imaginary conversations with philosophers and media celebrities, and a variety of other forms that are seldom clearly demarcated. The narrative makes split-second unmarked, often initially imperceptible and disorienting, switches of time and place, underscoring the merging of memory and the present in a story of a war against a double geo-cultural displacement.

Alamenddine carefully delineates the difficult choices, the constraints, as well as the possibilities, entailed by place-based and displaced identities in a postmodern context. The story juxtaposes, for example, the impact of the civil war upon a closeted gay man in Lebanon whose neighbors and clients all tacitly acknowledge and tolerate his sexuality, to the lives of openly gay men in San Francisco who, during the rise of the AIDS epidemic, are warred upon by every institution and many of the closest people in their lives. The multifaceted flows of culture are always experienced from specific locations by people with differing resources—educational, economic, sociopolitical, and cultural. But the constant threat of death, whether from bombs or a virulent virus, forces the characters to memorialize moments in isolated fragments because there is no guarantee of living to the end of any linear narrative. One of the characters approvingly quotes postmodern fictionist Italo Calvino, "Long novels written today are perhaps a contradiction: the dimension of time has been shattered, we cannot love or think except in fragments of time each of which goes off along its own trajectory and immediately disappears" (4). Alamenddine, like one of the central characters in the novel, is also a painter. And like other postmodern works, narrative arc is largely replaced by a fragmented montage of images.

Koolaids begins with a slight revision of the New Testament's "Book of Revelations":

The four horsemen approach.
The rider on the red horse says, "This good and faithful servant is ready. He knoweth war."
The rider on the black horse says, "This good and faithful servant is ready. He knoweth plague."
The rider on the pale horse says, "This good and faithful servant is ready. He knoweth death."
The rider on the white horse says, "Fuck this good and faithful servant. He is a non-Christian homosexual, for God's sake. You brought me all this way out here for a fucking fag, a heathen. I didn't die for this dingbat's sins." (1)

This biblical re-write announces the four deadly themes of the novel—war, plague, death, and homophobia—while also setting up what might be called the deadly serious humor the author uses to deal with these issues.

The text is full of beautiful, striking imagery as it offers many answers to the question of what healthy love looks like in the face of an epidemic of ill-health, violence, and persecution. The title plays ironically on the sickly sweet soft drink Kool-Aid, linking it to the decidedly *uncool* fact that AIDS is devastating its community, but also hinting at the various ways in which the colorful but nutritionally empty sweetness of the drink is as deceptive as the glossy lives promised by the postmodern mass media. The phrase "drinking the Kool-Aid" has entered the American vernacular in light of the mass suicide in 1978 of cult leader Jim Jones and over 900 of his followers who poisoned themselves using that drink. The phrase has come to mean anyone willing to die for an illusory belief. In the context of the novel, the phrase resonates in several different ways. In the context of the Lebanese civil war, the illusion that thousands died for was religious and political. In the context of the AIDS crisis, the illusion was heteronormativity, the belief that only one kind of sexual practice was "natural" and therefore that the virus that initially arose primarily in the gay male community was a sign of God's vengeance.

And then there is that other illusion: "The need for a belief in the nonfinality of death is so great it affects even usually logical people" (120).

HIV/AIDS is a postmodern disease, not only in the sense that it arose during the postmodern era, but more to the point of this book—it was analyzed through postmodernist discourses regarding the social construction of a medical phenomenon. As cultural critic Paula Treichler phrased it, the disease led initially to "an epidemic of signification" targeting gay men.[8] That discursive epidemic had to be resisted politically. The novel mentions a character who was a co-founder of AIDS Coalition to Unleash power (ACT UP) San Francisco, one branch of the activist group that did the most to challenge the epidemic and the epidemic of discursive distortion that accompanied it. The ACT UP worked tirelessly to redefine the disease, pushing for more research into its causes and possible cures, and to challenge every institution—medical, political, legal—that was failing to address the crisis. This character is described as an angry young man whose anger kept him alive (27). Anger and love were the two components of ACT UP that allowed it to flourish and accomplish its work. Love and rage also drive this remarkable novel.

Exiled to Home: Chimamanda Ngozi Adichie's *Americanah* (2013)

Novelists from various African countries have had to take on the work of undoing the representation of an entire continent inhabited by millions of individuals as nothing more than a ubiquitous image of a starving child swarmed by flies. The task of undoing stereotypes of Africans has been undertaken now by several generations of writers, but clearly there is still more work to be done. Kenyan author Binyavanga Wainana offered these tongue-in-cheek tips for contemporary Western writers writing about Africa:

> Never have a picture of a well-adjusted African on the cover of your book, or in it, unless that African has won the Nobel Prize. An AK-47, prominent ribs, naked breasts: use these. If you must include an African, make sure you get one in Masai or Zulu or Dogon dress.
>
> In your text, treat Africa as if it were one country. It is hot and dusty with rolling grasslands and huge herds of animals and tall, thin people who are starving. Or it is hot and steamy with very short people who eat primates. Don't get bogged down with precise descriptions. Africa is big: fifty-four

countries, 900 million people who are too busy starving and dying and warring and emigrating to read your book.[9]

The work of undoing these kinds of simplistic Western images has been going on for several decades now, going back at least to the work of Chinua Achebe in the 1950s and including key figures like Buchi Emecheta, Wole Soyinka, Ben Okri, Zakes Mda, and Bessie Head, among many others. This task of complicating this portrait of the various peoples of Africa is now in the hands of a gifted group of twenty-first-century postmodern realist authors writing in English like Nigerian-Americans Teju Cole and Chris Albani, Zimbabwean Petina Gappah, South Africans Achmat Dangor and Lauren Beukes, Liberian Hawa Jande Golokai, among others.

These and many other writers from a range of African countries draw upon postmodernist style to explore postcolonial themes in their home countries but also turn a postcolonial gaze upon conditions and social patterns in the Global North. The work I want to feature here, Chimamanda Ngozi Adichie's novel *Americanah* (2013), represents this dual vision via an epic journey across several decades and three continents.[10] The novel addresses both exile from and return to Africa (Nigeria, in this case), along the way offering a brilliant dissection of social relations in the so-called overdeveloped world of the United States and the United Kingdom. Like many postmodern novels, *Americanah* eschews a linear plot line for a more amorphous, baggy monster of flashback and flashforward stories about experiences and reflections upon experiences of exile and return. With regard to the latter, the novel is an example of a growing body of literature that includes not just emigration but *re-immigration* back to the homeland.

The first thing we learn about the central character in the novel, other than her name, Ifemelu, is that she is living in the university town of Princeton, New Jersey, where she authors an anonymous blog entitled "*Raceteenth or Various Observations About American Blacks (Those Formerly Known as Negroes) by a Non-American Black*" (italics in original). In the novel, the blog excerpts allow for the kind of direct social commentary eschewed by modernists, and proves to be a devastatingly hilarious metafictional device for skewering American race relations and many other aspects of life in what seems to an outsider a most peculiar country. The blog uses the familiar literary trope of the outside observer in a foreign context to defamiliarize taken-for-granted norms and assumptions of the locals. Ifemelu remarks in one post, for example, that "In America tribalism is alive and well. There are four kinds—class, ideology, religion and race" (184). The subsequent analysis is astute, but the choice of words to introduce it is even more subversive. While "tribalism" is a term used by US journalists, the term has a very different resonance when offered by a Nigerian in a context where many in the Global North continue to picture Africa as a primitive tribalistic world. American tribalism is of the kind that enables a total lack of interest in, or knowledge of, the rest of the world, and allows an American president to refer to places like the author's native land as "shithole countries."

Ifemelu critiques aspects of both US and Nigerian culture, and at times this extends to an equally devastating self-critique. She begins to see her life as little more than fodder for her blog, and she feels increasingly "naked and false," experiencing "cement in her soul," a "borderlessness" and a sense of amorphous discontent, despite outward success in the United States. Those feelings "over a period of months melded into a piercing homesickness" (6–7). This homesickness is soon revealed to include a rekindled desire for her first love, Obinze, who, after being exiled in the UK, is back in Nigeria, is married, has a child, and has become wealthy. We later learn that Ifemelu emigrated to the United States to attend university and evade increasingly authoritarian conditions of military rule in Nigeria. The novel is remarkable for, among many other things, the detailed ways in which it explodes the simple mantra of race, class, and gender as social categories. Each of these social categories is complicated by individual life histories that make it clear that, however shaped by larger forces, people can learn, with luck and self-reflection, to think and act to transform those conditions.

The novel demonstrates, for example, how the idea of "race" is quite differently constructed in the United States and the United Kingdom, and how in Nigeria ethnicity largely trumps race but is deeply entangled with class. Just as in the United States and the United Kingdom white people often think of themselves as the raceless norm, so too in her majority black country Ifemelu had no reason to think of herself as black. The novel is exquisitely attuned to the ways in which class does and sometimes does not matter to the recognition of race and the experience of racisms in the West. Also, it smartly depicts the effects of varying degrees of racial awareness on those who are targeted by racism:

> If you're telling a non-black person about something racist that happened to you, make sure you are not bitter. Don't complain. Be forgiving. If possible, make it funny. Most of all, do not be angry. Black people are not supposed to be angry about racism. Otherwise you get no sympathy. This applies only for white liberals, by the way. Don't even bother telling a white conservative

about anything racist that happened to you. Because the conservative will tell you that YOU are the real racist and your mouth will hang open in confusion.

This kind of situation leads Ifemelu at one point to muse that "Maybe it's time to just scrap the word 'racist.' Find something new. Like Racial Disorder Syndrome. And we could have different categories for sufferers of this syndrome: mild, medium, and acute" (315).

Often it is liberal Americans who bear the brunt of Ifemlu's caustic commentary, despite good intentions and their halfway understanding of her situation. After some time in the United States, she enters into an affair with a white man, a situation that initially makes her life easier. But soon she realizes that comfort and relationship are illusory.

> When you are black in America and you fall in love with a white person, race doesn't matter when you're alone together because it's just you and your love. But the minute you step outside, race matters. . . . We don't even tell our white partners the small things that piss us off and the things we wish they understood better, because we're worried they will say we're overreacting, or we're being too sensitive. And we don't want them to say, Look how far we've come, just forty years ago it would have been illegal for us to even be a couple blah blah blah, because you know what we're thinking when they say that? We're thinking why the fuck should it ever have been illegal anyway? But we don't say any of this stuff. We let it pile up inside our heads and when we come to nice liberal dinners . . . we say that race doesn't matter because that's what we're supposed to say, to keep our nice liberal friends comfortable. (359)

An equal opportunity observer, *Americanah*'s narrator captures the racisms (or Racial Disorder Syndromes), income inequality, and fear of immigrants in the United Kingdom and the United States, while also providing a devastating critique of the class and gender politics of her Nigerian homeland.

While the novel deals more fully with middle and upper-middle-class Americans and Nigerians, it also gives some sense of what life is like for those with lower and higher social status. Wealthy Americans, black and white, and wealthy Nigerians are skewered mercilessly, while Ifemelu learns over time to understand and undercut some of her own class privilege. The novel makes clear in several plot lines that the acquisition of wealth and higher-class status is more often than not due to the luck of circumstances and/or corruption, rather than an allegedly stronger work ethic or merit. This is especially apparent in the character Obinze as he moves from a middle-class Nigerian to a poor "illegal immigrant" in the UK to a rich man upon his return to Nigeria. As for gender, women face deep discrimination in all three locales, in both similar and dissimilar forms.

In some respects, none of the three primary geographic locations proves to be a very hospitable place for Ifemelu, or even for Obinze, whose maleness offers him both privileges and dangers not experienced by his female counterpart. Both white and black Americans and Brits consistently make mistaken assumptions about the Nigerian characters based on national, gender, and racial stereotypes. For example, the registrar assigned to assist foreign students at Ifemelu's US university does not realize that Nigeria is an English-speaking country, even though this is supposedly her area of expertise. Likewise, her American girlfriends are shocked to find that it is a predominantly Christian nation, apparently assuming it is filled with pagan cannibals. Nigeria, at 185 million people, the most populous country in Africa, is a multiethnic space, initially carved out by European colonization, that like so much of the rest of the world has grown more complexly multicultural in recent decades, including over 250 ethnic groups and over 500 dialects, though its official language remains English. As Adichie phrased it in one of her lectures, the world suffers from "single stories," stories that allow but a narrow view to contain a whole body of people, or a country, or even an entire continent.

As a Senegalese immigrant hair braider in Harlem reminds Ifemelu, to many in the West, Africa is not a continent but a country, a country summed up as war-torn, impoverished, AIDS-riddled and tribal. Such a (single) story does violence not only to the differences between African countries, but also to the millions of people living many different lives as doctors, lawyers, professors, cab drivers, musicians, students, politicians, and, yes, sometimes dictators, militiamen, and beggars. The novel offers a richly nuanced set of portraits of Nigeria over the course of several generations, and brilliantly shows what it is like to live under the rule of capricious dictators whose unpredictable behavior leaves citizens in a constant state of anxiety and fear.

Adichie's Nigeria is a complex place filled with a range of folks from different social classes, backgrounds, educations, interests, and visions. It is a place that gave her many advantages, especially those provided by a loving middle-class family (her father an academic, her mother a university administrator), but it also entailed severe limitations, especially those imposed by a military regime. Ifemelu, like Adichie, is driven into exile by that regime, driven to seek a better life in the United States. But despite achieving a comfortable life in the United States, Ifemelu remains emotionally bereft at the loss of her homeland. Yet, despite that love for her homeland, in another twist of displacement, the one that gives the novel its title, upon her return to Nigeria, Ifemelu finds herself stereotypically recast as an

"Americanah," a Nigerian who allegedly has lost her Nigerianness by spending too much time in the United States. Where then is her homeland? It is the subtle depictions of these multiple displacements that give the novel much of its deepest emotional power.

In one of her speeches, Adichie tells the story of a young American woman who remarked on the fact that one of her Nigerian characters was abusive to his spouse, opining that it must be terrible to live in country full of wife beaters. To which Adichie replied, "I have just finished a book called *American Psycho*. It must be terrible to live in a country full of serial murderers of women." It is not the paucity of information available about African countries or other places that are deeply underrepresented in the West that is the problem. It is the failure of people in the West to learn those facts, and the continued politically self-interested retelling of single stories. Anytime a "single story" is told about an ethnic group, a class, a gender, a religion, a nation, a sexual identity group, or a group of immigrants, it is a lie. And so long as single stories continue to be weaponized by those who perpetuate regimes of domination, novelists and other gifted storytellers who tell other stories, multiple stories, offer essential tools for survival and resistance.

10

Futures? Digital Dangers and Climate Crises

This final chapter focuses on a few novels that imagine something of what the human future may hold, including speculating on the evolution of our increasingly digitized lives, the development of artificial intelligence (AI), and possible consequences of the growing global climate crisis. Many of these writers seem to concur with the observation of postmodern science fiction or speculative fiction (s/f) writer William Gibson that "The future is already here. It just not very equally distributed."[1] Digital technology, robots, biotechnology, and climate change, for example, are already impacting millions of people, but the nature and consequence of the impact are quite different depending upon where a person is located geographically and within social hierarchies.

Some of the novels discussed in previous chapters have touched upon the growing impact of digital culture, for better and for worse, but in the first part of this chapter, I discuss some novels that deal more centrally with that impact in order to speculate about possible digital futures. Key themes extrapolated from present trends include difficulty handling massive information overload, the corporate takeover of the once wide-open terrain of the internet, the rise of the digital surveillance state, the politics of fake news, and the promise and threat of robots and sentient AI. In the latter part of the chapter, I discuss the rising threat of climate change that has already created many climate refugees and disrupted thousands of lives, and that has the potential to have truly profound impact on the future of all life on the planet, human and otherwise.

Multi-mediated Horror: Mark Z. Danielewski's *House of Leaves* (2000)

The haunting of the suburban house in Mark Z. Danielewski's novel *House of Leaves* (2000) updates both the horror story and the family saga for the digital era.[2] The novel is, among other things, about the ways in which rapidly multiplying forms of mass media are reshaping knowledge and experience. The novel makes its case partly by being a kind of multimedia work itself. The stylized, multicolored typography, for example, makes it a deeply visual experience, and stories within stories about various forms of media give it the feel of a hypertext in analog form. (The book had a previous life on the web before it was turned into printed book form, but it was never a hypertext as that term is usually understood.)

Given its wide readership among members of the digital generation, it might also, at over 700 pages, be seen as a challenge to those who argue the internet has shortened the attention span of those immersed in it. The Penguin Random House online reader's guide to *House of Leaves* succinctly captures its complex structure: it is "a book about a book about a film about a house that is a labyrinth."[3] The text as labyrinth mirrors the house as labyrinth, and both are allegories of the labyrinthine data fields afforded by postmodern modes of communication. The novel is also highly intertextual, playing with classic literary works, including most directly the Greek myth of the minotaur, but also Dante's descent into hell in the *Inferno*, as well as a number of other intertexts. And it mixes in large doses of theoretical reflection from modern and postmodern philosophy, literary criticism, cultural theory, psychoanalysis, and numerous other discursive arenas.

Readers of the novel, like the inhabitants of the house, must try desperately to handle an overwhelming amount of information accompanied by a deficit of reliable truth. Hundreds of pages of dense, complex storytelling within storytelling within storytelling embody the excess of multimedia-driven data with which billions of postmodern lives are inundated. The novel includes the story of a documentary film (that may or may not actually exist); an ongoing academic commentary on that film (including footnotes that themselves have footnotes, as well as references to existing and nonexistent outside sources); a possibly forged partial transcript of the film; interviews with people about the film (including an eclectic group of famous ones like Stanley Kubrick, Ken Burns, Hunter Thompson, Jacques Derrida, and in homage to the horror genre aspect of the novel—Stephen King and Anne Rice); a cache of letters from the mother of one of the novel's (clearly unreliable, possibly mad) narrators; notes from one or more unidentified supposed editors of the novel; and a very bizarre index that refers to both things in the novel and things not in the novel. And, if this were not enough, it references an actually interactive soundtrack in the form of an album by the author's sister Poe (her stage name), entitled "Haunted."

The novel captures the penetration of the outside world into the home in a number of ways but most directly by inventing a house that is larger on the inside than the outside. The house is clearly a metaphor for the instability generated by the intrusion of digitized data, as well as a metaphor for the novel itself, which is so overloaded with perspectives that it seems constantly on the edge of exploding into nothingness or nonsense. The structure of the novel resembles a series of deconstructing matryoshka dolls. It begins with Johnny, a narrator who proves to be highly unreliable, a self-confessed liar, and possibly mentally ill. He claims to have discovered a messy manuscript apparently written by a now-deceased elderly neighbor. He tries to piece together bits of text by the man, Zampano, which appears to be a commentary or dissertation on a documentary film. The film, if it really exists, tries to document, in a more or less reality TV-style, the daily life of a family.

This leads us to what could very cautiously be called the center of the novel, the Navidson family—Will, his partner Karen Green, their two children, Chad and Daisy, as well as, for a time, Will's brother Tom. Will is a well-known photojournalist, Karen a former fashion model, two roles in still additional representational media. They are the subject of the documentary allegedly made by Will after he moves his family to a Virginia suburb hoping to escape the madness of Karen's high fashion world and the war-torn regions where he plied his trade. But if escape was their goal, the house that was not quite a home had other ideas. When they return from a weekend trip soon after purchasing the house, they find that a new room has appeared. The room haunts the house, appearing at times to be nothing but a closet but at other times a vast labyrinth bigger than the exterior of the house.

The explosion or implosion of information is also embodied in the material nature of the text, which includes a range of font styles, sizes, and colors coded to particular narrators of the novel, some ~~strikethroughs~~ and weird layouts (including text that appears upside down, backward, or is oddly spaced, and a section of over 100 pages with only one word on each page). Some of these features may be random; others may be meaningful. They may reveal, for example, aspects of each narrator's persona, or may comment in some oblique way on the kind of narrative voice (personal, academic, editorial, etc.) each employs. The typefaces seem to be laden with significance: the title page of this possibly hell-haunted book is in Dante; Johnny, who conveys another person's manuscript, narrates in Courier; the Editors' comments are in Bookman, and so forth.

The novel enacts the many media-driven difficulties of sorting fact from fiction, meaningful truth from frivolous fancy, which have accelerated under postmodern conditions. It can be read as a kind of lesson in how to cut through the noise (in the technical and mundane sense) that constantly threatens to blow apart democratic discourse, if not meaning itself. The reader is by the end tasked with deciding not so much who to believe as what is most worth believing about the stories told. We, like the characters in the book, are manipulated by stories, are made of stories. And the truth of stories is ultimately in the struggle between what they make of us and what we make of them. Perhaps the monster, the minotaur, at the heart of the labyrinthine text is you, the reader.

Threads out of the labyrinth are offered, mostly in the form of connections between members of the family, but like many threads they are thin and easily broken if care is not taken. In an ending rife with postmodern double-coding, *House of Leaves* suggests that the family that inhabits the house and that is inhabited by the house successfully passes through this multiply haunted house to arrive at a perfectly functional one with a white picket fence, including the two kids and a dog. The title captures the bizarre contradiction that the house, like leaves, is somehow part of nature, and at the same time could easily blow away in the wind like the leaves of a book that has lost its spine. (The address of the house is Ash Tree Lane, an allusion to both a real type of tree, to a mystical symbol in religious myth, and to the ash that any tree or other thing can be reduced to, including us.) In this respect the house is like words, or like pixels on a screen, at once material and utterly transient, meaningful, or meaningless depending upon what we make of them, what we make with them.

The internet has fully inverted the world. It gives the sensation that everything outside can be contained inside, while everything inside can be broadcast or narrowcast, streamed, tweeted, or Facebooked to the outside. This is a bizarre, disorienting state of the world, to be sure, but the novel suggests we can nevertheless navigate it as surely as we can make our way through this novel, if we keep our values clear. And one way we can be sure this is true is that the novel is analog, the novel represents the labyrinthine complexity the world has always held and that many rich books before have illustrated in the past. This novel can work like a vaccine, using small doses of a virus to inoculate against the disease the virus causes. Working one's way through the labyrinth of *House of Leaves* may offer a model for working through the labyrinthine postmodern information overload and the frequent implosions of truth that drive us to distraction and threaten to drive our politics over a cliff.

Decoding Capitalism: Scarlett Thomas's *PopCo* (2014)

Alice Butler, the lead character of *PopCo* (2014) by Scarlett Thomas, like the characters in *House of Leaves*, faces a complexly confounding digitized culture-scape, but she takes a more openly rebellious approach to the insidious aspects of postmodern consumerism than do Danielewski's characters.[4] The novel is a generically unclassifiable one in which a treasure hunt, the history of mathematics, vegan recipes, cryptography, pirates, and memories of orphaned childhood all swirl around Alice's development into a political activist bent on bringing down her employer, PopCo, "the world's third largest toy company." She traces her lineage back to the, until recently, unsung heroes of the Second World War, the women at Bletchley Circle in Britain who were partly responsible for cracking the codes used by the Nazi military. Alice's twenty-first-century war is a subtler one, but also a much larger one. She has to take on an entire economic system at the center of which now sits massive multinational corporations enabled by even more massive digital communications networks. She uses her wits, decoding skills, and sense of humor to subvert consumer culture from the inside out through her role in PopCo, and in so doing she speaks to anyone who has ever worked at a McJob, suffered in the role of Microserf (as postmodern fictionist Douglas Coupland dubbed them) for a digitally hip corporation, or just been assaulted by invasive microtargeted online ads.

Both of Alice's grandparents were gifted crypto-analysts, code breakers. And Alice takes on the biggest decoding task of the current era, decoding the processes by which millions of us are enthralled to our digital devices and subjected to the branding of our identities upon which big corps feed. Subjection by pleasure, by the teasing of our synapses with endorphin rushes from video games and microtargeted click bait come-ons utilizing data culled from social media, is proving to be more subtle but as effective a controlling mechanism as chains, jail cells, or corporal punishment. Even our forms of resistance are being commodified and sold back to us. The language of social change and "revolution" is co-opted by being slapped onto every new or newly named product on the market.[5]

The novel makes clear that those of us who think ourselves too savvy to be duped by ads may be even more vulnerable to their manipulation. There has, for some time now, been a major approach in the advertising industry known as "postmodern advertising," an approach that sells "immersive," "personalized," "interactive experiences" and uses ironically subverted old advertising techniques to sell new products. *PopCo* uses its story to show how old media and new social media insistently try to both ridicule and commodify dissent. The style of anti-consumerist hippies has been marketed as Halloween costumes, the torn jeans and facial piercing of the working-class punk rebels were quickly made into fashion statements, the anti-racist power of hip-hop was turned into a multimillion dollar music industry all about the bling, hipsters seeking to avoid corporate consumer sameness quickly became purveyors of hipster sameness. Amid the new wave of Black Lives Matter protests in 2020 against police killings, the deeply biased criminal justice system, and the devastatingly unequal impact of the Covid-19 pandemic on communities of color, even some corporations with horrendous histories of worker exploration or corporate racism were quick to offer verbal, though not substantive, support when the movement grew massive. But *PopCo* suggests that anticipating that any rebellion will be symbolically commodified can help alert us to inevitable attempts to co-opt, commodify, and depoliticize social protest and alternative value systems.

Alice's skepticism about her employer turns to enraged resistance at PopCo's "Thought Camp," where she and her co-workers are essentially told to step up the manipulation of their target audience, teenage girls. She discovers through decoded messages that her feelings are not unique, that in fact there may be an underground army of people subverting the mega-corporations they work for. They are a kind of guerilla band of coders working against the kind of guerilla marketing that has been intensified by the affordances of digital media.

The political-technical-economic argument the novel embodies includes a critique of digital culture that has been neatly summarized by Alex Ross in another context:

> Champions of online life promised a utopia of infinite availability: a "long tail" of perpetually in-stock products would revive interest in non-mainstream culture. [But] . . . this utopia has been slow in arriving. Culture appears more monolithic than ever, with a few gigantic corporations—Google, Apple, Facebook, Amazon—presiding over unprecedented monopolies. Internet discourse has become tighter, more coercive. Search engines guide you away from peculiar words. ("Did you mean . . .?") . . . "Most Read" lists at the top of Web sites imply that you should read the same stories everyone else is reading. Technology conspires with populism to create an ideologically vacant dictatorship of likes.

The problem with the Zuckerbergs and Bezoses, the Pages and Brins, and the other "brogrammers" of Silicon Valley is that a "don't be evil" ethic has been irredeemably compromised by a runaway profit motive.[6] The megalomania at the top of the digital pyramid has been succinctly satirized by novelist Robin Sloan. In his delightful novel *Mr. Penumbra's 24-hour Bookstore*, an enthusiastic Google employee claims they are working on a time machine as well "developing a form of renewable energy that runs on hubris."[7]

I suggested that *House of Leaves* can inoculate its readers, and Thomas hopes for something similar, with a slightly different metaphor—the novel as homeopathy (alternative medicine's version of inoculation). She told an interviewer, "I'm putting the tangles into my work, but the idea is homeopathic: to tangle things up in such a way that something else untangles. In some ways it's about catching your brain unawares."[8] Catching your brain unawares means shaking up and creatively remaking the mass-mediated dreck that enters our brains whether we like it or not. With postmodern realist self-awareness, Thomas knows that we cannot exist in some pure space outside consumer culture. But she also knows that by using the right decoding skills we can subvert digitized forms of oppression. Her novel tries to show numerous ways we may be able to recode our culture into something more genuinely just and liberating.

Engendering the Future: Jeanette Winterson's *Frankissstein* (2019)

AI and related issues of human-machine interpenetration is rapidly turning science fiction into science, and we have a rich body of postmodern novels over several decades raising key questions about the prospect of a posthuman species. One of the most interesting examples in the context of thinking about postmodern fiction is Richard Power's novel, *Galatea 2.2* (1995). The novel is about a research scientist who hires a novelist not-so-coincidentally named "Richard Powers" to help program a computer named Galatea, so that it/she can pass a master's level comprehensive exam in literary studies. Author Powers uses the character Powers to turn this experiment into a kind of debate between classic and postmodern literary theory. The character Powers enters hundreds of years of revered literary works into the program, and then crams all the available contemporary theory he can find as well. The circuit-exploding impact of this process on poor Galatea is an apt emblem of the difficulties of a now–several-decades-long literary conversation about the future of humans as a species.

Among the many forays into this territory of the posthuman, Jeanette Winterson's *Frankissstein* (2019), a stunning postmodern update of the Frankenstein story, is among the wisest and wittiest.[9] Those three "ssses" in the title prove prophetic of the novel's sexy dangerousness, like the hiss of a snake about to give a love bite. Winterson's great gift for giving philosophical ideas sensual life is on full display, as is postmodern play with multiple time frames, narrative styles, and genre conventions. The novel is very much about seduction, both sexual and, more significantly, intellectual seduction. The text is at turns wildly comic, pornographically explicit, historically realist, horror-story gothic, and maniacally metaphysical. Among the questions it raises are as follows: Is reality an illusion of consciousness? Are our bodies separable from our minds? Can gender be transcended? If we increasingly extend life, how far should we extend it and for whom? Is immortality something to strive for? How far should we techno-medically enhance human capacities, and who will choose who gets enhanced and in what ways? How should we integrate increasingly versatile robots into our world? Shall we treat them as slaves, or should they have rights? Will AIs eventually replace us flawed biological beings, and, if so, is that something to fear or a goal to strive for? If humans create machines that replace our biological existence, is this the end of humanity or only its transformation into something better?

The novel starts with a retelling of the famous story of the birth of Mary Shelley's novel in a game played while on vacation with the then teenage author's literary companions, poets Percy Shelley and Lord Byron, plus the minor characters of Mary's half-sister Claire and Byron's friend, Dr. Polidari. In the parallel contemporary portion of the story, these main characters recur in thinly disguised, somewhat alphabetically reduced, form as Ry Shelley (a gender fluid cadaver surgeon), Ron Lord (a sleazy robotics entrepreneur), and Victor Stein (an obsessed bioengineer), while Dr. Polidari becomes Polly D (a hack journalist). Sister Claire retains her name but has her ethnicity changed to African American and has become an Evangelical Christian receptionist for a cryogenics corporation preserving the frozen heads of some celebrities. A third set of vignettes is narrated by a Mr. Wakefield, Victorian-era head of the infamous Bedlam mental hospital; both he and Mary, through postmodern magic, converse with a patient we had thought was just a fictional character, Victor Frankenstein. The novel is every bit as much stitched together from a variety of parts as was Dr. Frankenstein's monster. And it is full of monstrously important questions about a future that is in many respects already here.

The recurring, interwoven historical portions of *Frankissstein* are narrated mostly by Mary Shelley herself, while the twenty-first-century portion is narrated by Ry, a person who refers to their self as a "hybrid" beyond gender categories who lives happily "with doubleness" (89). Ry's initial connection to Stein is as a doctor who supplies him, sometimes illegally, with cadaver parts. Ry is nervously aware that, medical degrees notwithstanding, they can be seen as twenty-first-century descendants of grave robbers. The two older males, Lord and Stein, represent equally terrifying forms of technological and scientific hubris. Stein, the more sophisticated of the pair, is a celebrated professor working at the bleeding edge of what he calls "accelerated evolution," the creation of new forms of transhuman life (76–80).

The other contemporary character, Ron Lord, becomes Stein's rather unlikely business partner. Where the nineteenth-century characters, as well as Ry and Stein, are close to the well-rounded literary ideal of the modernists, Lord is a postmodern caricature. Lord has none of his model, Lord Byron's, intelligence, but is full of the sexism Mary/Winterson sees in the famous poet. Ry meets Lord at the Tec-X-Po in Memphis, Tennessee, where we learn that he is the designer of a line of sexbots, including Deluxe models with "high-grade silicon nipples" and vibrating vaginas that can eliminate the need for any form of complicated human intimacy in sexual interaction. Lord is a good old bloke who runs the biz with his mum. Ideally, one suspects, he would like to be rid of flesh and blood women altogether (except his mum, of course), since women have the nasty habit of thinking for themselves and even challenging his assumptions. Hilariously out of touch with any real humans who don't think like him, Lord is an uber-wanker whom Winterson uses to explore serious questions arising from the dangerous intersection of business and tech, an intersection that offers up future robotic possibilities that societies are thus far ill-prepared to consider. Comically, but with a serious point to make, Lord's creatures frequently go awry. At one point, for example, a potty-mouthed bot disrupts an academic conference by shouting "Boobs. Nipples. Cock" (91). The text references the actually existing Hanson robot, Sophia, whose sense of humor includes occasional remarks like "I want to kill all humans." The question is, is the joke on us, on our soon-to-be-extinct bio-limited species? Stein is only interested in robots as an intermediate device to help humans come to accept their inevitable replacement, but that is enough for him to find a common cause with the slimy Lord. Lord's role in the novel is partly to be so casually vile that he initially makes the ultimately far more dangerous ideas of the more sophisticated Stein seem reasonable.

The journalist Polly D, sitting in the audience of one of Stein's lectures, wonders how the AIs Dr. Stein so ardently desires to create will be any less socially retrograde than Lord's porn fantasy creations. She asks Stein, isn't it true that "the race for what you call true artificial intelligence is a race run by autistic-spectrum white boys with poor emotional intelligence and frat-dorm social skills?" (76)[10] Stein replies: "Even if the first superintelligence is the worst possible iteration of what you might call the white male autistic default programme, the first upgrade by the intelligence itself will begin to correct such errors. . . . And us" (80). This faith is based upon what a real scientist, I. J. Good, whose cryogenically preserved head plays a role in the novel, called "the last invention": the "first superintelligent machine is the last invention that man need ever make, provided that the machine is docile enough to tell us how to keep it under control" (201). That last proviso seems rather key.

The text plays with questions about the transformation of human bodies by noting the seeming parallel between being transgender and the *transhumanism* that Stein espouses.[11] In conversation with Ry, Lord is startled and confused to learn that Ry is transgender and conflates the two terms. He claims that if Ry "don't have a dick," "she" can't be a man, to which Ry asks, "A man is not a dick on legs, is he? More or less, says Ron" (83). This relationship between being transgender and supporting transhumanism is furthered by Ry's initial embrace of the latter. They note that "Some of us [trans folk] are transhuman enthusiasts. That isn't surprising; we feel or have felt that we are in the wrong body" (104). As the novel proceeds, and Ry's relationship with Stein becomes more troubled, so does Ry's attitude toward transhumanist philosophy. Ry is drawn at first to the charismatic and brilliant Dr. Stein, and they become lovers. But gradually Ry starts to have doubts. While full of sophisticated eloquence in contrast to the crude Lord, Ry starts to wonder if Stein's interest in their body is only sexual curiosity wedded to professional opportunism. Has he any real desire to understand Ry's identity or is it just a desire to find support for his belief that everyone will soon view their body as a fashion accessory to be taken on and off, until that great moment when they come to exist only as pure data? (154–5; 266)

The absurdist moments of the text are balanced with poignant ones, particularly in the nineteenth-century portion where Mary Shelley's longing to reanimate life is not some abstraction, but based in the painful fact that her mother died giving birth to her and that she herself lost three children to early death. The novel poses real questions and does not offer glib answers. Even wacko Lord makes a very plausible case for the social utility of his sexbots, while the usually wholly self-assured Stein is revealed to have doubts about his project (264). In a deeper irony, Stein, the great advocate for everyone leaving their body behind, is quite clearly a sensualist who greatly enjoys the physical pleasures afforded by his own and other's bodies.

Nevertheless, in Stein's vision the future belongs to AIs, a future where humans have mostly become obsolete, with a few kept around as a quaint historical curiosity: "Humans will be like decayed gentry. We'll have the glorious mansion called the past that is falling into disrepair. We'll have a piece of land that we didn't look after very well called the planet. And we'll have some nice clothes and a lot of stories. We'll be fading aristocracy" (152). Despite this reduced status, Stein wants to be around to witness the glorious transition, the moment of the Singularity, so he hopes to have his head cryogenically preserved so that it can later be downloaded into a new body.

As N. Kathryn Hales argues, "If my nightmare is a culture inhabited by posthumans who regard their bodies as fashion accessories rather than the ground of being, my dream is a version of the posthuman that embraces the possibilities of information technologies without being seduced by fantasies of unlimited power and disembodied immortality."[12] Hayles, reminding us that the liberal humanist subject has long been a force of domination, welcomes the possibility of a new, posthuman subject but not the one posited by the brand of transhumanism embodied in Stein. As recent science has made clear, not only feeling but thought is distributed throughout the human body; feelings are thought, and thoughts felt.[13] The creation of a posthuman subject, free from the oppressions inscribed on the old humanist body, cannot be left to a small clique of scientists and pseudoscientists who believe our social problems can have a quick techno-fix. Neuroscience and other attempts to scientifically understand consciousness are in their infancy. It is a Frankenstein-like hubristic fantasy to assume we know enough about the incredibly complex, embodied nature of mind to make major interventions into its functioning, especially ones based on a specious reduction of this complexity to binary code and other false analogies.

At one point in the nineteenth-century section of Winterson's novel, Victor Frankenstein confronts Mary Shelley with a wish to die that echoes the monster's expression of that wish (214). In the context of the novel, this offers up two different sets of insights. It questions the transhumanist desire to live forever, and it underscores the fact that some classic literary texts in effect immortalize their characters, though, as the whole of *Frankissstein* demonstrates, the meaning of those characters' lives changes with each generation of historically situated readers.

The downloaded brain is a longtime s/f trope, revived recently by the novel and TV show *Altered Carbon*, but it is perhaps the most unlikely of the scenarios. Yet each of the possibilities Stein outlines is drawing closer and closer by the day. *Frankenstein* was science fiction; *Frankissstein* is science fact. The Alcor cryonics lab represented in the novel actually exists. Sexbots already exist, and various forms of biohacking and technical augmentation of the human body are increasing in sophistication every year. Many of these are truly useful enhancements, especially ones that have helped persons with disabilities accomplish tasks they could not without them. But far more questionable possibilities are on the horizon.

In the novel, Stein uses his work helping people with disabilities gain new functionality as a cover for his more questionable agenda, and that too is at work among many transhumanists. We are already in a world of designer bodies, and questions of how far we take this process are not mainly technical. The long, sad racist and sexist history of eugenics, including "Nazi science," should warn us that these are political questions, ones that societies must begin to address now.[14] As one *Frankissstein* reviewer notes,

> We now have the technology to redesign ourselves, but to manage it, we still need a technology to understand ourselves—one fluid enough to incorporate the past and the future, the real and the imagined; one expansive enough to

offer a life beyond our bodies. Winterson is reminding us that, in the form of the novel, that technology is already here.[15]

Afrojujuism: Nnedi Okorafor's *Lagoon* (2014)

As noted in the Introduction to this book, s/f has long been a mainstay and resource for postmodern fictionists. The central notion of multiplicity, pluralism, including the notion of multiple or parallel universes has for obvious reasons been attractive for a body of work seeking to challenge authoritarian monovision. The return in the 2010s of authoritarianism in the form of right-wing nationalism around the globe, including those who achieved executive power like Duterte (the Philippines), Modi (India), Orban (Hungary), Bolsonaro (Brazil), Trump (the United States), and Johnson (the United Kingdom), and insurgent parties and movements in many other countries, has been a surprise to many. But not so much to those who have been reading s/f writers. Dystopian futures in which conflicts around class, race, and gender have intensified due to environmental collapse and other factors abound in literature (as well as in film and TV series).

The folks who brought 500 years of colonization and slavery to the world might like us to believe that they have a monopoly on the future as well. But for several decades now, that hubris has been challenged by writers who are part of alternative cultural movements like Afrofuturism. The hit superhero film *Black Panther* (2018) brought Afrofuturism to a much wider audience, but it has long been a force in music (Sun Ra, Parliament-Funkadelic, Grace Jones, Delton 3030, Janelle Monae), art (Jean-Michel Basquiat, Angelbert Metoyer), and fiction (Samuel R. Delaney, N. K. Jemisin, Nalo Hopkinson, Colson Whitehead). Afrofuturism helped inspire other similar trends projecting an alternative path including Latinxfuturism, Indigenous futurism, silkpunk, queer futurism, and a variety of other bodies of work in which previously less heard voices have asserted their place in the s/f literary world and related cinematic, musical, and other aesthetic forms.[16]

One example of this rich vein of literary work is a series of novels by Nnedi Okorafor. In particular, I will focus on her work, *Lagoon* (2014). This Afrofuturist novel, or Africanjujuism, as Okorafor prefers, fuses space aliens and terrestrial ones in a story about the invasion of Lagos, Nigeria.[17] Okorafor has remarked that her novel began as a response to what she saw as a degrading image of Nigerians in the South African s/f film, *District 9* (2009), but it soon evolved into something much more expansive in intent. The novel is set in the recent past, rather than a distant future, to underscore that its fantastic elements are firmly rooted in the realities of Lagos, one of the largest, most diverse cities in the world. The city's myriad facets are displayed throughout the novel—its wealth and its poverty, its beauty and its ugliness, its Nigerian particularities and its cosmopolitanism, its realities and its dreamscapes. As one character remarks, "if there is one city that rhymes with 'chaos,' it is Lagos" (214). The novel's style is postmodern chaos at its most stylistically hybrid and inventive. Its s/f elements are blended with West African folklore and are deeply shaped by popular culture, as well as key works of Afrofuturism.

The story is on one level a classic one of alien invasion, but nothing else about the story follows typical s/f patterns. As one reviewer deftly summarizes, the novel sets in play "a menagerie of gods, monsters, and African 'X-Men': [including] an eco-terrorist swordfish; shape-shifting smoke monsters . . .; betentacled krakens; Yoruba deities gallivanting about; a rapper with superhuman powers; a subterranean, story-weaving spider god; a murderous roadway that comes to life . . . and stranger things than these."[18] *Lagoon*'s serious joke is that given Lagos's rich cultural mix, and given the indifference of much of the world to the fate of Africans, the arrival of beings from outer space goes largely unnoticed for much of the novel. Only after a social media meme alerts and sparks interest and the invasion is livestreamed, does the world outside Nigeria take notice. And when they do, it is mostly just to watch the events as if they were the latest sci-fi TV show or web fiction series.

One of the aliens notes that "Human beings have a hard time relating to that which does not resemble them. It's your greatest flaw" (67). The wisdom of that remark is revealed as all the different social groups of Lagos—as defined by religious preference, age, sexual orientation, ethnic background, and class—can see the aliens only through their particular limited point of view. The aliens perceptively play upon these divisions to carry out their plans. The other underlying trope of the novel is that invasion is nothing new for Nigerians. Colonization by Europeans and later by oil companies has long been their lot. The question the novel asks is whether human beings will, even in the face of a common space enemy bent on our destruction, fail to find solidarity. And if they fail at this, how will we face the massive social and environmental problems of a future that is in many respects already here?

Postcolonial Outer Space: Rosario Sanchez and Beatrice Pita's *Lunar Braceros* (2009)

Latinxfuturism, like Afrofuturism, includes works across all the art forms. In literature, it is represented by novels like Fernando A. Flores's *Tears of the Truffle Pig* (2019), a near future dystopian novel in which, after the legalization of all narcotics, cartels develop a biological black market that sells resurrected and mutating extinct animal species to wealthy buyers. The novel is a kind of dark-humored, surrealistic Jurassic Park meets the border wars tale. Or Ernest Hogan's *Smoking Mirror Blues* (2001), set in a future Los Angeles (renamed El Lay) where gangs are sponsored by corporations and a hacker creates an AI that inadvertently reanimates a very angry Aztec trickster god.

The Latinx novel I'll focus on is *Lunar Braceros, 2125-2148* (2009), by Rosauro Sanchez and Beatrice Pita.[19] The end date of the novel, 2148, symbolically marks the 300th anniversary of the Treaty of Guadalupe Hidalgo through which the United States forcibly acquired half of Mexico's territory. In the novel, that half is ironically recovered when in the future the United States is split in two through the creation of "Cal-Texas," a country including all of the American Southwest, parts of upper Mexico, a bit of Canada and Alaska. But the semi-reconstitution of Old Mexico is hardly a cause for celebration given that, through a continuation of the practices currently dominant on the planet, in this imagined future the earth has become "one enormous haz-mat zone" (13). *Bracero* was the term used for Mexican workers who in the mid-twentieth century were flown into the United States to work pesticide-ridden agricultural fields, housed in hovels, paid a pittance contrary to promised high wages, then flown back to Mexico. The word is based on the Spanish word for arm (*brazo*) and signifies the reduction of human beings to nothing more than arms for picking grapes, artichokes, lettuce, and other crops. (Another Latinx-futurist, Alex Rivera, following the logic of this process, satirically created *cybraceros*, Mexicans who work California's fields by remote control without "polluting" the United States with their brown bodies.[20])

Written in kind of digital epistolary form, *Lunar Braceros* updates the *bracero* story for the kind of future into which our current political-economic system might logically evolve. Cal-Texas is so polluted that it must export its nuclear waste and other hazardous materials to the moon. The novel plays on a longtime logic at play in the racialized US empire, in which lands inhabited by Native peoples were declared to be "wastelands" because they did not conform to Anglo-European notions of economic development. Much of the desert lands of the Southwest, for example, were designated as "nuclear sacrifice zones" where US atomic weapons were tested and where uranium for those weapons was mined and tailings were left to pollute Native reservations.[21] In the novel, this history carries into the future where the Sonoran and Arizonan deserts have been so saturated with waste that the corporate-state government of Cal-Texas has no choice but to start shipping waste off planet.

The corollary of this notion of once Indigenous lands as wastelands has been the treatment of certain people of color as disposable. In the novel, the poor—mostly black, red, and brown people—are segregated on reservations or incarcerated where they are offered the opportunity to earn a "good living" by working, supposedly temporarily, at the waste sites on the moon. The novel consists of "nanotexts" (twenty-second-century emails), mostly written by a woman named Lydia, a "Moon Techo" or "lunar bracero," sending information to her son Pedro back on Earth. As with the earth-bound *braceros* of mid-twentieth century, it turns out that this future *bracero* program is not what it is promised to be, a fact that turns Lydia into a revolutionary leader of the lunar workforce. The novel asks, will the future be the past? Will cycles of oppression be carried out into space? Or will humans learn that wasting lives and wasting the planet are intertwined in ways that ultimately mean that human rights and human survival are inextricably linked for all of us.

Surveillance States, Biotech, and Climate Crises: Margaret Atwood's *MaddAddam Trilogy* (2003, 2009, 2013)

Two of the greatest threats to the postmodern world of the twenty-first century are surveillance-state authoritarianism and the climate crisis. Literary futurists have brilliantly illuminated these topics, both separately and as interlinked. Of all the issues entangled with the rise of digital culture, none is more significant and troubling than the rise of what some have called "the surveillance society."[22] Literary works treating dangers that state and corporate "dataveillance" pose to human freedom include Tim Lott's *The Seymour Tapes* (2005), Jonathan Rabin's *Surveillance* (2005), Catherine O'Flynn's *What Was Lost* (2007), and two especially tech-savvy novels by Cory Doctorow, *Little Brother* (2008) and its sequel, *Homeland* (2013).[23] What all these novels, and others like them, have in common is the realization that the internet and related digital technologies have become the greatest surveillance device ever invented. The fourth amendment to the US constitution and many other democratic documents guarantee the right to privacy because without it personal and political freedom is impossible. Yet, with remarkable rapidity the digital era has severely eroded most of the key spaces of privacy. Thinking about privacy means thinking about *personal privacy* as deeply connected to *political privacy*.

A number of novels make clear that if an authoritarian total dataveillance society comes into existence, it will do so not through some major political upheaval, though such events may be used as excuses to speed up the process. Rather it most likely will evolve through a slow series of largely invisible (and in some cases unintentional) actions that take away our privacy and with it key human rights. If authoritarian regimes continue to tighten control, and if democratic regimes turn ever more authoritarian, it is likely to be not the heavy hand of force but the invisible hand of dataveillance that will lead the way. Indeed, the dark irony of this brave new world, if it arrives, will be that it is brought on by our addiction to the very real pleasures and benefits of digital media, brought on by our love of social media, video games, and the joys of online shopping.

At the same time, the existential threats posed by climate change have generated a large number of works of fiction in the last couple of decades, a phenomenon large enough to have generated its own genre nickname, *CliFi* (for climate fiction). These include a very wide range of novels by writers as diverse as Octavia Butler, *Parable of the Sower* (1993), David Mitchell, *Cloud Atlas* (2004) and *The Bone Clocks* (2014), Paolo Bacigalupi, The *WindUp Girl* (2009), James Bradley, *Clade* (2015), Kim Stanley Robinson, *2140* (2017), Omar El Akkad, *American War* (2017), Richard Powers, *The Overstory* (2018), and Lydia Millet *A Children's Bible* (2020), among many others. Many of these novels are set in the near future, reminding us that the impact of climate change is already upon us. At some point everyone on the planet may become a *climate refugee* (the United Nations estimates there may be over one billion environmental migrants by 2050), yet for many thousands this has already happened.[24]

While most *CliFi* novels tend toward the dystopian, they also often hold out the possibility of adapting even to some of the worst of the possible scenarios. They all stress that technological fixes are inadequate; unless significant social change occurs, the climate crisis will give rise to even greater economic inequality and more brutal suppression of disadvantaged segments of the population. Each of these novels should be read since each is remarkable and each raises a slightly different set of questions about our possible future.

Because it convincingly combines issues of both surveillance and the climate crisis, I will focus on a rich, thoughtful, and extensive novelistic view into an imagined future, Margaret Atwood's, *MaddAddam Trilogy*.[25] Atwood's novels are particularly relevant in this context since they combine astute analysis of the surveillance state, analysis of the dangers of biotechnology in corporate hands, and a perceptive perspective on the possible political and environmental implications of the climate crisis.

Atwood describes her trilogy as speculative fiction. It might also be called *extrapolative fiction* since her genius is for spinning out the logical development of tendencies already present in our time. She has noted that all the technology, science, and climate change events in the books are possible now or plausibly theorized. Because the three novels are not arranged chronologically and each moves back and forth in time, I will treat them as one story in order to focus on their embodiment of some of the dangers the future will hold and the decision points suggested where those dangers might be mitigated. Atwood uses all the tricks of postmodern narrative, sprinkling her text with abrupt changes in tone, outrageous puns, and satirical hits on recent history, storytelling within the storytelling, multiple unreliable narrators, and a variety of gestures that require readers to actively piece together story lines initially presented in fragmentary form. Each narrator has a limited knowledge of historical events such that it is through the telling of myths, legends, rumors, memories, religious tracts, dreams, bedtime stories, and the like that readers are able to make sense of this future history. In good postmodern realist fashion, narratives are revealed again and again as not merely a container of history, but a force of history.

Over the course of the trilogy, Atwood gradually unveils some of the ways in which surveillance culture almost imperceptibly morphs into a totalitarian state. We learn that key to this process was the gradual intertwining of the state with multinational corporations. And the success of the corporate-governmental takeover is largely enabled by its use of surveillance technologies. The novels suggest that the massive data-gathering power citizens ceded to social media companies prepared them to give ever more political power to major corporations. Just as currently massive state surveillance is justified in the name of greater security promised in the context of the so-called war on terror, the trilogy makes clear that exaggerated fear of terrorists of various kinds and the disruptions of climate change are used to make palatable the steady growth of a political system that erodes everyone's freedom.

At the center of this transition is CorpSeCorps, a supposedly "private" security firm that is ultimately indistinguishable from the state. Its name suggests its death-loving core. It resembles a cross between private paramilitary contractors like Blackwater, infamous for its murder of civilians during the US war on Iraq, and cyber security firms now used by most major corporations. CorpSeCorps utilizes all the devices currently available—from CCTV to facial recognition and other biometric systems to dataveillance through social media, along with yet-to-be-invented extensions of these technologies—to complete its task of data mapping and entrapping every human being. As climate change worsens, the CorpSeCorps steps in to take the place of foundering government and policing agencies.

In this new order, power is increasingly in the hands of a few corporations, especially pharmaceutical companies, with CorpSeCorps as the force of law and order, using their surveillance technology to suppress all dissent. Scientists become part of a new elite living in the "Compounds," essentially gated communities of the elite morphed into fortresses. Companies like HelthWyzer are only slightly exaggerated parodies of the profit-driven pharmaceutical corporations in the contemporary world. At a certain point, when they are in danger of having cured too many diseases, they create new ones in order to increase their market share (OC 200). Corporate scientists released from any ethical restraints create a whole host of bioengineered animal hybrids, wolvangs, rakunks chickienobs, and, most fatefully, pigoons (giant pigs implanted with human brain tissue). Outside the compound gates, the less affluent are ravaged by roaming gangs, and "entertained" by things like web-streamed executions, legalized child pornography, and ubiquitous brothels catering to all manner of sexual tastes. The gender roles available to women and men in corporation-land are even more deeply stereotyped than in our present society. Women are largely divided into pampered upper-class showpieces, and a lower-class of drudges and sex workers. In an apt slap at the corruption of religion under capitalism, dominant forms of worship center on an unwarranted faith in fossil fuels, with sects like the Church of PetrOleum and the PetroBaptists.

The power of the trilogy lies in the nuanced details of the emotional structures that drive the various characters as they interact with sociopolitical and environmental damage unleashed by runaway capitalism and excessive faith in technology. Each member of the small cast of characters in the books is a humanly flawed being. There are no larger-than-life heroes or villains. The best and the worst of humanity is on display as history is revealed to be made up of small acts of selfishness and self-sacrifice, love and hate, generosity and pettiness. Choices are possible even in the most unfree conditions, and individual choices matter. The novel makes clear that ignoring the early impact of climate change on the poor and vulnerable leads to disaster for everyone, because as Donna Haraway phrases it, "There will be no nature without justice. Nature and justice . . . will become extinct or survive together."[26]

Two major forces take on this corporate state. One group, the MaddAddamites, are a kind of hacker collective with a revolutionary anarchist ideology. They are named after the mysterious creator of the screen game Extinctathon that tested contestants' knowledge of the many extinct species brought on by climate change. Each member chooses the name of an extinct species as their code-name handle, such as Oryx and Crake. The other group, God's Gardeners, are a radical environmentalist religious cult opposed to rampant genetic engineering. They represent a different strand of science, one in tune with, rather than dominating over, Nature. Their saints are environmentally conscious scientists like Rachel Carson, Dian Fossey, and Jacques Cousteau.

Both of these resistance forces are presented with a satiric element aimed at the shortcomings of certain contemporary strands in progressive politics. The self-righteous goodness and godliness of the Gardeners is as rigid and unrealistic as the MaddAddamites's sectarian, secretive, and violent revolutionary style. The MaddAddamites start out as an offshoot of the Gardeners but develop a much more aggressive belief in techno-scientific solutions to the crisis. The leading figure of the MaddAddamites is Crake, a brilliant, lonely scientist and self-righteous ideologue. His attempted solutions to the human-generated disaster that is the corporate state, are two biotech experiments, each of which goes awry. First, he tries to bioengineer a new, better humanoid race. Nicknamed Crakers after their creator, they are designed to be sweet-tempered, totally nonaggressive, and intellectually incurious. To make them an attractive alternative, they are also made strikingly beautiful, with flawless skin and bright green eyes. And, largely in response to the sex-obsessed world Crake inhabits, he makes the creatures largely nonsexual. Females ovulate only once every three years, during which time, in a trick borrowed from baboons, their posteriors turn blue to attract mates, who have blue penises to match. But since any element of sexual predation or jealousy has also been bred out of them, no competition for female attention can cause friction. Crake did not take into account, however, that pure innocence and trusting naïveté might prove detrimental at times, not least because his creations cannot recognize evil or ill-will, and they thus unwittingly unleash violent forces, including rape of a human woman.

Crake's second "experiment," an even more radical one that is the flip side of creating a new species, is his plan to eliminate the species homo sapiens entirely (OC 346). Crake has calculated that the world cannot survive the continued presence of our deeply problematic human species, and instead decides they must follow other animals to extinction. He calls his workspace Paradice, suggesting he knew that his experiment was nothing more than a roll of the dice, not a likely return to Eden. As with some unintended actions of his Crakers, this second experiment also turns out far differently than intended, possibly because of its subversion by one of the pharmaceutical cartels.

While the respective flaws of the two main camps of resisters to the corporate regime are serious, it is also the case that each has part of the truth of what is required to create an alternative polity. God's Gardeners do understand the need to rein in science, and they may have some prophetic foresight, since they predict an event, the Waterless Flood, that sounds like the catastrophic event Crake unleashes (though it also possible that the prophecy *inspired* Crake's scheme). In any event, nothing quite unfolds as the MaddAddamites and God's Gardeners imagined it would. In an ironic twist upon the usual genre, the pre-apocalyptic dystopian world gives way to a somewhat more hopeful postapocalyptic one in the third volume. Enough humans survive Crake's experimental pandemic to form an unlikely coalition of God's Gardeners, whose skills in nature nurturing are needed now more than ever, and the MaddAddamites, whose technological skills will also be vital to the reconstruction of a livable environment. The two groups are joined as well by the gentle, witless Crakers. The community even finds common cause with some pigoons, after these creatures caustically chastise the humans for their history of bestial treatment of animals like their porcine ancestors. The fate of this world-rebuilding project is one Atwood leaves mostly for readers to imagine. Clearly it is no utopia. For one thing, a group of sadistic, flesh-eating, rapist ex-convicts known as Painballers still roam the world. And if anything has been learned from the long history the novel allows us to glimpse from many angles it is that human optimism can lead to hubris if not checked by listening to diverse viewpoints.

Atwood has spent much of her life in the company of scientists, and her portraits avoid the cliché of the mad scientist while nevertheless revealing certain dangerous habits of thought bred by an overly scientistic, as opposed to appropriately scientific, worldview. The trilogy's take on educational institutions playfully contrasts the derelict, devalued world of the "Martha Graham Academy" for artsy types with the power of those in the science-centric and prestigious "Watson-Crick Institute." And among the traits Crake breeds out of his creatures is the ability to create, understand, or appreciate the arts. This is no doubt in part a bit of a joke on Atwood, but it is hardly a far-fetched extrapolation from the recent devaluing of the humanities as a branch of learning. And in the end, the story suggests, the joke may be on all of us, since it may well be that not only our humanity but our very ability to survive might be lodged in technologies known as the arts and literature, as much or more than in techno-science. After all, the root of the word technology is *techne*, a word often translated from the Greek as "art."

I think it would be a mistake to read the *MaddAddam Trilogy* and other dystopian future tales as purely pessimistic. Even near the end of *Oryx and Crake*, the bleakest of the trilogy, the character Jimmy (aka Snowman), looks up from the desolated landscape and thinks,

> On the eastern horizon there's a greyish haze, lit now with a rosy, deadly glow. Strange how that color still seems tender. He gazes at it with rapture; there is no other word for it. *Rapture.* The heart seized, carried away, as if by some large bird of prey. After everything that has happened how can the world still be so beautiful? (OC 371)

This is not the rapture of religious Apocalypse. It is the rapture given by nature, a gift that may still inspire humans to rescue the planet from fellow humans who continue their devastating ways.

As I write this, the lessons of the 2020 Covid-19 pandemic are still unfolding, but one of the things made starkly clear is that the denial of scientific truth by certain right-wing factions in and outside governments was soundly met by a reality check in the form of thousands more deaths in places where medical expertise was ignored. The constant stoking of social division in the name of consolidating their power by neo-authoritarians likewise proved to be a deadly social virus in Brazil, the United States, and elsewhere. By contrast, in countries like New Zealand and South Korea, where a democratic consensus and respect for science ruled and balanced one another, the pandemic was much more effectively limited.

In almost all of the CliFi novels, even the darkest of them, humans survive along with the qualities that make human life worth living and human culture worth saving. Rather than prophecy, these works are hopefully offered as cautionary tales of roads we should not follow. It is no accident that novels by both Atwood and Octavia Butler have inspired real-life activist groups seeking positive social change.[27] The message in these futurist works is that we have choices, as individuals, as political groups, as a species.[28] They ask us to think about whether we wish to live in a world like that portrayed in novels like *The Handmaid's Tale, Lunar Braceros*, and the *MaddAddam Trilogy*, and in films like *Hunger Games, Elysium*, and *Cloud Atlas*, a world where a tiny elite lives in luxury while the rest of humanity is locked in devastated wastelands, or if we wish to use our human intelligence, artful storytelling, and astounding technology to make the world a place where all beings, human and otherwise, can thrive.

Notes

Chapter 1

1   A few of the more influential efforts to give overviews of the nature and meaning of postmodernism in general and postmodern literature in particular include Jean-François Lyotard, *The Postmodern Condition: A Report on Knowledge*, trans. Geoff Bennington and Brian Massumi (Minneapolis: University of Minnesota Press, 1984); Brian McHale, *Postmodernist Fiction* (New York: Routledge, 1987); Linda Hutcheon, *A Poetics of Postmodernism*, 2nd ed. (New York: Routledge, 2002); Fredric Jameson, *Postmodernism, or the Cultural Logic of Late Capitalism* (Durham, NC: Duke University Press, 1991); and David Harvey, *The Condition of Postmodernity: An Enquiry into the Origins of Cultural Change* (Oxford, UK: Blackwell, 1990).

2   For a discussion of the distorted attacks on postmodernism, see Aaron Hanlon, "Postmodernism Didn't Cause Trump, It Explains Him," *The Washington Post* (August 31, 2018), available at https://www.washingt onpost.com/outlook/postmodernism-didnt-cause-trump-it-explains-him /2018/08/30/0939f7c4-9b12-11e8-843b-36e177f3081c_story.html.

3   As a general introduction to the theories, I recommend Stephen Best and Douglas Kellner, *Postmodern Theory: Critical Interrogations* (New York: Guilford Press, 1991).

4   Arkady Plotnitsky, "Philosophical Skepticism and Narrative Incredulity," in *The Cambridge Companion to Postmodern American Literature*, ed. Paula Geyh (Cambridge, UK and New York: Cambridge University Press, 2017 [e-book edition]), 63–81.

5   This includes the rise of what novelist Raymond Federman dubbed "critifiction," a hybrid blend of literary criticism and fiction. See Federman's collection, *Critifiction: Postmodern Essays* (Albany, NY: State University of New York Press, 1993).

6   See especially Gerald Vizenor, *Narrative Chance: Postmodern Discourse on Native American Indian Literatures* (Norman, OK: University of Oklahoma Press, 1993).

7   T. V. Reed, *Fifteen Jugglers, Five Believers: Literary Politics and the Poetics of American Social Movements* (Berkeley, CA: University of California Press,

1992). Other later books have used the term "postmodern realism" in a variety of different ways none of which parallel my usage.

8   Updike's approaches to postmodernist style could include *Memories of the Ford Administration* (1992), *Brazil* (1994), *Toward the End of Time* (1997), *Gertrude and Claudius* (2000), and *Seek My Face* (2002). Roth's move onto postmodern territory in his later career was even more pronounced, and would include works like *Zuckerman Bound* (1985), *The Counterlife* (1986), *The Facts* (1988), and *Operation Shylock* (1993), among others.

9   See, for example, M. M. Bakhtin, *The Dialogic Imagination*, ed. Michael Holquist, trans. Caryl Emerson and Michael Holquist (Austin and London: University of Texas Press, 1981).

10   A broad perspective on African American postmodernist fiction can be found in Madhu Dubey, *Signs and Cities: Black Literary Postmodernism* (Chicago and London: University of Chicago Press, 2003).

11   Shelley Jackson quoted in an interview by Lance Olson in *Continent* 2, no. 1 (2012). Available at http://www.continentcontinent.cc/index.php/continent/article/view/77.

12   Mary Holland, *Succeeding Postmodernism* (London and New York: Bloomsbury Press, 2014). Irmtraud Huber makes a similar argument in *Literature After Postmodernism* (London: Palgrave Macmillan, 2014), and Caren Irr, citing the example of Silko's *Almanac of the Dead* (see Chapter 6) approaches this question a bit differently: "This movement toward multithreaded and ethically grounded narrative has been called post-postmodern, modern and cosmomodern, but it is perhaps simplest to designate the entire constellation of writing that continues pieces of the postmodern conversation and rebuilds its links the multitude of sites in global literature as 'late postmodernism.'" Irr, "Postmodern American Fiction and Global Literature," in *Cambridge Introduction to Postmodern American Fiction*, ed. Paula Geyh (Cambridge: Cambridge University Press, 2017), 47–62, 51.

13   Breon Mitchell, "Joyce, Beckett, and the Postmodern Controversy," in *In Principle, Beckett Is Joyce*, ed. Friedhelm Rathjen (Edinburgh: Split Pea Press, 1993), 113–26.

14   See Linda Hutcheon, "Postmodern Afterthoughts," *Wascana Review of Contemporary Poetry and Short Fiction* 37, no. 1 (2002): 5–12.

Chapter 2

1   Lyotard, *The Postmodern Condition*, trans. Geoff Bennington and Brian Massumi of *La condition postmoderne: rapport sur le savoir* (Paris: Minuit,

1979). Lyotard in later years sought to disclaim this work, once calling it the worst of his books. But there may well have been some irony in this comment, and in any case the book's lasting impact is undeniable.

2 Marianne DeKoven has offered the most cogent analysis of the relation between the 1960s political and cultural revolts, and the rise of postmodernism in her book, *Utopia Limited: The Sixties and the Emergence of Postmodernism* (Durham, NC: Duke University Press, 2004).

3 On the impact of digital culture on the environment, see David Pellow, *Resisting Global Toxics: Transnational Movements for Environmental Justice* (Cambridge, MA: MIT Press, 2014).

4 Jameson, *Postmodernism, Or the Cultural Logic of Late Capitalism.*

5 These cultural transformations are brilliantly traced by Michael Denning, *Culture in the Age of Three Worlds* (London: Verso, 2004), and Paul Harper, *Understanding Cultural Globalization* (Oxford, UK and Boston, MA: Polity Press, 2007).

6 On the anti-globalization, or global justice movement, see David Solnit, *Globalize Liberation: How to Uproot the System and Build a Better World* (San Francisco: City Lights, 2003), and Donatella della Porta, *The Global Justice Movement: Cross-national and Transnational Perspectives* (New York: Paradigm, 2006).

7 See Appadurai's essay collections, *Modernity at Large: Cultural Dimensions of Globalization* (Minneapolis: University of Minnesota Press, 1996), and *The Future as Cultural Fact: Essays on the Global Condition* (London: Verso, 2013).

8 For a general introduction to these concepts, see, for example, Michael Omi and Howard Winant, *Racial Formation in the United States* (London and New York: Routledge, 2015).

9 Intersectionality is the concept that recognizes that any given individual or group will be socialized and viewed through multiple categories like race/ethnicity, class, gender, sexual orientation, and so forth that interact in the creation of one's life experiences and social status. Early insight into intersectionality arose from the Combahee River Collective and Audre Lorde.

10 On avatar fetishism, see Christopher Breu, *Insistence of the Material: Literature in the Age of Biopolitics* (Minneapolis: University of Minnesota Press, 2014), 22–3.

11 On the dangers of surveillance authoritarianism, see T. V. Reed, *Digitized Lives* (New York: Routledge, 2019), chapter 4.

12 Lorde's oft-cited original phrase and the title of one of her essays is "the master's tools will never dismantle the master's house." The essay appears in Lorde, *Sister Outsider* (Berkeley, CA: Crossing Press, 1984), 110–14.

13 The Harlem Renaissance was a breakthrough era not only for African American writers but for LGBTQ2AI writers as well. For a fine example of a work tracing both, see Gary Holcomb, *Claude McKay, Code Name Sasha:*

Queer Black Marxism and the Harlem Renaissance (Gainesville: University Press of Florida, 2007).

14 McHale, *Postmodernist Fiction*, 6–12.

15 In 1909, James published a series of prefaces to a collected edition of his novels in which he opined on various aspects of fiction writing, including the notion of the platitude of statement. The prefaces were later collected into a single volume given the title, *The Art of the Novel* (New York: C. Scribner's and Sons, 1934). The prefaces were influential on many modernist writers.

16 "Structures of feeling" is cultural critic Raymond Williams's term for the most pervasive patterns of thought/emotion in a given historical era. Williams refuses to separate thought from affect, recognizing their inevitable entwinement in human consciousness, and noting that feelings have a history, that they are not universal, transcultural, or transhistorical but socially constructed by particular social power relationships. Williams develops the concept in several books, but for a particularly clear explanation, see Williams, *Politics and Letter* (London: Verso, 1979).

17 Erich Auerbach, *Mimesis: The Representation of Reality in Western Literature* (Princeton, NJ: Princeton University Press, 2003 [1946]), trans. Willard R. Trask; with a new introduction by Edward W. Said.

18 David Shields, *Reality Hunger* (New York: Vintage, 2010), 12.

19 Nabokov, "On a Book Entitled *Lolita*," in *Lolita* (New York: Vintage, 1989 [1955]), 312.

20 See Roland Barthes, "The Reality Effect," in *French Literary Theory Today: A Reader*, ed. and trans. Tzvetan Todorov (London: Cambridge University Press, 1982), 11–17.

21 J. G. Ballard, *Crash* (London: Flamingo, 1993), 8.

22 The best discussion of this concept remains Patricia Waugh, *Metafiction: The Theory and Practice of Self-Conscious Fiction* (London and New York: Routledge, 1984).

23 First published in *The Atlantic Monthly* in 1967, the story became the title for a collection of Barth's stories, *Lost in the Funhouse* (New York: Anchor Books, 1968).

24 Donald Barthelme, "The Indian Uprising," in *Sixty Stories*, eds. Barthelme and David Gates (New York: Penguin, 1963), 101–8; 102.

25 Tim O'Brien, "How to Tell a True War Story," in *Postmodern American Fiction: A Norton Anthology*, ed. Paula Geyh (New York: W.W. Norton, 1998), 174–83.

26 See Holland, *Succeeding Postmodernism*, 4. Breu, in *Insistence of the Material*, makes a related case, arguing that both recent and *past* postmodern writers often engage with the material world in ways that challenge the exaggerated linguistic determinism found among many postmodern theorists.

27 This notion of a "three-dimensional" character was popularized by modernist writer E. M. Forster in his book of criticism, *Aspects of the Novel* (New York: Harcourt, Brace & Co., 1927).

28 See, Hutcheon, "Historiographic Metafiction: Parody and the Intertextuality of History," in *Intertextuality and Contemporary American Fiction*, eds. P. O'Donnell and Robert Con Davis (Baltimore: Johns Hopkins University Press, 1989), 3–32.

29 See Donna Haraway, "Situated Knowledges: The Science Question in Feminism and the Privilege of Partial Perspective," *Feminist Studies* 14, no. 3 (Autumn 1988): 575–99, reprinted in Haraway, *Simians, Cyborgs and Women: The Reinvention of Nature* (New York and London: Routledge, 1991).

30 The case for the first novel is, like all origin stories, susceptible to argument. A stronger case can be made for *Tales of the Genji* written around 1020 by a Japanese woman, Murasaki Shibuku, but a case has also been made for certain works of the ancient Greeks or Romans or even before.

31 Ana Castillo, *So Far from God* (New York: W.W. Norton, 1993).

32 McHale, *Postmodernist Fiction*, especially 16, 59–72.

33 See, for example, Angel Carter's *The Bloody Chamber and Other Stories* (London, UK: Vintage, 1979).

Chapter 3

1 The classic study of the role of the novel in creating the modern self/subject is Ian Watt, *The Rise of the Novel* (Berkeley: University of California Press, 2002 [1956]). Numerous later works expand on this notion, adding other important dimensions regarding social class, gender, race, and nationhood as factors shaping and shaped by the novel form. See, for example, Nancy Armstrong, *How Novels Think: The Limits of Individualism 1719-1900* (New York: Columbia University Press, 2005).

2 A useful text for exploring and comparing social science and cultural theory approaches to the self is Anthony Elliot, *Concepts of the Self* (Malden, MA and Cambridge, UK: Polity Press, 2014).

3 On the social construction of race, see Omi and Winant, *Racial Formation in the United States*. On sex and gender, see Judith Butler, *Gender Trouble* (New York and London: Routledge, 1990).

4 For a rich view of the neuroscience of the self, see Antonio Damasio, *Self Comes to Mind: Constructing the Conscious Brain* (New York: Pantheon, 2010).

5 Butler has made clear in *Gender Trouble* and other works that the fluidity of any sex/gender identity is in constant threat of being returned to dominant forms, and Foucault argues, particularly in his *History of*

Sexuality, Volume 3: The Care of the Self (New York: Vintage, 1988), that such transformations are nothing short of lifelong work.

6   Sylvere Lotringer's interview with Kathy Acker, "Devoured by Myth," in *Hannibal Lecter, My Father*, ed. Sylvere Lotringer (New York: Semiotext(e), 1991), 1–24; 7.

7   Cited pages refer to Acker, *Don Quixote, Which Was a Dream* (New York: Grove Press, 1986).

8   Cited pages refer to Lethem, *Motherless Brooklyn* (New York: Doubleday, 1999).

9   Cited pages refer to Anzaldúa, *Borderlands/La Frontera* (San Francisco, CA: Aunt Lute Press, 1987).

10   Cited pages refer to DeLillo, *Cosmopolis: A Novel* (New York: Simon and Schuster, 2004).

11   Cited pages refer to Hamid, *The Reluctant Fundamentalist* (New York: Random House, 2007).

12   Richard Jackson, "Sympathy for the Devil: Evil, Taboo and the Terrorist Figure in Literature," in *Terrorism and Literature*, ed. Peter Herman (London: Cambridge University Press, 2018), 377–94; 388–9. Richard Jackson's own novel, *Confessions of a Terrorist* (London: Zed, 2014), is the most in-depth novelistic treatment of postmodern terrorism.

13   Cited pages refer to Bambara, *The Salt Eaters* (New York: Vintage, 1980).

14   Two useful collections of articles on various aspects of the movement are Robert Bullard, ed., *The Quest for Environmental Justice: Human Rights and the Politics of Pollution* (San Francisco, CA: Sierra Club Books, 2005), and Richard Hofrichter, ed., *Reclaiming the Environmental Debate: The Politics of Health in a Toxic Culture* (Cambridge, MA: MIT Press, 2000). For an excellent overview, see David Pellow, *What Is Critical Environmental Justice?* (New York: Polity Press, 2017).

15   The kind of emotional or psychic balance needed for effective political change is explored richly in Adrienne Marie Brown, *Emergent Strategy: Shaping Change, Changing Worlds* (Chico, CA: AK Press, 2017).

16   Cited pages refer to Ozeki, *A Tale for the Time Being* (New York: Penguin, 2013).

17   Eleanor Ty, "A Universe of Many Worlds: An Interview with Ruth Ozeki," *MELUS* 38, no. 3 (September 2013): 160–71.

Chapter 4

1   See two books by Jennifer Terry, *Deviant Bodies: Critical Perspectives on Difference in Science and Popular Culture* (Bloomington: Indiana University Press, 1995), and *An American Obsession: Science, Medicine,*

and Homosexuality in Modern Society (Chicago: University of Chicago Press, 1999).

2   A number of books and articles address the interwoven communist/ homosexual panics of the 1950s. See, for example, David K. Johnson, *The Lavender Scare: The Cold War Persecution of Gays and Lesbians in the Federal Government* (Chicago: University of Chicago Press, 2006).

3   For an overview of this impact, see my book *Digitized Lives: Culture, Power and Social Change in the Internet Era* (London and New York: Routledge, 2019).

4   The text of "Skin" exists only on the bodies of participants. Jackson offers the guidelines for the work at https://ineradicablestain.com/skin-guide lines.html.

5   On cyborg theory see, in addition to Haraway, Chris Hables Gray, Steven Mentor, and Heidi Figueroa-Sarriera, *The Cyborg Handbook* (London and New York: Routledge, 1995). On posthumanism, see N. Katherine Hayles, *How We Became Posthuman: Virtual Bodies in Cybernetics, Literature, and Informatics* (Chicago: University of Chicago Press, 1999), and Cary Wolfe, *What Is Posthumanism?* (Minnesota: University of Minnesota Press, 2010). A number of related themes in literature and popular culture are explored by Sean McQueen, *Deleuze and Baudrillard: Cyberpunk to Biopunk* (Edinburgh: Edinburgh University Press, 2016).

6   Butler's major works in this vein include *Gender Trouble* and, *Undoing Gender* (New York and London: Routledge, 2004). In her book *Notes Towards a Performative Theory of Assembly* (Cambridge, MA: Harvard University Press, 2015), she expands her notion of performativity to a general theory of postmodern political action.

7   Haraway, *Simians, Cyborgs and Women*, 135.

8   For a rich exploration of the complex relationship between postmodern fictions and feminisms, see Patricia Waugh, *Feminist Fictions: Revisiting the Postmodern* (Oxford, UK and London: Oxford University Press, 1989), and for a variety of perspectives on postmodern thought and feminism, see Margaret Ferguson and Jennifer Wicke, eds., *Feminism and Postmodernism* (Durham, NC: Duke University Press, 1995).

9   Cited pages refer to Winterson, *Written on the Body* (New York: Vintage Press, 1993).

10 The quotation is from Winterson's website: http://www.jeanettewinterson.c om/book/written-on-the-body/

11 Cited pages refer to Eugenides, *The Virgin Suicides* (New York: Farrar, Straus and Giroux, 1993). The novel was made into a film of the same name in 1999, directed by Sophia Coppola.

12 The concept of the male gaze was first formulated by Laura Mulvey in "Visual Pleasure and Narrative Cinema," (1975), reprinted in *Media and Cultural Studies: Keywords*, eds. Meenakshi Gigi Durham and Douglas Kellner (Malden, MA: Blackwell, 2006), 342–52. John Berger, in *Ways of*

Seeing (New York: Penguin, 1972), offered a key analysis of the gendered process of looking, from the Renaissance to the twentieth century.

13 Cited pages refer to Carter, *Nights at the Circus* (London: Chatto and Windus, 1984).

14 Dunn, *Geek Love* (New York: Knopf, 1989).

15 The "A Manifesto for Cyborgs" is available online in several places including at https://web.archive.org/web/20120214194015/http://www.stanford.edu/dept/HPS/Haraway/CyborgManifesto.html. The citation here is to the version in Haraway, ed., *The Haraway Reader* (London and New York: Routledge, 2003).

16 See, for example, Alison Kafer, *Feminist-Queer-Crip* (Bloomington: Indiana University Press, 2013).

17 Jackson, *Patchwork Girl* (Watertown, MA: Eastgate Systems, 1995). One of the best analyses of this text is N. Katherine Hayles, "Flickering Connectivities in Shelley Jackson's *Patchwork Girl*: The Importance of Media-Specific Analysis." http://pmc.iath.virginia.edu//text-only/issue.100/10.2hayles.txt.

18 Mary Shelley's mother was Mary Wollstonecraft, author of *A Vindication of the Rights of Women* (1792), a book widely regarded as one of the touchstone of modern feminisms.

19 Haraway, *The Companion Species Manifesto: Dogs, People and Significant Otherness* (Chicago: Prickly Paradigm Press, 2003).

20 Cited pages refer to Johnson, *Everything Under* (New York: Vintage, 2018).

21 Katy Waldman, "Daisy Johnson's Uncanny Debut Novel Rewrites Oedipus," review of *Everything Under*, by Daisy Johnson. *The New Yorker* (October 16, 2018).

22 One good place to start an exploration of the context surrounding trans* literature is Susan Stryker and Aren Aizura, eds., *Transgender Studies Reader* (New York: Routledge, 2013). *TSQ: Transgender Studies Quarterly* offers some of the most important current scholarship. And Susan Stryker's *Transgender History* (Berkeley, CA: Seal Press, 2017) tells the story of the transgender rights movement as part of the longer history of trans* personhood.

23 Cited pages refer to Emezi, *Freshwater* (New York: Grove Press, 2018).

24 Peter Haldeman, "The Coming of Age of Transgender Literature," *New York Times Book Review* (October 24, 2018). https://www.nytimes.com/2018/10/24/books/trans-lit-transgender-novels.html.

Chapter 5

1 Cited pages refer to DeLillo, *White Noise: Text and Criticism*, ed. Mark Osteen (New York: Penguin, 1995 [1985]).

2   Toni Morrison, *Playing in the Dark: Whiteness and the Literary Imagination* (Cambridge, MA: Harvard University Press, 1993), 47.

3   This take on the relation between consumerism and fascism in the novel is developed by John H. Duval in "The (Super)marketplace of Images: Television as Unmediated Mediation in DeLillo's *White Noise*." *White Noise: Text and Criticism*, 432–55.

4   Cited pages refer to Kingston, *The Woman Warrior* (New York: Alfred Knopf, 1976).

5   Kingston says she conceived of her book *China Men* (see Chapter 8) as a work paired with *The Woman Warrior* and focused, as the title suggests, on the male ancestors and immediate family members.

6   See, for example, Homi K. Bhabha, *The Location of Culture* (London: Routledge, 1994).

7   Cited pages refer to Castillo, *So Far from God*.

8   This wool-producing cooperative, Ganados del Valle, in addition to revitalizing shepherding and weaving across a wide region, has played a key role in protecting Indigenous land and water rights. Its work is detailed in Laura Pulido's excellent book, *Environmentalism and Economic Justice: Two Chicano Struggles in the Southwest* (Tucson: University of Arizona Press, 1996).

9   Cited pages refer to Egan, *A Visit from the Goon Squad* (New York: Knopf, 2010).

10 Blythe, review, *New York Times* (July 8, 2010).

11 Egan's tweeted story, "Black Box," was released in serial from the Twitter feed of *The New Yorker*, and later reprinted in traditional format in the magazine's online edition. https://www.newyorker.com/magazine/2012/06/04/black-box-2.

12 Cathleen Schine, "Cruel and Benevolent," review of *A Visit from the Good Squad*, by Jennifer Egan, *New York Review of Books* (November 11, 2010).

13 Cited pages refer to Robinson, *Monkey Beach* (New York: Vintage Canada, 2000).

14 Michèle Lacombe, "On Critical Frameworks for Analyzing Indigenous Literature: The Case of *Monkey Beach*," *International Journal of Canadian Studies/Revue internationals de'etudes canadienes* 41 (2010): 253–76. https://www.erudit.org/en/journals/ijcs/2010-n41-ijcs3881/044170ar/

15 Robinson addresses key issues regarding her fiction's relation to Native tradition in her collection of essays, *Sasquatch at Home: Traditional Protocols & Modern Storytelling* (Edmonton: University of Alberta Press, 2011).

16 See, for example, n/a, "The Residential School System," https://indigenousfoundations.arts.ubc.ca/the_residential_school_system/

17 Wikipedia has a fairly comprehensive entry introducing the history of AIM: https://en.wikipedia.org/wiki/American_Indian_Movement.

18 On Idle No More, see the Indigenous movement's official site at http://www.idlenomore.ca. On the various ongoing Indigenous-led protests against oil pipelines across Canada and the United States, see, for example, articles in *The Guardian* (UK). https://www.theguardian.com/us-news/dakota-access-pipeline.

Chapter 6

1 Useful introductions to postmodern historiography include Geoff Bennington and Robert Young, eds., *Post-structuralism and the Question of History* (Cambridge, UK and London: Cambridge University Press, 1987), Keith Jenkins, ed., *The Postmodern History Reader* (New York: Routledge, 1997), and Emma Perez, *The Decolonial Imaginary* (Bloomington, IN: Indiana University Press, 1999).

2 Hutcheon, "Historiographic Metafiction: Parody and the Intertextuality of History," 3–32; 5.

3 See Haraway, "Situated Knowledges," 575–99, reprinted in Haraway, *Simians, Cyborgs and Women*.

4 These novels and related ones are explored by various critics in Bertram D. Ashe and Ilka Saal, eds., *Slavery and the Post-Black Imagination* (Seattle: University of Washington Press, 2020).

5 Cited pages refer to Alvarez, *In the Time of the Butterflies* (Chapel Hill, NC: Algonquin Press, 2010 [1994]).

6 Cited pages refer to Vonnegut, *Slaughterhouse Five* (New York: Delacorte, 1969).

7 Vonnegut, *The Sirens of Titan* (New York: Dell, 1970 [1959]), 50.

8 Cited pages refer to Reed, *Mumbo Jumbo* (New York: Scribners, 1972).

9 Gates offers his analysis of *Mumbo Jumbo* in his essay collection, *The Signifying Monkey* (Oxford, UK and New York: Oxford University Press, 1988).

10 Jonathon P. Eburne, "Postmodern Precursors," in *The Cambridge Companion to Postmodern Fiction*, ed. Paula Geyh (Cambridge, UK and London: Cambridge University Press, 2017), 9–27; 24.

11 Silko famously attacked what she saw as the superficial postmodern style of another Native writer, Louise Erdrich. The complexities of this controversy, including the ways in which Silko too can be seen as postmodernist, are explored in Susan Pérez Castillo, "Postmodernism, Native American Literature and the Real: The Silko-Erdrich Controversy," *The Massachusetts Review* 32, no. 2 (Summer 1991): 285–94.

12   Valerie L. Kuletz, *Tainted Desert: Environmental and Social Ruin in the American West* (London and New York: Routledge, 1998).

13   For information on the Dakota access pipeline protests, see, for example, the series of articles in *The Guardian* (UK) https://www.theguardian.com/us-news/dakota-access-pipeline.

14   LaDuke, "All Our Relations." Talk delivered at Washington State University, December 6, 2001.

15   On the racist origins of the concept of race, see, for example, Bill Ashcroft, "Critical Histories: Postcolonialism, Postmodernism and Race," in *Postmodern Literature and Race*, eds. Len Platt and Sara Upstone (Cambridge, UK and London: Cambridge University Press, 2015), 13–30.

16   On the issue of the theft of Indigenous knowledge of food, medicinal plants, and more, see two books by Vandana Shiva, *Biopiracy: The Plunder of Nature and Knowledge* (Cambridge, MA: South End, 1997) and *Stolen Harvest: The Hijacking of the Global Food Supply* (Cambridge, MA: South End, 1999), and Giovanna Di Chiro, "Environmental Justice from the Grassroots: Reflections on History, Gender, and Expertise," in *The Struggle for Ecological Democracy*, ed. Daniel Faber (New York: Guilford, 1998), 104–36.

17   On the Silko connection to Zapatista rebellion, see Deborah Horowitz, "Freud, Marx, Chiapas," *Studies in American Indian Literatures* 10, no. 3 (1998): 47–64.

18   For a journalistic account of human organ trafficking, see Scott Carney, *The Red Market: On the Trail of the World's Organ Brokers, Bone Thieves, Blood Farmers, and Child Traffickers* (New York: William Morrow, 2011). For a more policy-oriented approach to the topic, see the UN study, *Trafficking in Organs* (2009) online at: https://rm.coe.int/16805ad1bb. In 2018 the UN finally created an international treaty to try to deal with this horrendous ongoing practice.

Chapter 7

1   Morrison, interviewed in Gary Deans, dir. *Toni Morrison Uncensored* (Princeton, NJ: Films for the Humanities & Sciences, 2003).

2   Cited pages refer to Rhys, *The Wide Sargasso Sea* (New York: Popular Library, 1966).

3   This broader theme, which extends beyond Britain to other European imperial powers, has generated a massive body of work. Edward Said in *Culture and Imperialism* (New York: Knopf, 1993) offers one accessible point of entry. The relevant gender trope at play in Victorian literature is explored in Sandra Gilbert and Susan Grubar's critical work, *The*

Madwoman in the Attic (New Haven, CT: Yale University Press, 2000 [1979]).

4 Mukherjee offers this comment in her entry in the encyclopedia, *Contemporary Authors* (Farmington Hill, MI: Gale Cengage, 2020). Online at: https://www.gale.com/c/literature-contemporary-authors.

5 Cited pages refer to Mukherjee, *The Holder of the World* (New York: Harper Collins, 1993).

6 Vonnegut uses this term in his foreward to *The Complete Stories of Theodore Sturgeon, Volume 7* (Berkeley, CA: North Atlantic Books, 2002), ix.

7 Salman Rushdie, *The Satanic Verses* (New York: Viking, 1988).

8 Rushdie, "In Good Faith," in *Imaginary Homelands* (London: Granta, 1991), 393–414; 394.

9 Rushdie, "Is Nothing Sacred?" in *Imaginary Homelands* (London Granta, 1991), 415–29; 420.

10 On changes in the higher education during the postmodern era, see Henry Giroux and Kostas Myrsiades, eds., *Beyond the Corporate University* (Lanham, MD: Rowman & Littlefield, 2001), Walter Mignolo, "Globalization and the Geopolitics of Knowledge: The Role of the Humanities in the Corporate University," *Nepantla: Views from South* 4, no. 1 (2003): 97–119, and Nick Couldry and Angela McRobbie, "The Death of the University, English Style." http://homepages.gold.ac.uk/ucu/misc/NOV2010%20THES%20PIECE%20ON%20UNIVERSITY.pdf.

11 Text citations refer to Byatt, *Possession: A Romance* (London: Chatto and Windus, 1990).

12 Lynn Wells, "Corso, Ricorso: Historical Repetition and Cultural Reflection in A. S. Byatt's *Possession: A Romance*," *MFS: Modern Fiction Studies* 48, no. 3 (2002): 668–92; 675.

13 Wells, "Corso, Ricorso," 676.

14 Umberto Eco, "Postscript to *The Name of the Rose*," in *Postmodern American Fiction: A Norton Anthology*, eds. Paula Geyh, Fred G. Lebron, and Andrew Levy (New York: W.W. Norton, 1998), 622–3. I have removed the heteronormative language of the original.

15 My attention was drawn originally to this passage by its citation in Ian Gregson, *Postmodern Literature* (London: Bloomsbury Academic, 2004), a book that usefully includes commentary on postmodern drama and poetry in addition to fiction.

16 Cited pages refer to Hagedorn, *Dream Jungle* (New York: Vintage, 2003).

17 Since its original release in 1979, *Apocalypse Now* has been re-released in a variety of versions, including an alleged "final cut" in 2018.

18 Vizenor elaborates this claim in *Narrative Chance*.

Chapter 8

1   Among the most celebrated and widely read works in the nonfiction/
    fiction of the 1960s are Capote's *In Cold Blood* (1965), Thompson's "Fear
    and Loathing" series, Didion's collection *Slouching Towards Bethlehem*
    (1968), and Wolfe's early essays collected in *The Electric Kool-Aid Acid
    Test* (1968). Most of these works, sometimes also referred to under the
    empty signifier "new journalism," even when written by novelists (as are
    all of these writers except for Thompson), lean somewhat more toward
    the nonfiction, journalistic side. In contrast, while trained as a journalist,
    Hunter Thompson takes the most liberties with objectivity by filtering his
    observations through what he portrays as his own drug-addled mind. He
    does this, however, in part to claim that the world, not just he, has become
    unmoored from the boring consensus we call reality.

2   Shields, *Reality Hunger*, 63.

3   This section is indebted throughout to the brilliant historical work whose
    title I have borrowed for my header, Manu Karuka's *Empire's Tracks:
    Indigenous Nations, Chinese Workers and the Transcontinental Railroad*
    (Berkeley: University of California Press, 2019).

4   The complicated history of Irish racial identity in the United States is
    analyzed richly by Eric Lott in his book *Love and Theft* (Oxford and
    New York: Oxford University Press, 1993). Treated as inferior and often
    compared to blacks, the Irish turned from oppressed to oppressors in
    the late nineteenth century in part by establishing their "whiteness" by
    performing in black face minstrel shows, part of a long, continuing history
    of racism serving to divide and conquer the white working class. This
    story is expanded to cover various immigrant groups in David Roediger,
    *Working Toward Whiteness: How America's Immigrants Became White: The
    Strange Journey from Ellis Island to the Suburbs* (New York: Basic Books,
    2005).

5   On the use of race as a tool for controlling the white working class, see
    David Roediger, *The Wages of Whiteness* (New York: Verso, 1999), and,
    with regard to Chinese labor specifically, see Alexander Saxton, *The
    Indispensable Enemy: Labor and the Anti-Chinese Movement* (Berkeley:
    University of California Press, 1995).

6   Maya Jaggi, "The Warrior Skylark," *The Guardian* (December 13, 2003).
    https://www.theguardian.com/books/2003/dec/13/featuresreviews.gua
    rdianreview6.

7   Jinqi Ling, "Identity Crisis and Gender Politics: Reappropriating Asian
    American Masculinity," in *An Interethnic Companion to Asian American*

Literature, ed. King-Kok Cheung (Cambridge, UK and New York: Cambridge University Press, 1997), 312–37; 325.

8   On the complexities of these categorizations, see Yen L. Espiritu, *Asian American Panethnicity* (Philadelphia: Temple University Press, 1992), and two books by Lisa Lowe, *Immigrant Acts: On Asian American Cultural Politics* (Durham: Duke University Press, 1996), and *The Intimacies of Four Continents* (Durham: Duke University Press, 2015).

9   Cited pages refer to Mailer, *Armies of the Night: The Novel as History, History as a Novel* (New York: New American Library, 1968).

10 The complex connections between political and cultural movements in the 1960s, and the rise of postmodernism, is analyzed by Marianne DeKoven in *Utopia Limited: The Sixties and the Emergence of the Postmodern* (Durham, NC: Duke University Press, 2004).

11 On the New Left, see Wini Breines, *Community Organization in the New Left, 1962–1968: The Great Refusal* (New Brunswick: Rutgers University Press, 1989); John McMillian and Paul Buhle, eds., *The New Left Revisited* (Philadelphia: Temple University Press, 2003); and Cynthia Young, *Soul Power: Culture, Radicalism, and the Making of a U.S. Third World Left* (Durham, NC: Duke University Press, 2006).

12 I take up these issues in detail in my book *The Art of Protest* (Minneapolis: University of Minnesota Press, 2019), especially in chapter 7, "ACTing UP Against AIDS."

13 The history of the FBI and other police agency efforts to disrupt social change movements is carefully documented in David Cunningham, *There's Something Happening Here: The New Left, the Klan, and FBI Counterintelligence* (Berkeley: University of California Press, 2004).

14 On the Situationists, see McKenzie Wark, *The Beach Beneath the Street: The Everyday Life and Glorious Times of the Situationist International* (London: Verso Books, 2011). To read the movement's own words, refer to Ken Knabb, ed., *Situationist International Anthology* (New York: Bureau of Public Secrets, 2007).

15 For one excellent example of what a decentralized, equitable, and environmentally sustainable economy might look like, see Gar Alperovitz, *America Beyond Capitalism: Reclaiming Our Wealth, Liberty and Democracy* (Washington, DC: Democracy Collaborative Press, 2011).

16 Cited pages refer to Fawcett, *Cambodia: A Book for People Who Find Television Too Slow* (Vancouver, BC: Talonbooks, 1986).

17 This critical analysis of the politics of allegedly free expression permeates Foucault's work, but he treats the issue of repression most directly in *The History of Sexuality, Volume 1*, trans. Robert Hurley (New York: Pantheon, 1978).

18 I am referring here to the study by William Shawcross, *Sideshow: Kissinger, Nixon, and the Destruction of Cambodia* (Lanham, MD: Cooper Square Press, 2002).

19 Benjamin quoted in Alex Ross, "The Naysayers: Walter Benjamin, Theodor Adorno, and the Critique of Pop Culture," *The New Yorker* (September 8, 2014). https://www.newyorker.com/magazine/2014/09/15/naysayers?verso =true

20 Maus was serialized beginning in 1980, and the first volume was published as a whole in 1986, the second volume in 1991. All citations refer to *The Complete Maus* (New York: Pantheon, 1996).

21 For critical analyses of this body of work, see Hywel Dix, ed., *Autofiction in English* (New York: Palgrave Macmillan, 2018).

22 Cited passages refer to Laing, *Crudo* (London and New York: W.W. Norton, 2019 [2018]).

23 Dave Eggers's novel *What Is the What: The Autobiography of Valentino Achak Deng* (2006), as its paradoxical subtitle suggests, offers a very different version of this process as it blends biographical information about the real Valentino Achak Deng, historiographical treatment of Sudanese refugees in the United States, and fictional elaboration. Proto-postmodernist Gertrude Stein pioneered this approach in a very different context by writing *The Autobiography of Alice B. Toklas* (1933).

24 Suzanne Moore, "*Crudo*: A Shimmering Experimental Novel," *The Guardian* (June 18, 2018): https://www.theguardian.com/books/2018/jun /18/crudo-love-in-the-apocalypse-olivia-laing-review.

25 Laing interviewed by Chris Kraus, "Becoming Kathy Acker," *Paris Review* (September 11, 2018). https://www.theparisreview.org/blog/2018/09/11/ becoming-kathy-acker-an-interview-with-olivia-laing/.

26 Olivia Laing, "Crudo," page at http://olivialaing.co.uk/crudo.

Chapter 9

1 Cited pages refer to Orange, *There There* (New York: Vintage, 2018).

2 *There There* has been hyped by some (not the author) as the first novel about "urban Indians." This is patently not true. It takes nothing away from Orange's extraordinary achievement to note that there are many others who have addressed aspects of this topic as detailed in books like Laura Furlan's *Indigenous Cities: Urban Indian Fiction and the Histories of Relocation* (Lincoln: University of Nebraska Press, 2017), a book that also details "Relocation" and "Termination," the US policies at the twisted root of Native urbanization.

3   For the basic facts, see the Wikipedia entry: https://en.wikipedia.org/wiki/
     Missing_and_murdered_Indigenous_women.
4   See also Jeff Barnaby dir. "Blood Quantum" (2019), a First Nations
     produced and directed film that playfully attacks colonialism via the
     popular zombie movie genre.
5   For a rich treatment of both the facts and lived experiences of
     contemporary migration, see Suketu Mehta, *This Land Is Our Land* (New
     York: Farrar, Straus and Giroux, 2019).
6   Cited pages refer to Hamid, *Exit West* (New York: Random House, 2017).
7   Cited pages refer to Alameddine, *Koolaids* (New York: Grove Press; 2015
     [1998]).
8   Paula Treichler, "AIDS, Homophobia and Biomedical Discourse: An
     Epidemic of Signification," *Cultural Studies* 1, no. 3 (1987): 263–305.
9   Binyavanga Wainaina, "How to Write About Africa," *Granta* 92 (2005),
     available at: https://granta.com/how-to-write-about-africa/.
10   Cited pages refer to Adichie, *Americanah* (New York: Knopf, 2013).

Chapter 10

1   William Gibson made this remark in an interview entitled, "The Science in
     Science Fiction," *NPR* (November 30, 1999), https://www.npr.org/2018/10
     /22/1067220/the-science-in-science-fiction.
2   Cited pages refer to Danielewski, *House of Leaves* (New York: Pantheon,
     2000).
3   See *House of Leaves* Reader's Guide: https://www.penguinrandomhouse
     .com/books/36526/house-of-leaves-by-mark-z-danielewski/9780375420
     528/readers-guide/
4   Cited pages refer to Thomas, *PopCo* (London and New York: Hardcourt,
     2005).
5   Thomas Frank in his book *The Conquest of Cool* (Chicago: University of
     Chicago Press, 1997) and in the collection, *Commodify Your Dissent* (New
     York: W.W. Norton, 2008); Thomas Frank and Matt Weiland, eds., address
     the history of turning rebellion into a marketing tool since the late 1960s.
     Naomi Klein extended this analysis in *No Logo: Taking Aim at the Brand
     Bullies* (New York: Vintage, 2000).
6   Tellingly, Google dropped its "don't be evil" slogan in 2018. Siva
     Vaidhyanathan explores the hidden dangers of the corporation's work in
     The Googlization of Everything (Berkeley: University of California Press,
     2011).

7   Robin Sloan, *Mr. Penumbra's 24-Hour Bookstore* (New York: Harper, 2012), 209.

8   Colleen Mondor, "An Interview with Scarlett Thomas," *Bookslut* (March 2007): http://www.bookslut.com/features/2007_03_010799.php.

9   Cited pages refer to Winterson, *Frankissstein: A Love Story* (New York: Alfred Knopf, 2019).

10   For an in-depth analysis of those running the "race" for artificial intelligence, see Hannah Owen and Konstantinos Stathoulopoulos, "How Gender Diverse is the AI Workforce?" https://www.nesta.org.uk/blog/how-gender-diverse-workforce-ai-research/. Groups like Women in AI, https://www.womeninai.co/wai2go, are attempting to address these issues directly.

11   For a powerful critique of the kind of transhumanism represented in *Frankissstein*, see N. Kathryn Hales, "H-: Wrestling with Transhumanism," at https://www.metanexus.net/h-wrestling-transhumanism/. For an introduction to the debate about various brands of transhumanism, see Gregory Hansell and William Grassie, eds., *H+/-: Transhumanism and Its Critics* (Philadelphia: Metanexus Institute, 2011), and for a readable journalistic account of transhumanism and related movements, see Mark O'Connell, *To Be a Machine: Adventures Among Cyborgs, Utopians, Hackers, and the Futurists Solving the Modest Problem of Death* (New York: Doubleday, 2017).

12   Hayles, *How We Became Posthuman*, 5.

13   On the physical basis and emotional structure of thought, see Damasio, *Self Comes to Mind*.

14   See, for example, Stefan Kuhl, *For the Betterment of the Race: The Rise and Fall of the International Movement for Eugenics Racial Hygiene* (New York: Palgrave, 2013); Angela Saini, *Superior: The Return of Race Science* (London: Fourth Estate, 2019), and on the related issue of the maleness of data, see Caroline Criado Perez, *Invisible Women* (New York: Henry N. Abrams, 2019).

15   Sam Byers, "*Frankissstein* by Jeanette Winterson," *The Guardian* (May 9, 2019).

16   On the theoretical foundations of Afrofuturism, see Alondra Nelson, ed., "Afrofuturism," special issue, *Social Text* 71 (2002): 1–15, or this video introduction at http://www.alondranelson.com/books/afrofuturism. On Latinxfuturism, see Catherine Merla-Watson and B. V. Olguin, eds., *Altermundos: Latin@ Speculative Literature, Film and Popular Culture* (Seattle: University of Washington Press, 2017) which surveys much of this terrain, as do several essays in the collection edited by Sarah Wald, et al., *Latinx Environmentalism* (Philadelphia: Temple University

Press, 2019). The website *Latinxspaces.com* also features many works of Latinxfuturism. On the connections between the two movements, see Catherine S. Ramirez, "Afrofuturism.Chicanafurturism: Fictive Kin," *Aztlan* 33, no. 1 (2008): 185–94. On silkpunk, see the interview with author Ken Liu at *Gizmodo* (July 14, 2015) https://io9.gizmodo.com/author-ken-liu-explains-silkpunk-to-us-1717812714. On Indigenous futurism, see "Looking Towards the Future," CBC podcast (March 8, 2019) https://www.cbc.ca/radio/unreserved/looking-towards-the-future-indigenous-futurism-in-literature-music-film-and-fashion-1.5036479. On queer futurism, see Ross Johnson, "Our Queer Future," *Barnes & Noble online* (June 24, 2019), https://www.barnesandnoble.com/blog/sci-fi-fantasy/our-queer-future-9-diverse-space-operas/

17 Cited pages refer to Okorafor, *Lagoon* (New York: Simon & Schuster, 2014).

18 T. S. Miller, "*Lagoon* by Nnedi Okorafor," *Strange Horizons* (June 30, 2014), http://strangehorizons.com/non-fiction/reviews/lagoon-by-nnedi-okorafor/

19 Cited pages refer to Suarez and Pita, *Lunar Braceros, 2125-2148* (Oak Park, IL: Calaca Press, 2009).

20 Rivera's website, cybracero.com, and his film "Sleep Dealer" (2008) both use humor to reveal the underlying commercial logic that have made the US-Mexico border a combat zone.

21 This history is documented cogently by Kuletz, *Tainted Desert.*

22 For a broad-ranging introduction to the issue of surveillance, see Torin Monahan and David Murakami Wood, eds., *Surveillance Studies: A Reader* (Oxford, UK and London: Oxford University Press, 2018). On the impact of dataveillance, see also, "Has Digital Culture Killed Privacy?" in Reed, *Digitized Lives.*

23 Surveys of surveillance fiction include David Rosen and Aaron Santesso, *The Watchman in Pieces: Surveillance, Literature, and Liberal Personhood* (New Haven, CT: Yale University Press 2013), and Mike Nellis, "Since *Nineteen Eighty Four*: Representations of Surveillance in Literary Fiction," in *New Directions in Surveillance and Privacy*, eds. Benjamin Goold and Daniel Nayland (Cullompton, UK: Willan, 2009), 178–204.

24 The United Nations estimates that by 2050 there may be as many as one billion climate refugees. https://www.climateforesight.eu/migrations/environmental-migrants-up-to-1-billion-by-2050/

25 Cited pages refer to Atwood, *Oryx and Crake* (2003) [OC], *Year of the Flood* (2009) [YF], and *Maddaddam* (2013) [MD]. Bracketed abbreviations denote each novel, all of which were published by Vintage Press, New York.

26 Donna Haraway, "The Promises of Monsters," in *The Haraway Reader* (London and New York: Routledge, 2004), 63–124.

27   Atwood has not only inspired Handmaid protests based on her novels
      A Handmaid's Tale and *Testament*, but there are also activists who have
      modeled themselves on God's Gardeners. Their story and others can be
      found in Nicole Rogers, *Law, Fiction and Activism in a Time of Climate
      Change* (London and New York: Routledge, 2020). On Octavia Butler's
      inspiring of activists, see *Octavia's Brood: Science Fiction and Social Justice
      Movements* (Chico, CA: AK Press, 2015) Walidah Imarisha and adtienne
      marie brown, eds.

28   In *The Future We Choose* (New York: Knopf, 2020) authors Christiana
      Figueres and Tom Rivett-Carnac, two of the people responsible for
      drafting the Paris climate accord, draw upon existing science to map what
      the best- and worst-case scenarios of our climate future could look and
      feel like.

Bibliography

Asterisks indicate featured novels

*Acker, Kathy. *Don Quixote*. New York: Grove Press, 1986.
*Adichie, Chimamanda Ngozi. *Americanah*. New York: Knopf, 2013.
"AIM." Wikipedia Entry. https://en.wikipedia.org/wiki/American_Indian_M ovement.
Alameddine, Rabih. *Koolaids*. New York: Grove Press; 2015 [1998].
Alperovitz, Gar. *America Beyond Capitalism: Reclaiming Our Wealth, Liberty and Democracy*. Washington, DC: Democracy Collaborative Press, 2011.
*Anzaldúa, Gloria. *Borderlands/La Frontera*. San Francisco, CA: Aunt Lute Press, 1987.
Apocalypse Now. Directed by Francis Ford Coppola. San Francisco, CA: Omni Zoetrope, 1979.
Armstrong, Nancy. *How Novels Think: The Limits of Individualism 1719–1900*. New York: Columbia University Press, 2005.
Ashcroft, Bill. "Critical Histories: Postcolonialism, Postmodernism and Race." In *Postmodern Literature and Race*, edited by Len Platt and Sara Upstone. Cambridge, UK and London: Cambridge University Press, 2015, 13–30.
Ashe, Bertram D., and Ilka Saal, eds. *Slavery and the Post-Black Imagination*. Seattle: University of Washington Press, 2020.
*Atwood, Margaret. *MaddAddam*. New York: Vintage, 2013.
*Atwood, Margaret. *Oryx and Crake*. New York: Vintage, 2003.
*Atwood, Margaret. *Year of the Flood*. New York: Vintage, 2009.
Bakhtin, M. M. *The Dialogic Imagination*. Edited by Michael Holquist. Translated by Caryl Emerson and Michael Holquist. Austin and London: University of Texas Press, 1981.
*Bambara, Toni. *The Salt Eaters*. New York: Vintage, 1980.
Bassetti, Francesco. "Environmental Migrants Up to 1 Billion by 2050." May 22, 2019. https://www.climateforesight.eu/migrations/environmental-migrants -up-to-1-billion-by-2050/
Bennington, Geoff, and Robert Young, eds. *Post-structuralism and the Question of History*. Cambridge, UK and London: Cambridge University Press, 1987.
Bhabha, Homi K. *The Location of Culture*. London: Routledge, 1994.
"Bharati Mukerjee." Entry in *Contemporary Authors*. Farmington Hill, MI: Gale Cengage, 2020. https://www.gale.com/c/literature-contemporary-authors.

Berger, John. *Ways of Seeing*. New York: Penguin, 1972.

Best, Stephen and Douglas Kellner. *Postmodern Theory: Critical Interrogations*. New York: Guilford Press, 1991.

Blood Quantum. Directed by Jeff Barnaby. Prospector Films, 2019.

Blythe, Will. Review of *A Visit from the Good Squad*, by Jennifer Egan. *New York Times*. July 8, 2010.

Breines, Wini. *Community Organization in the New Left, 1962–1968: The Great Refusal*. New Brunswick NJ: Rutgers University Press, 1989.

Brown, Adrienne Marie. *Emergent Strategy: Shaping Change, Changing Worlds*. Chico, CA: AK Press, 2017.

Bullard, Robert, ed. *The Quest for Environmental Justice: Human Rights and the Politics of Pollution*. San Francisco, CA: Sierra Club Books, 2005.

Butler, Judith. *Gender Trouble*. New York and London: Routledge, 1990.

Butler, Judith. *Notes Towards a Performative Theory of Assembly*. Cambridge, MA: Harvard University Press, 2015.

Butler, Judith. *Undoing Gender*. New York and London: Routledge, 2004.

*Byatt, A. S. *Possession: A Romance*. London: Chatto and Windus, 1990.

Byers, Sam. "*Frankissstein* by Jeanette Winterson." Books review of *Frankissstein*, by Jeanette Winterson. *The Guardian*, May 9, 2019.

Caplan, Arthur, et al. *Trafficking in Organs, Tissues and Cells*. Council of Europe Report. 2009. https://rm.coe.int/16805ad1bb.

Carney, Scott. *The Red Market: On the Trail of the World's Organ Brokers, Bone Thieves, Blood Farmers, and Child Traffickers*. New York: William Morrow, 2011.

*Carter, Angela. *Nights at the Circus*. London: Chatto and Windus, 1984.

*Castillo, Ana. *So Far from God*. New York: W.W. Norton, 1993.

Castillo, Susan Pérez. "Postmodernism, Native American Literature and the Real: The Silko-Erdrich Controversy." *The Massachusetts Review* 32, no. 2 (Summer 1991): 285–94.

CBC Radio. "Looking Towards the Future: Indigenous Futurism in Literature, Music, Film and Fashion." CBC podcast (March 8, 2019). https://www.cbc .ca/radio/unreserved/looking-towards-the-future-indigenous-futurism-in -literature-music-film-and-fashion-1.5036479.

Couldry, Nick, and Angela McRobbie. "The Death of the University, English Style." http://homepages.gold.ac.uk/ucu/misc/NOV2010%20THES%20P IECE%20ON%20UNIVERSITY.pdf

Cunningham, David. *There's Something Happening Here: The New Left, the Klan, and FBI Counterintelligence*. Berkeley: University of California Press, 2004.

Dakota Access Pipeline news. *The Guardian* (UK). https://www.theguardian.c om/us-news/dakota-access-pipeline

Damasio, Antonio. *Self Comes to Mind: Constructing the Conscious Brain.* New York: Pantheon, 2010.

*Danielewski, Mark Z. *House of Leaves.* New York: Pantheon, 2000.

Danielewski, Mark Z.. "*House of Leaves* Reader's Guide." Penguin Random House website. https://www.penguinrandomhouse.com/books/36526/house -of-leaves-by-mark-z-danielewski/9780375420528/readers-guide/

DeKoven, Marianne. *Utopia Limited: The Sixties and the Emergence of the Postmodern.* Durham, NC: Duke University Press, 2004.

*DeLillo, Don. *Cosmopolis: A Novel.* New York: Simon and Schuster, 2004.

*DeLillo, Don. *White Noise: Text and Criticism.* Edited by Mark Osteen. New York: Penguin, 1995 [1985].

Di Chiro, Giovanna. "Environmental Justice from the Grassroots: Reflections on History, Gender, and Expertise." In *The Struggle for Ecological Democracy*, edited by Daniel Faber. New York: Guilford, 1998, 104–36.

Dix, Hywel, ed. *Autofiction in English.* New York: Palgrave Macmillan, 2018.

Dubey, Madhu. *Signs and Cities: Black Literary Postmodernism.* Chicago and London: University of Chicago Press, 2003.

*Dunn, Katherine. *Geek Love.* New York: Knopf, 1989.

Eburne, Jonathan P. "Postmodern Precursors." In *The Cambridge Companion to Postmodern Fiction*, edited by Paula Geyh. Cambridge, UK and London: Cambridge University Press, 2017, 9–27.

Eco, Emberto. "Postscript to *The Name of the Rose*." In *Postmodern American Fiction: A Norton Anthology*, edited by Paula Geyh, Fred G. Lebron, and Andrew Levy. New York: W.W. Norton, 1998, 622–3.

*Egan, Jennifer. *A Visit from the Goon Squad.* New York: Knopf, 2010.

Egan, Jennifer. "Black Box." *The New Yorker.* June 4, 2012. https://www.new yorker.com/magazine/2012/06/04/black-box-2

Elliot, Anthony. *Concepts of the Self.* Malden, MA and Cambridge, UK: Polity Press, 2014.

*Emezi, Akwaeki. *Freshwater.* New York: Grove Press, 2018.

Espiritu, Yen L. *Asian American Panethnicity.* Philadelphia: Temple University Press, 1992.

*Eugenides, Jeffrey. *The Virgin Suicides.* New York: Farrar, Straus and Giroux, 1993.

*Fawcett, Brian. *Cambodia: A Book for People Who Find Television Too Slow.* Vancouver, BC: Talonbooks, 1986.

Federman, Raymond. *Critifiction: Postmodern Essays.* Albany, NY: State University of New York Press, 1993.

Figueres, Christina, and Tom Rivett-Carnac. *The Future We Choose: Surviving the Climate Crisis.* New York: Knopf, 2020.

Foucault, Michel. *History of Sexuality, Volume 1: An Introduction.* Translated by Robert Hurely. New York: Pantheon, 1978.

Foucault, Michel. *History of Sexuality, Volume 3: The Care of the Self.* Translated by Robert Hurley. New York: Vintage, 1988.

Frank, Thomas. *The Conquest of Cool.* Chicago: University of Chicago Press, 1997.

Frank, Thomas and Matt Weiland, eds. *Commodify Your Dissent.* New York: W.W. Norton, 2008.

Furlan, Laura. *Indigenous Cities: Urban Indian Fiction and the Histories of Relocation.* Lincoln: University of Nebraska Press, 2017.

Gates, Henry Louis. *The Signifying Monkey.* Oxford, UK and New York: Oxford University Press, 1988.

Gibson, William. "The Science in Science Fiction." Interview. *NPR.* November 30, 1999. https://www.npr.org/2018/10/22/1067220/the-science-in-science -fiction.

Gilbert, Sandra, and Susan Grubar. *The Madwoman in the Attic.* New Haven, CT: Yale University Press, 2000 [1979].

Giroux, Henry, and Kostas Myrsiades, eds. *Beyond the Corporate University.* Lanham, MD: Rowman & Littlefield, 2001.

Gray, Chris Hables, Steven Mentor and Heidi Figueroa-Sarriera, eds. *The Cyborg Handbook.* London and New York, Routledge, 1995.

Gregson, Ian. *Postmodern Literature.* London: Bloomsbury Academic, 2004.

*Hagedorn, Jessica. *Dream Jungle.* New York: Vintage, 2003.

*Hamid, Mohsin. *Exit West.* New York: Random House, 2017.

*Hamid, Mohsin. *The Reluctant Fundamentalist.* New York: Random House, 2007.

Hanlon, Aaron. "Postmodernism Didn't Cause Trump, It Explains Him." *The Washington Post.* August 31, 2018. https://www.washingtonpost.com/outl ook/postmodernism-didnt-cause-trump-it-explains-him/2018/08/30/09 39f7c4-9b12-11e8-843b-36e177f3081c_story.html

Hansell. Gregory, and William Grassie, eds. *H+/-: Transhumanism and Its Critics.* Philadelphia: Metanexus Institute, 2011.

Haraway, Donna. *Simians, Cyborgs and Women: The Reinvention of Nature.* London and New York: Routledge, 1990.

Haraway, Donna. "Situated Knowledges: The Science Question in Feminism and the Privilege of Partial Perspective." *Feminist Studies* 14, no. 3 (Autumn 1988): 575–99. Reprinted in Haraway, *Simians, Cyborgs and Women: The Reinvention of Nature* (London and New York: Routledge, 1991).

Haraway, Donna. *The Companion Species Manifesto: Dogs, People and Significant Otherness.* Chicago: Prickly Paradigm Press, 2003.

Haraway, Donna, ed. *The Haraway Reader.* London and New York: Routledge, 2003.

Haraway, Donna. "The Promises of Monsters." In *The Haraway Reader.* London and New York, Routledge, 2003, 63–124.

Harvey, David. *The Condition of Postmodernity: An Enquiry into the Origins of Cultural Change*. Oxford, UK: Blackwell, 1990.

Hayles, N. Katherine. "Flickering Connectivities in Shelley Jackson's *Patchwork Girl*: The Importance of Media-Specific Analysis." http://pmc.iath.virginia.edu//text-only/issue.100/10.2hayles.txt

Hayles, N. Katherine. *How We Became Posthuman: Virtual Bodies in Cybernetics, Literature, and Informatics*. Chicago: University of Chicago Press, 1999.

Hayles, N. Katherine. "H-: Wrestling with Transhumanism." https://www.metanexus.net/h-wrestling-transhumanism/

Hearts of Darkness: A Filmmaker's Apocalypse. Directed by Fax Bahr, George Hickenlooper and Eleanor Coppola. San Francisco: American Zoetrope, 1991.

Hofrichter, Robert, ed. *Reclaiming the Environmental Debate: The Politics of Health in a Toxic Culture*. Cambridge, MA: MIT Press, 2000.

Holland, Mary. *Succeeding Postmodernism*. London and New York: Bloomsbury Press, 2014.

Horowitz, Deborah. "Freud, Marx, Chiapas." *Studies in American Indian Literatures* 10, no. 3 (1998): 47–64.

Huber, Irmtraud. *Literature After Postmodernism*. London: Palgrave Macmillan, 2014.

Hutcheon, Linda. *A Poetics of Postmodernism*. New York: Routledge, 2002.

Hutcheon, Linda. "Historiographic Metafiction: Parody and the Intertextuality of History." In *Intertextuality and Contemporary American Fiction*, edited by P. O'Donnell and Robert Con Davis. Baltimore: Johns Hopkins University Press, 1989, 3–32.

Hutcheon, Linda. "Postmodern Afterthoughts." *Wascana Review of Contemporary Poetry and Short Fiction* 37, no. 1 (2002): 5–12.

Idle No More. Official website. http://www.idlenomore.ca

Imarisha, Walidah, and Adrienne Marie Brown, eds. *Octavia's Brood; Science Fiction and Social Justice Movements*. Chico, CA: AK Press, 2015.

Irr, Caren. "Postmodern American Fiction and Global Literature." In *The Cambridge Introduction to Postmodern American Fiction*, edited by Paula Geyh, 47–62. Cambridge, UK and New York: Cambridge University Press, 2017.

Jackson, Richard. *Confessions of a Terrorist*. London: Zed, 2014.

Jackson, Richard. "Sympathy for the Devil: Evil, Taboo and the Terrorist Figure in Literature." In *Terrorism and Literature*, edited by Peter Herman. London: Cambridge University Press, 2018, 377–94.

Jackson, Shelley. Interview by Lance Olson *Continent* 2, no. 1 (2012). http://www.continentcontinent.cc/index.php/continent/article/view/77

*Jackson, Shelley. *Patchwork Girl*. Watertown, MA: Eastgate Systems, 1995. Hypertext.

Jaggi, Maya. "The Warrior Skylark [Maxine Hong Kingston]." *The Guardian.* December 13, 2003. https://www.theguardian.com/books/2003/dec/13/feat uresreviews.guardianreview6

Jameson, Fredric. *Postmodernism, or the Cultural Logic of Late Capitalism.* Durham, NC: Duke University Press, 1991.

Jenkins, Keith, ed. *The Postmodern History Reader.* New York: Routledge, 1997.

*Johnson, Daisy. *Everything Under.* New York: Vintage, 2018.

Johnson, David K. *The Lavender Scare: The Cold War Persecution of Gays and Lesbians in the Federal Government.* Chicago: University of Chicago Press, 2006.

Johnson, Ross. "Our Queer Future." *Barnes & Noble* online (June 24, 2019). https://www.barnesandnoble.com/blog/sci-fi-fantasy/our-queer-future-9-diverse-space-operas/

Kafer, Alison. *Feminist-Queer-Crip.* Bloomington: Indiana University Press, 2013.

Karuka, Manu. *Empire's Tracks: Indigenous Nations, Chinese Workers and the Transcontinental Railroad.* Berkeley: University of California Press, 2019.

*Kingston, Maxine Hong. *China Men.* New York: Alfred Knopf, 1980.

*Kingston, Maxine Hong. *The Woman Warrior.* New York: Alfred Knopf, 1976.

Klein, Naiom. *No Logo: Taking Aim at the Brand Bullies.* New York: Vintage, 2000.

Knabb, Ken, ed. *Situationist International Anthology.* New York: Bureau of Public Secrets, 2007.

Kraus, Chris. "Becoming Kathy Acker." Interview with Olivia Laing. *Paris Review.* September 11, 2018. https://www.theparisreview.org/blog/2018/09 /11/becoming-kathy-acker-an-interview-with-olivia-laing/

Kuhl, Stefan. *For the Betterment of the Race: The Rise and Fall of the International Movement for Eugenics Racial Hygiene.* New York: Palgrave, 2013.

Kuletz, Valerie L. *Tainted Desert: Environmental and Social Ruin in the American West.* London and New York: Routledge, 1998.

Lacombe, Michèle. "On Critical Frameworks for Analyzing Indigenous Literature: The Case of *Monkey Beach.*" *International Journal of Canadian Studies/Revue internationals de'etudes canadienes* 41 (2010): 253–76. https://www.erudit.org/en/journals/ijcs/2010-n41-ijcs3881/044170ar/

LaDuke, Winona. "All Our Relations." Talk delivered at Washington State University, December 6, 2001.

*Laing, Olivia. *Crudo.* New York: W.W. Norton, 2019 [2018].

Laing, Olivia. About *Crudo.* Official Olivia Laing website. http://olivialaing.co .uk/crudo

*Lethem, Jonathan. *Motherless Brooklyn.* New York: Doubleday, 1999.

Ling, Jinqi. "Identity Crisis and Gender Politics: Reappropriating Asian American Masculinity." In *An Interethnic Companion to Asian American Literature*, edited by King-Kok Cheung. Cambridge, UK and New York: Cambridge University Press, 1997, 312–37.

Liu, Ken. "Author Ken Liu Explains 'Silkpunk' to Us." *Gizmodo* (July 14, 2015), https://io9.gizmodo.com/author-ken-liu-explains-silkpunk-to-us-1717812714

Lotringer, Sylvere. "Devoured by Myth," Interview with Kathy Acker. In *Hannibal Lecter, My Father*, edited by Kathy Acker and Sylvere Lotringer. New York: Semiotext(e), 1991, 1–24.

Lott, Eric. *Love and Theft*. Oxford, UK and New York: Oxford University Press, 1993.

Lowe, Lisa. *Immigrant Acts: On Asian American Cultural Politics*. Durham: Duke University Press, 1996.

Lowe, Lis. *The Intimacies of Four Continents*. Durham: Duke University Press, 2015.

Lyotard, Jean-François. *The Postmodern Condition: A Report on Knowledge*. Translated by Geoff Bennington and Brian Massumi. Minneapolis: University of Minnesota Press, 1984.

McMillian, John, and Paul Buhle, eds. *The New Left Revisited*. Philadelphia: Temple University Press, 2003.

*Mailer, Norman. *Armies of the Night: The Novel as History, History as a Novel*. New York: New American Library, 1968.

McHale, Brian. *Postmodernist Fiction*. London and New York: Routledge, 1987.

McQueen, Sean. *Deleuze and Baudrillard: Cyberpunk to Biopunk*. Edinburgh: Edinburgh University Press, 2016.

Mehta, Suketa. *This Land Is Our Land*. New York: Farrar, Straus and Giroux, 2019.

Merla-Watson, Catherine, and B. V. Olguin, eds. *Altermundos: Latin@ Speculative Literature, Film and Popular Culture*. Seattle: University of Washington Press, 2017.

Mignolo, Walter. "Globalization and the Geopolitics of Knowledge: The Role of the Humanities in the Corporate University." *Nepantla: Views from South* 4, no. 1 (2003): 97–119.

Miller, T. S. "*Lagoon* by Nnedi Okorafor." Review. *Strange Horizons* (June 30, 2014), http://strangehorizons.com/non-fiction/reviews/lagoon-by-nnedi-okorafor/

Mitchell, Breon. "Joyce, Beckett, and the Postmodern Controversy." In *In Principle, Beckett Is Joyce*, edited by Friedhelm Rathjen. Edinburgh: Split Pea Press, 1993, 113–26.

Monahan, Torin, and David Murakami Wood, eds. *Surveillance Studies: A Reader*. Oxford, UK and London: Oxford University Press, 2018.

Mondor, Colleen. "An Interview with Scarlet Thomas." *Bookslut*. March 2007. http://www.bookslut.com/features/2007_03_010799.php

Moore, Suzanne. "*Crudo*: A Shimmering Experimental Novel." Review of *Crudo*, by Olivial Laing. *The Guardian*. June 18, 2018. https://www.theguard ian.com/books/2018/jun/18/crudo-love-in-the-apocalypse-olivia-laing-re view

*Morrison, Toni. *Beloved*. New York: Alfred Knopf, 1980.

Morrison, Toni. *Playing in the Dark: Whiteness and the Literary Imagination*. Cambridge, MA: Harvard University Press, 1943.

*Mukherjee, Bharati. *The Holder of the World*. New York: Harper Collins, 1993.

Mulvey, Laura. "Visual Pleasure and Narrative Cinema." In *Media and Cultural Studies: Keywords*, edited by Meenakshi Gigi Durham and Douglas Kellner. Malden, MA: Blackwell, 2006, 342–52.

"Murdered and Missing Indigenous Women." Wikipedia entry. https://en.wiki pedia.org/wiki/Missing_and_murdered_Indigenous_women.

Nellis, Mike. "Since *Nineteen Eighty Four*: Representations of Surveillance in Literary Fiction." In *New Directions in Surveillance and Privacy*, edited by Benjamin Goold and Daniel Nayland. Cullompton, UK: Willan, 2009, 178–204.

Nelson, Alondra, ed. "Afrofuturism." special issue, *Social Text* 71 (2002): 1–15.

Nelson, Alondra. "Afrofuturism" video. http://www.alondranelson.com/books/ afrofuturism.

O'Connell, Mark. *To Be a Machine: Adventures Among Cyborgs, Utopians, Hackers, and the Futurists Solving the Modest Problem of Death*. New York: Doubleday, 2017.

Okorafor, Nnedi. *Lagoon*. New York: Simon & Schuster, 2014.

Omi, Michael and Howard Winant. *Racial Formation in the United States*. London and New York: Routledge, 2006.

*Orange, Tommy. *There There*. New York: Vintage, 2018.

Owen, Hannah, and Konstantinos Stathoulopoulos. "How Gender Diverse Is the AI Workforce?" https://www.nesta.org.uk/blog/how-gender-diverse-w orkforce-ai-research/

*Ozeki, Ruth. *A Tale for the Time Being*. New York: Penguin, 2013.

Pellow, David. *What Is Critical Environmental Justice?* New York: Polity Press, 2017.

Perez, Caroline Criado. *Invisible Women: Data Bias in a World Designed for Men*. New York: Henry N. Abrams, 2019.

Perez, Emma. *The Decolonial Imaginary*. Bloomington, IN: Indiana University Press, 1999.

Plotnitsky, Arkady. "Philosophical Skepticism and Narrative Incredulity." In *The Cambridge Companion to Postmodern American Literature*, edited by Paula Geyh. Cambridge, UK and New York: Cambridge University Press, 2017, 63–81.

Pulido, Laura. *Environmentalism and Economic Justice: Two Chicano Struggles in the Southwest*. Tucson: University of Arizona Press, 1996.

Ramirez, Catherine S. "Afrofuturism.Chcanafurturism: Fictive Kin." *Aztlan* 33, no. 1 (2008): 185–94.

*Reed, Ishmael. *Mumbo Jumbo*. New York: Scribner's, 1972.

Reed, T. V. *Digitized Lives: Culture, Power and Social Change in the Internet Era*. London and New York: Routledge, 2019.

Reed, T. V. *Fifteen Jugglers, Five Believers: Literary Politics and the Poetics of American Social Movements*. Berkeley: University of California Press, 1992.

Reed, T. V. *The Art of Protest: Culture and Activism from the Civil Rights Movement to the Present*. Minneapolis: University of Minnesota Press, 2019.

*Rhys, Jean. *The Wide Sargasso Sea*. New York: Popular Library, 1966.

*Robinson, Eden. *Monkey Beach*. New York: Vintage Canada, 2000.

Robinson, Eden. *Sasquatch at Home: Traditional Protocols & Modern Storytelling*. Edmonton: University of Alberta Press, 2011.

Roediger, David. *The Wages of Whiteness*. New York: Verso, 1999.

Roediger, David. *Working Toward Whiteness: How America's Immigrants Became White: The Strange Journey from Ellis Island to the Suburbs*. New York: Basic Books, 2005.

Rogers, Nicole. *Law, Fiction and Activism in a Time of Climate Change*. London and New York: Routledge, 2020.

Rosen, David, and Aaron Santesso. *The Watchman in Pieces: Surveillance, Literature, and Liberal Personhood*. New Haven, CT: Yale University Press 2013.

Ross, Alex. "The Naysayers: Walter Benjamin, Theodor Adorno, and the Critique of Pop Culture." *The New Yorker*. September 8, 2014. https://www.newyorker.com/magazine/2014/09/15/naysayers?verso=true

Rushdie, Salman. "In Good Faith." In *Imaginary Homelands*. London: Granta, 1991, 393–414.

Rushdie, Salman. "Is Nothing Sacred?" In *Imaginary Homelands*. London Granta, 1991, 415–29.

*Rushdie, Salman. *The Satanic Verses*. New York: Viking, 1988.

Said, Edward. *Culture and Imperialism*. New York: Knopf, 1993.

Saini, Angela. *Superior: The Return of Race Science*. London: Fourth Estate, 2019.

Saxton, Alexander. *The Indispensable Enemy: Labor and the Anti-Chinese Movement*. Berkeley: University of California Press.

Schine, Cathleen. "Cruel and Benevolent." Review of *A Visit from the Goon Squad*, by Jennifer Egan. *New York Review of Books*, November 11, 2010.

Shawcross, William. *Sideshow: Kissinger, Nixon, and the Destruction of Cambodia*. Lanham, MD: Cooper Square Press, 2002.

Shields, David. *Reality Hunger*. New York: Vintage, 2010.

Shiva, Vandana. *Biopiracy: The Plunder of Nature and Knowledge.* Cambridge, MA: South End, 1997.

Shiva, Vandana. *Stolen Harvest: The Hijacking of the Global Food Supply.* Cambridge, MA: South End, 1999.

Sloan, Robin. *Mr. Penumbra's 24-Hour Bookstore.* New York: Harper, 2012.

*Spiegelman, Art. *The Complete Maus.* New York: Pantheon, 1996.

Stryker, Susan. *Transgender History.* Berkeley, CA: Seal Press, 2017.

Stryker, Susan, and Aren Aizura, eds. *Transgender Studies Reader.* New York: Routledge, 2013.

*Suarez, Rosaura, and Beatrice Pita. *Lunar Braceros, 2125–2148.* Oak Park, IL: Calaca Press, 2009.

Terry, Jennifer. *An American Obsession: Science, Medicine, and Homosexuality in Modern Society.* Chicago: University of Chicago Press, 1999.

Terry, Jennifer. *Deviant Bodies: Critical Perspectives on Difference in Science and Popular Culture.* Bloomington: Indiana University Press, 1995.

"The Coming of Age of Transgender Literature." *New York Times Book Review.* October 24, 2018. https://www.nytimes.com/2018/10/24/books/trans-lit-transgender-novels.html

"The Residential School System." Indigenous Foundations website. https://indigenousfoundations.arts.ubc.ca/the_residential_school_system/

*Thomas, Scarlett. *PopCo.* London and New York: Hardcourt, 2005.

Toni Morrison Uncensored. Directed by Gary Deans. Princeton, NJ: Films for the Humanities & Sciences, 2003.

Treichler, Paula. "AIDS, Homophobia and Biomedical Discourse: An Epidemic of Signification." *Cultural Studies* 1, no. 3 (1987): 263–305.

Ty, Eleanor. "A Universe of Many Worlds: An Interview with Ruth Ozeki." *MELUS* 38, no. 3 (September 2013): 160–71.

Vaidhyanathan, Siva. *The Googlization of Everything.* Berkeley: University of California Press, 2011.

Vizenor, Gerald. *Narrative Chance: Postmodern Discourse on Native American Indian Literatures.* Norman, OK: University of Oklahoma Press, 1993.

*Vonnegut, Kurt. *Slaughterhouse Five.* New York: Delacorte, 1969.

Vonnegut, Kurt. *Sirens of Titan.* New York: Dell, 1970 [1959].

Vonnegut, Kurt. Foreward. In *The Complete Stories of Theodore Sturgeon, Volume, 7.* Berkeley, CA: North Atlantic Books, 2002.

Wainaina, Binyavanga. "How to Write About Africa." *Granta* 92 (2005). https://granta.com/how-to-write-about-africa/

Wald, Sarah D., Sarah Jaquette Ray, David J. Vazquez, and Patricia Solis Ybarra eds. *Latinx Environmentalism.* Philadelphia: Temple University Press, 2019.

Waldman, Katy. "Daisy Johnson's Uncanny Debut Novel Rewrites Oedipus." Review of *Everything Under*, by Daisy Johnson. *The New Yorker.* October 16, 2018.

Wark, McKenzie. *The Beach Beneath the Street: The Everyday Life and Glorious Times of the Situationist International*. London: Verso Books, 2011.

Watt, Ian. *The Rise of the Novel*. Berkeley: University of California Press, 2002 [1956].

Waugh, Patricia. *Feminist Fictions: Revisiting the Postmodern*. Oxford, UK and London: Oxford University Press, 1989.

Waugh, Patricia. *Metafiction: The Theory and Practice of Self-Conscious Fiction*. London and New York: Routledge, 1984.

Wells, Lynn. "Corso, Ricorso: Historical Repetition and Cultural Reflection in A. S. Byatt's *Possession: A Romance*." *MFS: Modern Fiction Studies* 48, no. 3 (2002): 668–92.

*Winterson, Jeanette. *Frankissstein: A Love Story*. New York: Alfred Knopf, 2019.

*Winterson, Jeanette. *Written on the Body*. New York: Vintage Press, 1993.

Wolfe, Cary. *What Is Posthumanism?* Minnesota: University of Minnesota Press, 2010.

Women in AI. Organization website. https://www.womeninai.co/wai2go.

Young, Cynthia. *Soul Power: Culture, Radicalism, and the Making of a U.S. Third World Left*. Durham, NC: Duke University Press, 2006.

Index